Residential Burial: A Multiregional Exploration

Ron L. Adams and Stacie M. King, Editors

Contributions by

Ron L. Adams
Chureekamol Onsuwan Eyre
Susan D. Gillespie
Rosemary A. Joyce
Stacie M. King
Ayu Kusumawati
Nicola Laneri
Patricia A. McAnany
Christopher B. Rodning
Lynne P. Sullivan
Joyce C. White

2011
Archeological Papers of the
American Anthropological Association, Number 20

Residential Burial: A Multiregional Exploration

Ron L. Adams and Stacie M. King, Editors

1

Residential Burial in Global Perspective

Ron L. Adams
Simon Fraser University
and
Stacie M. King
Indiana University

ABSTRACT

While the study and interpretation of mortuary practices have long been important parts of archaeological analyses, rarely has residential burial – the practice of burying the deceased in and around houses – been a specific focus of investigation. Here, we examine some of the global contexts in which residential burial has occurred and discuss the different ways that archaeologists have interpreted residential burial. Though practices vary in time, place, and context, the presence of burials in residential settings compels archaeologists to carefully consider the relationship between the living and the dead and to explore the importance of social memory, social reproduction, relations of power, mortuary ritual, and social landscapes. [burial, ancestors, social reproduction, memory, landscapes]

Archaeologists have long considered burials and burial location pivotal to the examination of prehistoric social practices. Since early work that considered burials as reflections of prehistoric social orders (e.g., Binford 1971; Renfrew 1973, 1976; Saxe 1970) and as important to the analyses of the social practices of the living (e.g., Flemming 1973), mortuary analyses in archaeology have expanded in scope to explore topics related to social reproduction, social memory, social cohesion, and landscapes (e.g., Kuijt 2001, 2008; Parker Pearson 1999; Van Dyke 2003). Many studies of prehistoric mortuary practices have put specific emphasis on issues concerning burial placement when considering the relevance of burials to the social and symbolic worlds of the living (e.g., Ashmore and Geller 2005; McAnany 1995). The presence of human remains within residential areas forces a particular consideration of the role of the deceased in the lives of the living. Here termed "residential burial," this practice is spatially and temporally widespread and can entail entirely different meanings than cases of burials placed in locations far away from living quarters. The close proximity of the living and dead in residential contexts prompts a reexamination of the relationships between prehistoric peoples and their deceased forebears and the impact burials had on social relations in residential contexts.

What has been lacking up to this point is a comprehensive discussion of this important and growing topic of archaeological and anthropological inquiry. A desire to advance the discussion of residential burial and bring the topic to the forefront of anthropological discussions of funerary practices prompted the creation of this volume. Most of the essays in this volume were first presented in a symposium on the same topic at the 2007 Society for American Archaeology Annual Meeting in Austin, Texas. The primary goal of the symposium was to assemble a group of papers with a wide range of geographic and theoretical perspectives on the subject of residential burial. The chapters in this volume reflect this diversity. The themes discussed range from macro-level analyses looking at regional patterning and changes through time in burial practices to those examining the more localized meanings of residential burial in particular cases, ranging from Southeast Asia to Mesoamerica. Social memory, identity, power, and social reproduction

ARCHEOLOGICAL PAPERS OF THE AMERICAN ANTHROPOLOGICAL ASSOCIATION, Vol. 20, Issue 1, pp. 1–16, ISSN 1551-823X, online ISSN 1551-8248. DOI: 10.1111/j.1551-8248.2011.01024.x.

are among the topics discussed in these chapters. Despite the diversity of contexts and perspectives represented, all of the chapters are united by a focus on the various realms of meaning associated with burials in domestic contexts. Collectively, the contributions address how the practice of residential burial entails particular forms of sociality and has diverse social implications, yet also show which facets of residential burial seem to be unique and particular to particular peoples at particular times.

The chapters in this volume address themes that build on a long line of mortuary studies in archaeology and anthropology. Mortuary analyses in the first half of the twentieth century were influenced by the work of Kroeber (1927), who argued that mortuary behavior had little to do with other aspects of social life and, thus, could not provide clues to the nature of past societies. This view continued to have a major influence on mortuary archaeology as late as the 1960s (Ucko 1969). The advent of the "New Archaeology" led to a paradigm shift in relation to mortuary archaeology. The works of Saxe (1970) and Binford (1971) took a systematic and cross-cultural approach to the study of burials that sought to link burial and mortuary treatment to the social position of the deceased and the degree of complexity within a society. Burials and mortuary ritual were thus viewed as material manifestations of prehistoric social orders. Many researchers (e.g., Chapman 1981; Goldstein 1980; Peebles and Kus 1977; Morris 1991) have revised and expanded the general principles of the "Saxe-Binford approach" and the paradigm continues to influence current analyses of mortuary practices.

The Saxe-Binford approach has also drawn substantial criticism. Most critics caution against the universal application of this perspective on the social importance of burial patterning. Many of these criticisms have been considered to represent the overall outlook of a post-processual approach and have called attention to the historically contingent, contextual variability associated with burial and mortuary behavior (Hodder 1982; Parker Pearson 1982). The backlash against the Saxe-Binford perspective has also criticized the embedded assumption that mortuary treatment embodies the deceased's social position in life. Instead of being a static reflection of the social role of the deceased, many have argued, mortuary remains can be the result of funerary traditions in which social distinctions are idealized or masked (Carr 1995; Chesson 1999; Hodder 1990, 1994; McGuire 1983; Metcalf and Huntington 1991; Morris 1987; Schiller 1997). Examining cycles of mortuary behavior in different societies, Cannon (1989) has also shown how social distinctions are not always linked to mortuary elaboration and how the expression of social distinction in mortuary practice can change over time. Still others have observed that mortuary treatment has just as much, if not more, to do with the living and those who are participating in the mortuary rituals as it does with the deceased individual (e.g., Gillespie 2001).

Indeed, the importance of the living context of mortuary behavior is an issue that has come to the forefront of archaeological mortuary analysis (Laneri 2007). Such discussions of mortuary ritual highlight funerary practices and have shown that death and mortuary ritual are not only concerned with mourning and reverence but also can be occasions for the enhancement of group solidarity, the advancement of power, and the expression of a "symbolic discourse on life" (Humphreys 1981:9; Raharijaona and Kus 2001:64). Archaeologists and anthropologists have begun to explore the dynamics of identity and solidarity associated with mortuary ritual and how the rituals can reaffirm contexts of meaning within social groups. In many cases, mortuary rituals have been shown to possess integrative mechanisms by highlighting real or perceived links between individuals and groups (Berreman 1981; Flanagan 1989; Flanagan and Rayner 1988; Gerlach and Gerlach 1988; Kuijt 2001; McKinnon 1991, 1995; Paynter 1989; Rayner 1988).

Archaeologists have also begun to address the importance of funerals as venues for sociopolitical action among the living (Morris 2007; Pollock 1999, 2007; Schwartz 2007). Pollock (1999:216–217) has argued that death can be a "contested realm" in which the living competed for control of the dead in the same way they competed for the control of resources and labor. In the context of the third millennium C.E. in Mesopotamia, Pollock (1999:217) asserts that differences in burial treatment reflected political and socioeconomic differentiation and were part of strategies in establishing relations of dependency. Many archaeologists have addressed such social issues in relation to funerary feasts in South American contexts as well (Gummerman 2004; Hastorf 2003; Lau 2002; Shimada et al. 2004:383, 386). Ethnographic studies in Southeast Asia, Africa, Polynesia, and northwestern North America have illustrated how funerary rituals can be events at which individuals and groups are able to promote their interests and success through hosting lavish feasts and establishing important relationships of sociopolitical support (Adams 2004; Bond 1987; Clarke 2001; Hayden 2009; Hayden and Villeneuve n.d.; Perodie 2001).

While many chapters in this volume deal with similar issues related to the living context of funerary traditions and attempt to connect burial patterning to social patterning, the emphasis here is not on cross-cultural generalizations in the sense of the Saxe-Binford perspective. Instead, a more recent trend in mortuary archaeology that considers the spatial and social significance of burial placement influences the chapters of this volume. In particular, the overall discussion of this volume resonates well with previous works that have examined the placement of the dead and their relation to the living (e.g., Ashmore and Geller 2005; McAnany 1995; essays in Silverman and Small 2002). The in-depth look at residential burial from geographically diverse locales is what sets this volume apart. As is demonstrated in the following chapters, residential burial practices can take many forms, ranging from subfloor burials within houses to burials in front of or behind houses. The purpose of this volume is to explore the many ways in which residential burial and burial ritual are linked to the social and symbolic realms of the living. More specifically, it addresses how the placement of the dead in places so intimately connected to everyday life impacts the living and is reflective of an array of concerns for individuals and groups. This perspective on mortuary behavior is thus similar to previous discussions in which the dead and their treatment in burial have been viewed as the key to understanding past societies. The goal of this volume, however, is not to generate a grand theory that explains the phenomenon of residential burial in all cases, but rather to explore the complexities of the practice in a variety of contexts.

What Is Residential Burial?

As a topic currently lacking a major synthetic discussion, just what constitutes residential burial is a theme that is addressed throughout this volume (most intensively in the chapters by Gillespie and by Adams and Kusumawati). Residential burials can take on a variety of forms. Classic examples include the Great House burial rooms in pueblos of the U.S. Southwest (Akins 2003; Van Dyke 2004) and the subfloor burials of the ancient Near East (Kenyon 1981; Rollefson 1983, 1986). In past analyses of residential burial, "residential burial" or "intramural burial" has often been used to denote subfloor or other types of burials within residential structures, such as those within structure walls (e.g., Düring 2005; Kuijt 2000, 2008; Laneri 1999; Lull 2000). Burials designated as "residential" in this volume do not always adhere to the strict classification of burials that occur within the walls of a residential building. In this volume, burials within houses as well as burials in outdoor living areas, where everyday domestic activities occur and where a clear spatial relationship between the living area and the domestic structure exists, are considered residential. Although the issue has not been discussed comprehensively in the past, others have alluded to a similar designation of residential or intramural burial for interments located within domestic contexts, but outside of residential structures (e.g., Schwartz 2007). These kinds of burials can include tombs in the center of settlements (Schwartz 2007), graves in front of and beside houses (in this volume, Adams and Kusumawati, chapter 2; Sullivan and Rodning, chapter 6; White and Eyre, chapter 5), burials in platform mounds (Gillespie, chapter 7, this volume), and burials in patios (Gillespie, chapter 7, this volume). These residential contexts are clearly distinguishable from cemeteries and other types of burials, such as long barrows and other types of megalithic burials of the European Neolithic, that are spatially set apart from a domestic setting and therefore clearly represent "extramural burials." Chapters by Adams and Kusumawati, Gillespie, Sullivan and Rodning, and White and Eyre all deal with burials that are not necessarily found within residential structures but are nonetheless residential in their association with domestic structures and the meanings they convey.

Gillespie's (chapter 7, this volume) examination of burials both within and immediately adjacent to residential structures in Formative period Chalcatzingo, Mexico, provides an important discussion of the differences and similarities between within-house and other types of "residential" burial. Gillespie reworks her own earlier analysis of residential burial at Chalcatzingo from a synchronic perspective of shared practices and interrogates the ways in which residential burial is sequential, repeated, and changed through time. In examining the pattern of mortuary behavior at Chalcatzingo, Gillespie concludes that subfloor burial was not the only "normative" burial pattern in the area. Burials in patios and platform mounds outside of houses were also within the spatial domains of social houses and these more "public" burials were found to have many similarities with and to reference the same "citational network" as subfloor burials, challenging the notion that burials within residential structures represent the only burial practice that should be considered residential. Gillespie shows how both the burials within residential structures and those outside the structures were important for social reproduction and memory and how employing a practice-oriented approach focusing on the vertical connections between successive interments over time as well as the horizontal connections between interments across spatial scales can be useful heuristic tools in mortuary analysis.

Connecting the Living and the Dead

A major framework for the chapters in this volume is that the living and the dead are linked to one another through residential burial. Archaeologists have traditionally viewed the living and the dead in opposition to one another, entailing separate interpretations. Such a perspective is enhanced by the placement of the dead in cemeteries, away from the domestic contexts of the living. On the contrary, chapters in this volume view living societies in terms of their connection to deceased forebears in line with a paradigm that has been referred to as an "ancestral-descendant" perspective to mortuary analysis (Rakita and Buikstra 2005:8). According to this perspective, the social, material, and symbolic worlds of the living are shaped by their connection to and interaction with ancestors. Such a connection can be expressed through inherited claims to property and other material wealth (Ashmore and Geller 2005:84; Gillespie 2002; McAnany 1995). In this way, the spatial locale of burials creates a "genealogy of place that links descendants to that land" (McAnany 1995:65).

In many cases, the connections between the living and the dead can be extended to indicate an actual presence of the dead within the lives of the living. This perspective views the deceased as active agents in the lives of the living. In the context of Anglo-Saxon burial practices, Williams (2004:264) has argued that the dead can affect the actions and thoughts of the living. Ethnographically, beliefs that ancestors are essential to the well-being of the living are widespread (Raharijaona and Kus 2001:58). In some societies, this connection can be manifested in beliefs that the dead could haunt or cause misfortune to the living if certain rituals were not performed, as was the belief in Mesopotamia and second-millennium Syria (Lewis 1989:31). Similar beliefs are prevalent among groups in eastern Indonesia. In West Sumba, Indonesia, Kuipers (1990) has noted that performing large feasts is considered to be, in part, an obligation to ancestors to continue long-standing practices. Hardships are believed to result when such obligations are not fulfilled. By the same token, performance of certain rituals and proper care of the deceased can be considered beneficial for individuals and groups (Lewis 1989:31; Richardson 1999–2001:194). Thus, the real or perceived "agency" of the deceased can be viewed as altering or steering the behavior of the living.

Living groups' connections to deceased ancestors have also been examined in terms of the importance burial traditions and associated funerary practices have in creating an identity and social memory for individuals and groups (Chesson 2001; Hodder and Cessford 2004; Kuijt 2000, 2008). This perspective has been heavily influenced by the work of Connerton (1989) and moves beyond the material importance of rights and inheritance to address issues of social cohesion and reproduction. Connections to the past and to past ancestors exemplified in such things as burials, landscape, and architecture are what bring the discussion of social memory into archaeology (Van Dyke and Alcock 2003). Such material manifestations of collective memory are what Connerton (1989:75–79) referred to as "inscribed" memories. Situated within the space of everyday domestic activities, residential burials can serve as important mnemonic devices for collective and individual memories.

Rituals associated with the dead and the material remains they leave behind are aspects of commemoration that also become part of the archaeological record. In this sense, as ancient practices, the rituals associated with the deceased invoke the memory of past ancestors through their continued practice. This type of commemoration in relation to ritual practice was outlined by Connerton (1989:44–45) in his comprehensive discussion of social memory and is discussed in relation to the continuation of ancient mortuary practices in the context of eastern Indonesia in this volume (see Adams and Kusumawati, chapter 2). Archaeologically, the remnants of this kind of behavior can range from ceramic pot fragments and food refuse found in front of tombs of the European Neolithic (Hayden 2003:232, 233; Sherratt 1991:56) to large *menhir* stones traditionally erected on the occasion of large funerals in the Torajan highlands of eastern Indonesia (Crystal 1974).

In contemporary North America, the issues associated with NAGPRA further illustrate the continued importance of ancestors and social memory to descendant communities. Aside from the complexities, difficulties, and conflicts that have arisen and are perhaps best illustrated in the controversy surrounding the handling of the remains of Kennewick man (Watkins 2004), the NAGPRA legislation underscores the continued importance of the deceased in the lives of the living. NAGPRA has forced a reconsideration of the dead in the United States by addressing the obligations the living have to the deceased and their descendant communities (Colquhoun 2000). By facilitating the repatriation and reburial of Native American human remains, NAGPRA is a contemporary example of the importance of social memory for the collective meanings and identities of groups. The respectful reburial of archaeological skeletal remains in contemporary North America has not been limited to Native American communities. Although not an example of residential burial, the African Burial Ground investigations and reburial in New York resulted in the reclaiming of a nearly lost aspect of African American history with the potential to enhance the collective social memory and identity of the descendant communities involved (Perry et al. 2006). Importantly, not all descendant communities approve of mortuary analyses involving their deceased ancestors, an issue the authors in this volume are mindful of when approaching and presenting mortuary data.

Residential burials in archaeological contexts, particularly those under house floors, have been considered to give clear indications of the importance of social memory and identity in a variety of contexts (e.g., Hodder and Cessford 2004; Joyce 1999; Kuijt 2001, 2008). The placement of burials in residential contexts can provide the living with a direct, ongoing connection to ancestors and a constant reminder of their place in what can be a long line of descendants originating from the founding ancestor of a household or larger group. Several chapters in this volume explore such issues related to social memory and how it is manifested in residential burial practices (particularly Adams and Kusumawati, chapter 2, and King, chapter 4). In prehistoric coastal Oaxaca, Mexico, King (chapter 4, this volume) explores the role of residential burial in the construction of social memory during the Early Postclassic period (C.E. 975–1220) and presents a case in which she argues that residential subfloor burials both reinforced the collective identity of social groups and memorialized individual ancestors. From an ethnoarchaeological perspective, Adams and Kusumawati (chapter 2, this volume) illustrate how the memorial aspects of residential burial can be entwined with practical sociopolitical concerns of individuals and groups in the context of the megalithic residential burial tradition in West Sumba, Indonesia.

Other forms of monumental burial, although not residential, also exemplify the link between the living and deceased forebears. Large Mississippian burial mounds of the U.S. Southeast considered to contain the remains of powerful lineages are a cornerstone for North American interpretations of chiefdom societies as markers of the location of dominant settlements and symbols of their power (Beck 2003; Blitz 1993, 1999; Steponaitis 1978, 1991). Similarly, many archaeologists over the years have interpreted megalithic tombs in western Europe to be particularly symbolic of descent groups (Powell 2005; Sjögren 1986) and markers of territories or resources (Chapman 1981, 1995; Lidén 1995; Madsen 1982; Renfrew 1976). Whittle et al. (2007) examined long barrow and long cairn burials of southern Britain in the fourth millennium B.C.E. considering both their commemorative significance in connecting the living with deceased ancestors and the specific meanings that monument form may have had in referencing a deeper past when long houses were first constructed. This connection is also addressed by Hodder (1984, 1990). Adams and Kusumawati (chapter 2, this volume) present a case in which residential burials in West Sumba, Indonesia, reach monumental proportions and elucidate the similarities in the social meanings conveyed between these more elaborate forms of residential burial and simpler forms of residential burial, such as subfloor interments.

Continuity and Integration of Social Groups

As an extension to social memory, burial and mortuary practice can foster the integration of individuals and related households that form social groups and the continuity of these groups through time. Geertz (1980:32) has argued that one of the important ways in which relations of kin are expressed is through "rights and obligations" associated with mortuary practices. Archaeologically, intramural burial placement has been interpreted as a defining characteristic of practices linked to rights of inheritance and membership in social groups (Gillespie 2002; McAnany 1995). Kuijt (2001) considered subfloor burial practices and patterns of architectural renovation, which included design standardization, as exemplifying the social continuity and integration of communities in an analysis of southern Levantine Pre-Pottery Neolithic mortuary practices. In reference to this mortuary tradition, Kuijt noted that "architecture was continually linked to mortuary practices through the placement of burials inside of residential structures, highlighting elements of continuity and standardization in the design of residential and nonresidential structures over multiple generations, and anchoring the architecture to the social landscape as a geographical focus of ritual action" (Kuijt 2001:93).

Hodder and Cessford (2004) examined residential burial within a larger discussion of daily practices, social memory, and the generation of a *habitus* (Bourdieu 1977) at Çatalhöyük. Drawing upon Connerton's (1989) theories concerning social memory, Hodder and Cessford (2004) suggested that the presence of subfloor burials and repetitive practices that referenced the past, such as the standardized rebuilding of houses over time, contributed to the generation of social memory. According to Hodder and Cessford (2004), subfloor burials at particular houses, repetitive practices concerned with social memory, and standardized rebuilding of houses through time are suggestive of the presence of house societies (Lévi-Strauss 1983). As such, each symbolically elaborated residential structure at Çatalhöyük was linked to a particular social group whose connections to others were created and strengthened through shared practices in architectural spaces. The link between residential burial and house societies at Çatalhöyük was further discussed by Düring (2007), who argued that the high concentrations of subfloor burials in the more elaborate houses at Çatalhöyük were indicative of the presence of structures that served as the focal ritual locales of house society groups.

Beyond Çatalhöyük, the house society model has been widely applied in analyses of prehistoric social organization (see Beck 2007; Joyce and Gillespie 2000). The house society, as an analytical category for classifying social structures, was developed by Claude Lévi-Strauss. Lévi-Strauss developed the category of house society as an alternative to more traditional categories of social groups, such as lineages and clans. In simple terms, house societies are social groups associated with "an estate made up of both material and immaterial wealth" that is perpetuated by the "transmission of its name, its goods, and its titles down a real or imaginary line" (Lévi-Strauss 1982:151). Unlike lineages and clans, house societies do not necessarily follow strict rules of descent and inheritance. Instead, a house society can have more flexible membership rules and entail both exogamy and endogamy as well as variability in postmarital residence (Gillespie 2000a:7; Helms 1998:15). Importantly, members are linked to a specific named house or physical architectural space that defines their relationship not only with others in their group but with other house society groups as well (Beck 2007:7).

The utility of the house society concept in archaeology derives, in part, from its emphasis on material culture (e.g., residential architecture, property and material goods, and burial) and repeated practices, both of which are evident in archaeological contexts. The model allows for flexibility in the composition of social groups, since house members need not be defined through kinship alone. Most importantly, the house society model explicitly connects material practices to forms of social organization. Residential burial is thus a common way that ideas about house origins, collective memory, and the temporal and spatial continuity of the house are communicated. Gillespie's (2000b, 2000c) examination of prehistoric house societies among the Maya illustrates how residential burial and associated rituals can enhance the connections between the living and the dead and integrate individuals tied to houses and house compounds. Borić (2007) suggested that residential burial served to shape collective identity and spatial continuity of house societies in the Mesolithic and early Neolithic of the Upper Gorge of the Danube (Borić and Stefanović 2004). In the U.S. Southwest, Heitman (2007) explored the applicability of the house society model to Pueblo Bonito by examining various architectural elements, such as the cyclical replastering of kiva murals and episodes of reflooring in the Great House, and burials housed in the oldest portion of the pueblo. Heitman suggested that these practices fostered an anchoring of place, ancestor reverence, and a concern for the collective memory of the pueblo. In a reinterpretation of large burials in Mississippian Etowah Mound C in Alabama, Brown (2007) used the house society model as a heuristic tool to show how the burial evidence points to the presence of multiple rival decent groups at the society's top level as opposed to the traditional interpretation that there was a single paramount chiefly lineage.

The majority of contributors in this volume expand the discussion of residential burial within house societies (see Adams and Kusumawati, chapter 2; Gillespie, chapter 7; Joyce, chapter 3; King, chapter 4; Sullivan and Rodning, chapter 6). King (chapter 4) puts particular emphasis on house society dynamics and their relation to residential burial in her discussion of the role of residential burial in the construction of social "house" histories during the Early Postclassic (C.E. 975–1220) of Oaxaca. King argues that subfloor burials reinforced a collective identity and memory of house-based groups. Among these burials is variability in treatment of the deceased, whereby only adults were buried beneath house floors. The lack of children in subfloor burials, according to King, is indicative of a scenario in which full-fledged membership in certain houses was potentially age-dependent and only adults were able to serve as house ancestors and have access to rights and property of the house. The standardization associated with subfloor burials in terms of both placement and grave goods is also highly suggestive of a concern for maintaining the collective identity of houses, while individual ancestors were celebrated by giving them exclusive burial locations undisturbed by later interments. King argues that in this way residential burial commemorated specific and generalized ancestors at the same time and marked the house as the appropriate medium for individual and collective social practice.

Landscapes and Mortuary Practice

Apart from the obvious connection between the living and the dead manifested in residential burial, the practice is unique in terms of the cultural landscape that it creates. Analyses of prehistoric landscapes in relation to burial have for many years aided the development of theories related to the dynamics of complex Mississippian societies of the U.S. Southeast (Brown et al. 1978; Scarry 1996; Steponaitis 1978, 1991) and Neolithic Europe (Chapman 1981, 1995; Madsen 1982; Renfrew 1976). Regional analyses of broad patterns of sociopolitical development have continued to shape many archaeological studies of landscape (e.g., Martindale and Supernant 2009; Mizoguchi 2009; Munson and Macri 2009; Peterson and Drennan 2005; see also Rodning 2010). Archaeological studies utilizing a landscape approach have also begun to emphasize the way in which prehistoric people experienced and shaped their surroundings from a more symbolic perspective (Ashmore and Knapp 1999; Rodning 2010; Thomas 1999; Van Dyke 2003). This approach to cultural landscapes has highlighted the many ways that values, beliefs, and social entanglements can shape the way in which people perceive landscape (Bender 1998; Bender et al. 1997; Fowles 2009; Thomas 1999; Wesson 1998). In relation to the placement of the dead, such methods of analysis have led to a focus on the importance of the connections between the past and the present in terms of social reproduction as well as the materialization of kinship rights to property (Buikstra and Charles 1999; Parker Pearson 1999:124; Philip 2003:119, 122). A landscape approach to burial patterning has also been shown to illuminate the gender roles within prehistoric societies (Rodning 2001; Sullivan 2001). In some contexts, burials have been interpreted as creating a landscape of the dead symbolically distinct from the landscape of the living (Parker Pearson and Ramilisonina 1998). Residential burial connects the domains of the living and the dead in a unique landscape that forces archaeologists to consider the entanglements of the living and their deceased forebears.

The volume authors set out to make sense of this unique landscape and thereby expand the discussion of residential burial by looking at residential mortuary practices in geographically dispersed locales, while exploring new theoretical perspectives and broadening the scope of existing interpretations. Above all, the authors in this volume expose the varying reasons for and implications of residential burial in diverse settings and connect these practices to distinct historically specific traditions and changing sociopolitical structures in everyday social landscapes. Sullivan and Rodning (chapter 6, this volume) offer a specific examination of burial in relation to the larger cultural landscape in the context of the southern Appalachian region of North America during the mid-second millennium C.E. During this time, male burials tended to be situated in the public settings of platform mounds, while burials of women were more commonly placed within residences. Sullivan and Rodning demonstrate how this pattern of burial placement is indicative of women's leadership roles within house-based clan structures and men's roles as warriors and brokers of intercommunity relations and trade, while challenging the traditional view that only male roles were associated with social dominance and power in this context.

Likewise, White and Eyre (chapter 5, this volume) take a renewed look at the spatial patterning of burials in Metal Age Thailand (ca. 2000 B.C.E. to C.E. 500) and challenge previously held notions of burial and social structure. Contrary to traditional archaeological interpretations of Metal Age Thailand that have been grounded in the notion that the dead were buried in cemeteries, White and Eyre present evidence indicating that residential burial was also a common practice during this time. According to White and Eyre, this evidence forces not only a reinterpretation of Metal Age burial practices, but also a reevaluation of the social dynamics that are thought to have been in place during the Metal Age. White and Eyre argue for the existence of a social order characterized by heterarchy and group-oriented, corporate political dynamics that contrasts with the traditional view of the Metal Age as a time of hierarchical forms of sociopolitical organization in Thailand.

Diachronic Considerations

It has become an old adage that one of the benefits of archaeology as a subfield of anthropology is in its potential to analyze societal change over long periods of time. This diachronic orientation is at the heart of the field and is reflected in the organization of innumerable textbooks and works dealing with regional overviews. Archaeologists have frequently looked to burial in the analysis of macro-level changes in prehistoric societal organization, such as the emergence of particularly elaborate monumental burial practices as an indication of the emergence of new social orders (e.g., Bradley 1998; Hodder 1990; Mizoguchi 2002; Nelson 1999; Sherratt 1990, 1995; Steponaitis 1978). In residential burial contexts, significant changes in social structures have also been considered to accompany a shift in burial practices. For instance, the Argaric period (2250/200–1500 cal B.C.E) in southeastern Spain is marked by a shift from nonresidential, monumental communal burials of the earlier Copper Age to burials beneath the floors and within the walls of individual houses. This change in funerary customs is considered to have accompanied a change from a society in which social identity and power were associated with competing lineage groups to a more hierarchical society in which power was consolidated in a politically and economically dominant elite class, reflected in clear indications of wealth disparities between houses, and identity was based on membership in nuclear families (Chapman 1990, 2005, 2007; Lull 2000).

In this volume, essays by Joyce (chapter 3) and Laneri (chapter 8) also examine the emergence of residential forms of burial from other, earlier types of burial. Joyce explores the origins of residential burial in prehispanic Honduras. According to Joyce, the importance of residential burial in shaping identities and naturalizing claims to differential social status does not necessarily implicate these factors as being present in the minds of those who made the conscious decision to inter the deceased within their residences. To more closely examine the origins of residential burial, Joyce offers a long-term historical perspective on funerary practices at the site of Puerto Escondido in Honduras, where there is evidence for occupation extending from before 1600 B.C.E. to after C.E. 450. She shows that pre-residential burial practices at Puerto Escondido contain similar elements to those that were present when residential burial was adopted, including incorporation, disjunction, and commemoration. Incorporation refers to activities such as the caching of body ornamentation beneath house floors, which brings materials into constructed spaces. Disjunction refers to the separation of items from their surroundings and their placement in different locations (e.g., the placement of body ornaments in subfloor caches). Activities associated with commemoration are those that are consciously undertaken to evoke memories, such as rebuilding structures in the same locations. The long-term acceptance of practices of incorporation, disjunction, and commemoration at Puerto Escondido, according to Joyce, allowed for the ease with which these practices became associated with and incorporated into residential burial.

Nicola Laneri takes the discussion of residential burial to Mesopotamia in the third millennium B.C.E. with data from the site of Titriş Höyük in southeastern Turkey. It is during this time that very significant changes occurred in the socioeconomic landscape of the region that coincided with a shift from funerary customs associated with extramural cemeteries and mausolea to intramural tombs within private dwellings, palaces, and temples. According to Laneri, this change in burial practices was vital to the power consolidation of emerging elites during the mid-late third and early second millennia B.C.E. of Mesopotamia. Laneri offers a sociohistorical perspective on the subject and references the broader patterns throughout the region in which funerary practices and economic subsistence are viewed as being the result of long-term transformations in production and consumption.

Dealing with much smaller time scales, Adams and Kusumawati (chapter 2, this volume) explore the nuanced changes in the meanings that burials have over time to living people in their ethnoarchaeological study of residential tombs in West Sumba, Indonesia. Employing a biographical perspective, Adams and Kusumawati reveal a complexity attached to the emblemic significance of residential tombs that can undergo shifts in meaning from the time the tombs are erected to the time when they become long-lasting monuments, depending on the perspective of the agents involved in their creation. While initially tombs are primarily symbols of the power of individuals and clan groups, the monuments' significance in terms of the social memory of clan groups grows through time as they become not only symbols of power but also testimonials to prominent ancestors and the long-term continuity of groups.

Volume Organization and Goals

Within this overall framework of exploring the links between the living and the dead in residential burial, the chapters of this volume cover a great deal of contextual and theoretical variability. The goal of the volume is to advance the discussion of residential burial and give it deserved consideration as a central topic in current discussions of mortuary archaeology and anthropology. The case studies open with a discussion of the living residential burial tradition in West Sumba, Indonesia (Adams and Kusumawati, chapter 2), followed by an analysis of the origins of residential burial practices in prehispanic Honduras (Joyce, chapter 3). From these chapters dealing with the persistence of the practice in one context and its origin in another, the discussions shift to prehistoric settings in Postclassic Oaxaca, Mexico (King, chapter 4), Metal Age Thailand (White and Eyre, chapter 5), late prehistoric and early Cherokee cultures of the Southern Appalachians (Sullivan and Rodning, chapter 6), Formative period Chalcatzingo, Mexico (Gillespie, chapter 7), and ancient Mesopotamia (Laneri, chapter 8). Patricia McAnany (chapter 9) concludes the volume with a discussion of theoretical approaches to residential burial and the different kinds of residential burial presented in this volume. McAnany summarizes the themes that are addressed in this volume that cross-cut the variations in residential burial in case studies from across the globe and through time. She also provides a commentary on the successes and failures of these approaches, and helps to evaluate the contribution of this volume within mortuary archaeology.

In spite of the diversity of regions, years, and perspectives represented by the volume authors, all have a common belief that residential burial practices offer unique insights into how people in the past and in the contemporary world perceived and continue to perceive their relationships with their deceased ancestors and with one another. The authors are also united by the belief that a synthesis of the subject of residential burial is overdue and particularly relevant to many of the current discussions within archaeology and anthropology. It is hoped that this volume will inspire new ideas and further research into this important topic.

References

Adams, Ron L.
2004 An Ethnoarchaeological Study of Feasting in Sulawesi, Indonesia. Journal of Anthropological Archaeology 23:56–78.

Akins, Nancy
2003 The Burials of Pueblo Bonito. *In* Pueblo Bonito: Center of the Chacoan World. Jill E. Neitzel, ed. Pp. 94–106. Washington, DC: Smithsonian Institution Press.

Ashmore, Wendy, and Pamela L. Geller
2005 Social Dimensions of Mortuary Space. *In* Interacting with the Dead: Perspectives on Mortuary Archaeology for the New Millennium. Gordon F. M. Rakita, Jane E. Buikstra, Lane A. Beck, and Sloan R. Williams, eds. Pp. 81–92. Gainesville: University Press of Florida.

Ashmore, Wendy, and A. Bernard Knapp, eds.
1999 Archaeologies of Landscape: Contemporary Perspectives. Oxford: Blackwell.

Beck, Robin A., Jr.
2003 Consolidation and Hierarchy: Chiefdom Variability in the Mississippian Southeast. American Antiquity 68:641–661.
2007 The Durable House: Material, Metaphor, and Structure. *In* The Durable House: House Society Models in Archaeology. Robin A. Beck Jr., ed. Pp. 3–24. Occasional Paper 35. Carbondale: Center for Archaeological Investigations, Southern Illinois University.

Bender, Barbara, with Paul Aitken
1998 Stonehenge: Making Space. Oxford: Berg.

Bender, Barbara, Sue Hamilton, and Christopher Tilley
1997 Leskernick: Stone Worlds; Alternative Narratives; Nested Landscapes. Proceedings of the Prehistoric Society 63:147–178.

Berreman, Gerald D.
1981 Social Inequality: A Cross-Cultural Analysis. *In* Social Inequality: Comparative and Developmental Approaches. Gerald D. Berreman, ed. Pp. 3–40. New York: Academic.

Binford, Lewis R.
1971 Mortuary Practices: Their Study and Their Potential. *In* Approaches to the Social Dimensions of Mortuary Practices. James A. Brown, ed. Pp. 6–29. Memoirs of the Society for American Archaeology, 25. Washington, DC.

Blitz, John H.
1993 Ancient Chiefdoms of the Tombigbee. University of Alabama Press, Tuscaloosa.
1999 Mississippian Chiefdoms and the Fission-Fusion Process. American Antiquity 64:577–592.

Bond, George
1987 Ancestors and Protestants: Religious Coexistence in the Social Field of a Zambian Community. American Ethnologist 14:55–72.

Borić, Dušan
2007 The House Between Grand Narrative and Microhistory: A House Society in the Balkans. *In* The Durable House: House Society Models in Archaeology. Robin A. Beck Jr., ed. Pp. 97–129. Occasional Paper 35. Carbondale: Center for Archaeological Investigations, Southern Illinois University.

Borić, Dušan, and Sofija Stefanović
2004 Birth and Death: Infant Burials from Vlasac and Lepenski Vir. Antiquity 78:526–546.

Bourdieu, Pierre
1977 Outline of a Theory of Practice. Cambridge: Cambridge University Press.

Bradley, Richard
1998 The Significance of Monuments: On the Shaping of Human Experience in Neolithic and Bronze Age Europe. London: Routledge.

Brown, James A.
2007 The Social House in Southeastern Archaeology. *In* The Durable House: House Society Models in Archaeology. Robin A. Beck Jr., ed. Pp. 227–247. Occasional Paper 35. Carbondale: Center for Archaeological Investigations, Southern Illinois University.

Brown, James A., Robert E. Bell, and Don E. Wyckoff
1978 Caddoan Settlement Patterns in the Arkansas River Drainage. *In* Mississippian Settlement Patterns. Bruce D. Smith, ed. Pp. 169–200. New York: Academic.

Buikstra, Jane E., and Douglas K. Charles
1999 Centering the Ancestors: Cemeteries, Mounds and Sacred Landscapes of the Ancient North American

Midcontinent. *In* Archaeologies of Landscape: Contemporary Perspectives. Wendy Ashmore and A. Bernard Knapp, eds. Pp. 201–228. Oxford: Blackwell.

Cannon, Aubrey
1989 The Historical Dimension in Mortuary Expressions of Status and Sentiment. Current Anthropology 30:437–458.

Carr, C.
1995 Mortuary Practices: Their Social, Philosophical-Religious, Circumstantial, and Physical Determinants. Journal of Archaeological Method and Theory 2:105–200.

Chapman, Robert
1981 Archaeological Theory and Communal Burial in Prehistoric Europe. *In* Patterns of the Past: Studies in Honor of David Clarke. Ian Hodder, Glynn Isaac, and Norman Hammond, eds. Pp. 387–411. Cambridge: Cambridge University Press.
1990 Emerging Complexity: The Later Prehistory of South-east Spain, Iberia and the West Mediterranean. Cambridge: Cambridge University Press.
1995 Ten Years After—Megaliths, Mortuary Practices, and the Territorial Model. *In* Regional Approaches to Mortuary Analysis. Lane Anderson Beck, ed. Pp. 29–51. New York: Plenum.
2005 Mortuary Analysis: A Matter of Time? *In* Interacting with the Dead: Perspectives on Mortuary Archaeology for the New Millennium. Gordon F. M. Rakita, Jane E. Buikstra, Lane A. Beck, and Sloan R. Williams, eds. Pp. 25–40. Gainesville: University Press of Florida.
2007 Mortuary Rituals, Social Relations, and Identity in Southeast Spain in the Late Third to Early Second Millennia B.C. *In* Performing Death: Social Analyses of Funerary Traditions in the Ancient Near East and Mediterranean. Nicola Laneri, ed. Pp. 69–79. Oriental Institute Seminars 3. Chicago: Oriental Institute.

Chesson, Meredith S.
1999 Libraries of the Dead: Early Bronze Age Charnel Houses and Social Identity at Urban Bab edh-Dhra', Jordan. Journal of Anthropological Archaeology 18:137–164.

Chesson, Meredith S., ed.
2001 Social Memory, Identity, and Death: Anthropological Perspectives on Mortuary Rituals. Archeological Papers of the American Anthropological Association, 10. Arlington, VA: American Anthropological Association.

Clarke, Michael J.
2001 Akha Feasting: An Ethnoarchaeological Perspective. *In* Feasts: Archaeological and Ethnographic Perspectives on Food, Politics, and Power. Michael Dietler and Brian Hayden, eds. Pp. 144–167. Washington, DC: Smithsonian Institution Press.

Colquhoun, Justin
2000 Reburying the Dead: The Effects of NAGPRA on Our Relationships and Obligations to the Deceased. Anthropology of Consciousness 11(1–2):64–69.

Connerton, Paul
1989 How Societies Remember. Cambridge: Cambridge University Press.

Crystal, Eric
1974 Man and the Menhir: Contemporary Megalithic Practice of the Sa'dan Toraja of Sulawesi, Indonesia. *In* Ethnoarchaeology. Christopher B. Donnan and C. William Clewlow Jr., eds. Pp. 117–128. Los Angeles: Institute of Archaeology, University of California.

Düring, Bleda S.
2005 Building Continuity in the Central Anatolian Neolithic: Exploring the Meaning of Buildings at Aşikli Höyük and Çatalhöyük. Journal of Mediterranean Archaeology 18(1):3–29.
2007 The Articulation of Houses at Neolithic Çatalhöyük, Turkey. *In* The Durable House: House Society Models in Archaeology. Robin A. Beck Jr., ed. Pp. 130–153. Occasional Paper 35. Carbondale: Center for Archaeological Investigations, Southern Illinois University.

Flanagan, James G.
1989 Hierarchy in Simple "Egalitarian" Societies. Annual Review of Anthropology 18:245–266.

Flanagan, James G., and Steve Rayner, eds.
1988 Rules, Decisions, and Inequality in Egalitarian Societies. London: Gower.

Flemming, Andrew
1973 Tombs for the Living. Man 8(2):178–193.

Fowles, Severin M.
2009 The Enshrined Pueblo: Villagescape and Cosmos in the Northern Rio Grande. American Antiquity 74:448–466.

Geertz, Clifford
1980 Negara: The Theatre State in Nineteenth-Century Bali. Princeton, NJ: Princeton University Press.

Gerlach, Luther P., and Ursula M. Gerlach
1988 Egalitarianism, Collectivism, and Individualism: The Digo of Kenya. *In* Rules, Decisions, and Inequality in Egalitarian Societies. James G. Flanagan and Steve Rayner, eds. Pp. 113–144. London: Gower.

Gillespie, Susan D.
2000a Beyond Kinship: An Introduction. *In* Beyond Kinship: Social and Material Reproduction in House Societies. Rosemary A. Joyce and Susan D. Gillespie, eds. Pp. 1–21. Philadelphia: University of Pennsylvania Press.
2000b Maya "Nested Houses": The Ritual Construction of Place. *In* Beyond Kinship: Social and Material Reproduction in House Societies. Rosemary A. Joyce and Susan D. Gillespie, eds. Pp. 135–160. Philadelphia: University of Pennsylvania Press.
2000c Rethinking Ancient Maya Social Organization: Replacing "Lineage" with "House." American Anthropologist 102:467–484.
2001 Personhood, Agency, and Mortuary Ritual: A Case Study from the Ancient Maya. Journal of Anthropological Archaeology 20:73–112.
2002 Body and Soul among the Maya: Keeping the Spirits in Place. *In* The Space and Place of Death. Helaine Silverman and David B. Small, eds. Pp. 67–78. Archeological Papers of the American Anthropological Association, 11. Arlington, VA: American Anthropological Association.

Goldstein, Lynne G.
1980 Mississippian Mortuary Practices: A Case Study of Two Cemeteries in the Lower Illinois Valley. Scientific Papers 4. Evanston, IL: Northwestern University Archaeological Program.

Gummerman, George, IV
2004 Big Hearths and Big Pots: Moche Feasting on the North Coast of Peru. Paper presented at the Annual Meeting of the Society for American Archaeology, Montreal, March 31–April 4.

Hastorf, Christine
2003 Andean Luxury Foods: Special Food for the Ancestors, Deities and the Elite. Antiquity 77:545–554.

Hayden, Brian
2003 Shamans, Sorcerers and Saints: A Prehistory of Religion. Washington, DC: Smithsonian Books.
2009 Funeral Feasts: Why Are They so Important. Cambridge Archaeological Journal 19(1):29–52.

Hayden, Brian, and Suzanne Villeneuve.
N.d. Preliminary Report on Feasting in Futuna. http://www.sfu.ca/archaeology/dept/fac_bio/hayden/reports/futuna.pdf, accessed August 17, 2008.

Heitman, Carrie C.
2007 Houses Great and Small: Reevaluating the "House" in Chaco Canyon, New Mexico. *In* The Durable House: House Society Models in Archaeology. Robin A. Beck Jr., ed. Pp. 248–272. Occasional Paper 35. Carbondale: Center for Archaeological Investigations, Southern Illinois University.

Helms, Mary
1998 Access to Origins: Affines, Ancestors and Aristocrats. Austin: University of Texas Press.

Hodder, Ian
1982 Symbols in Action. Cambridge: Cambridge University Press.
1984 Burials, Houses, Women and Men in the European Neolithic. *In* Ideology, Power and Prehistory. Daniel Miller and Christopher Tilley, eds. Pp. 51–68. Cambridge: Cambridge University Press.
1990 The Domestication of Europe: Structure and Contingency in Neolithic Societies. Oxford: Basil Blackwell.
1994 Architecture and Meaning: The Example of Neolithic Houses and Tombs. *In* Architecture and Order: Approaches to Social Space. Michael

Parker Pearson and Colin Richards, eds. Pp. 73–86. London: Routledge.

Hodder, Ian, and Craig Cessford
2004 Daily Practice and Social Memory at Çatalhöyük. American Antiquity 69:17–40.

Humphreys, S. C.
1981 Introduction: Comparative Perspectives on Death. *In* Mortality and Immortality: The Anthropology and Archaeology of Death. S. C. Humphreys and Helen King, eds. Pp. 1–13. London: Academic.

Joyce, Rosemary A.
1999 Social Dimensions of Pre-Classic Burials. *In* Social Patterns in Pre-Classic Mesoamerica. David C. Grove and Rosemary A. Joyce, eds. Pp. 15–47. Washington, DC: Dumbarton Oaks.

Joyce, Rosemary A., and Susan D. Gillespie, eds.
2000 Beyond Kinship: Social and Material Reproduction in House Societies. Philadelphia: University of Pennsylvania Press.

Kenyon, Kathleen M.
1981 The Architecture and Stratigraphy of the Tell, vol. 3: Excavations at Jericho. T. Holland, ed. London: British School of Archaeology.

Kroeber, Alfred L.
1927 Disposal of the Dead. American Anthropologist 29:308–315.

Kuijt, Ian
2000 Keeping the Peace: Ritual, Skull Caching, and Community Integration in the Levantine Neolithic. *In* Life in Neolithic Farming Communities: Social Organization, Identity, and Differentiation. Ian Kuijt, ed. Pp. 137–164. New York: Kluwer Academic.
2001 Place, Death, and the Transmission of Social Memory in Early Agricultural Communities of the Near Eastern Pre-Pottery Neolithic. *In* Social Memory, Identity, and Death: Anthropological Perspectives on Mortuary Rituals. Meredith S. Chesson, ed. Pp. 80–99. Archeological Papers of the American Anthropological Association, 10. Arlington, VA: American Anthropological Association.
2008 The Regeneration of Life: Neolithic Structures of Symbolic Remembering and Forgetting. Current Anthropology 49:171–197.

Kuipers, Joel
1990 Power in Performance: The Creation of Textual Authority in Weyewa Ritual Speech. Philadelphia: University of Pennsylvania Press.

Laneri, Nicola
1999 Intramural Tombs: A Funerary Tradition in the Middle Euphrates Valley during the IIIrd Millennium B.C. Anatolica 25:221–241.

Laneri, Nicola, ed.
2007 Performing Death: Social Analyses of Funerary Traditions in the Ancient Near East and Mediterranean. Oriental Institute Seminars 3. Chicago: Oriental Institute.

Lau, George
2002 Feasting and Ancestor Veneration at Chinchawas, North Highlands of Ancash, Peru. Latin American Antiquity 13:279–304.

Lévi-Strauss, Claude
1982 The Way of the Masks. Sylvia Modelski, trans. Seattle: University of Washington Press.
1983 The Way of the Masks. London: Jonathan Cape.

Lewis, Theodore J.
1989 Cults of the Dead in Ancient Israel and Ugarit. Harvard Semitic Monographs 39. Atlanta: Scholars Press.

Lidén, Kerstin
1995 Megaliths, Agriculture, and Social Complexity: A Diet Study of Two Swedish Megalith Populations. Journal of Anthropological Archaeology 14:404–417.

Lull, Vicente
2000 Argaric Society: Death at Home. Antiquity 74:581–590.

McAnany, Patricia A.
1995 Living with the Ancestors: Kinship and Kingship in Ancient Maya Society. Austin: University of Texas Press.

McGuire, Randall H.
1983 Breaking Down Cultural Complexity: Inequality and Heterogeneity. Advances in Archaeological Method and Theory 6:91–142.

McKinnon, Susan
1991 From a Shattered Sun: Hierarchy, Gender, and Alliance in the Tanimbar Islands. Madison: University of Wisconsin Press.
1995 Houses and Hierarchy: The View from a South Moluccan Society. *In* About the House: Lévi-Strauss and Beyond. Janet Carsten and Stephen Hugh-Jones, eds. Pp. 170–188. Cambridge: Cambridge University Press.

Madsen, Torsten
1982 Settlement Systems of Early Agricultural Societies of East Jutland, Denmark: A Regional Study of Change. Journal of Anthropological Archaeology 1:197–236.

Martindale, Andrew, and Kisha Supernant
2009 Quantifying the Defensiveness of Defended Sites on the Northwestern Coast of North America. Journal of Anthropological Archaeology 28:191–204.

Metcalf, Peter, and Richard Huntington
1991 Celebrations of Death: The Anthropology of Mortuary Ritual. 2nd edition. Cambridge: Cambridge University Press.

Mizoguchi, Koji
2002 An Archaeological History of Japan: 30,000 B.C. to A.D. 700. Philadelphia: University of Pennsylvania Press.
2009 Nodes and Edges: A Network Approach to Hierarchisation and State Formation in Japan. Journal of Anthropological Archaeology 28:14–26.

Morris, Ellen F.
2007 Sacrifice for the State: First Dynasty Royal Funerals and the Rites at Macramallah's Rectangle. *In* Performing Death: Social Analyses of Funerary Traditions in the Ancient Near East and Mediterranean. Nicola Laneri, ed. Pp. 15–37. Oriental Institute Seminars 3. Chicago: Oriental Institute.

Morris, Ian
1987 Burial and Ancient Society: The Rise of the Greek City-State. Cambridge: Cambridge University Press.
1991 The Archaeology of Ancestors: The Saxe/Goldstein Hypothesis Revisited. Cambridge Archaeological Journal 1:147–169.

Munson, Jessica L., and Martha J. Macri
2009 Sociopolitical Network Interactions: A Case Study of the Classic Maya. Journal of Anthropological Archaeology 28:424–438.

Nelson, Sarah Milledge
1999 Megalithic Monuments and the Introduction of Rice into Korea. *In* The Prehistory of Food: Appetites for Change. Chris Gosden and Jon Hather, eds. Pp. 147–165. New York: Routledge.

Parker Pearson, Mike
1982 Mortuary Practices, Society, and Ideology: An Ethnoarchaeological Study. *In* Symbolic and Structural Archaeology. Ian Hodder, ed. Pp. 99–113. Cambridge University Press, Cambridge.
1999 The Archaeology of Death and Burial. College Station: Texas A&M University Press.

Parker Pearson, Mike, and Ramilisonina
1998 Stonehenge for the Ancestors: The Stones Pass on the Message. Antiquity 72:308–326.

Paynter, Robert
1989 The Archaeology of Equality and Inequality. Annual Review of Anthropology 18:369–399.

Peebles, Christopher S., and Susan M. Kus
1977 Some Archaeological Correlates of Ranked Societies. American Antiquity 42:421–448.

Perodie, James R.
2001 Feasting for Prosperity: A Study of Southern Northwest Coast Feasting. *In* Feasts: Archaeological and Ethnographic Perspectives on Food, Politics, and Power. Michael Dietler and Brian Hayden, eds. Pp. 185–214. Washington, DC: Smithsonian Institution Press.

Perry, Warren R., Jean Howson, and Barbara A. Bianco, eds.
2006 New York African Burial Ground Archaeology Final Report, vol. 1. Prepared for the United

States General Services Administration Northeastern and Caribbean Region. Washington, DC: Howard University.

Peterson, Christian E., and Robert D. Drennan
2005 Communities, Settlements, Sites, and Survey: Regional-Scale Analysis of Prehistoric Human Interaction. American Antiquity 70:5–30.

Philip, Graham
2003 The Early Bronze Age of the Southern Levant: A Landscape Approach. Journal of Mediterranean Archaeology 16(1):103–132.

Pollock, Susan
1999 Ancient Mesopotamia: The Eden That Never Was. Case Studies in Early Societies. Cambridge: Cambridge University Press.
2007 Death of a Household. *In* Performing Death: Social Analyses of Funerary Traditions in the Ancient Near East and Mediterranean. Nicola Laneri, ed. Pp. 209–222. Oriental Institute Seminars 3. Chicago: Oriental Institute.

Powell, Andrew B.
2005 The Language of Lineage: Reading Irish Court Tomb Design. European Journal of Archaeology 8(1):9–28.

Raharijaona, Victor, and Susan Kus
2001 Matters of Life and Death: Mortuary Rituals as Part of a Larger Whole among the Betsileo of Madagascar. *In* Social Memory, Identity, and Death: Anthropological Perspectives on Mortuary Rituals. Meredith S. Chesson, ed. Pp. 56–68. Archeological Papers of the American Anthropological Association, 10. Arlington, VA: American Anthropological Association.

Rakita, Gordon F. M., and Jane E. Buikstra
2005 Introduction. *In* Interacting with the Dead: Perspectives on Mortuary Archaeology for the New Millennium. Gordon F. M. Rakita, Jane E. Buikstra, Lane A. Beck, and Sloan R. Williams, eds. Pp. 1–11. Gainesville: University Press of Florida.

Rayner, Steve
1988 The Rules That Keep Us Equal: Complexity and Costs of Egalitarian Organization. *In* Rules, Decisions, and Inequality in Egalitarian Societies. James G. Flanagan and Steve Rayner, eds. Pp. 20–42. London: Gower.

Renfrew, Colin
1973 Monuments, Mobilization and Social Organization in Neolithic Wessex. *In* The Explanation of Culture Change. Models in Prehistory. Colin Renfrew, ed. Pp. 539–558. London: Duckworth.
1976 Megaliths, Territories and Populations. *In* Acculturation and Continuity in Atlantic Europe. Dissertationes Archaeologicae Gandenses 16:198–220.

Richardson, Seth.
1999–2001 An Assyrian Garden of Ancestors: Room 1, Northwest Palace, Kalhu. State Archives of Assyrian Bulletin 13:145–216.

Rodning, Christopher
2001 Mortuary Ritual and Gender Ideology in Protohistoric Southwestern North Carolina. *In* Archaeological Studies of Gender in the Southeastern United States. Jane M. Eastman and Christopher B. Rodning, eds. Pp. 77–100. Gainesville: University Press of Florida.
2010 Place, Landscape, and Environment: Anthropological Archaeology in 2009. American Anthropologist 112:180–190.

Rollefson, Gary O.
1983 Ritual Ceremony at Neolithic Ain Ghazal (Jordan). Paléorient 9(2):29–37.
1986 Neolithic Ain Ghazal (Jordan): Ritual and Ceremony, II. Paléorient 12(1):45–52.

Saxe, Arthur A.
1970 Social Dimensions of Mortuary Practices. Ph.D. dissertation, Department of Anthropology, University of Michigan.

Scarry, John F.
1996 Stability and Change in the Apalachee Chiefdom: Centralization, Decentralization, and Social Reproduction. *In* Political Structure and Change in the Prehistoric Southeastern United States. John F. Scarry, ed. Pp. 192–227. Gainesville: University Press of Florida.

Schiller, Anne
1997 Small Sacrifices: Religious Change and Cultural Identity among the Ngaju of Indonesia. New York: Oxford University Press.

Schwartz, Glenn M.
2007 Status, Ideology, and Memory in Third-Millennium Syria: "Royal" Tombs at Umm El-Marra. *In* Performing Death: Social Analyses of Funerary Traditions in the Ancient Near East and Mediterranean. Nicola Laneri, ed. Pp. 39–68. Oriental Institute Seminars 3. Chicago: Oriental Institute.

Sherratt, Andrew
1990 The Genesis of Megaliths: Monumentality, Ethnicity and Social Complexity in Neolithic North-west Europe. World Archaeology 22:147–167.
1991 Sacred and Profane Substances: The Ritual Use of Narcotics in Later Neolithic Europe. *In* Sacred and Profane. Paul Garwood, David Jennings, R. G. Skeates, and Judith Toms, eds. Pp. 50–64. Oxford: Institute of Archaeology.
1995 Instruments of Conversion? The Role of Megaliths in the Mesolithic/Neolithic Transition in North-west Europe. Oxford Journal of Archaeology 14:245–260.

Shimada, Izumi, Ken-ichi Shinoda, Julie Farnum, Robert Corruccini, and Hirokatsu Watanabe
2004 An Integrated Analysis of Pre-Hispanic Mortuary Practices. Current Anthropology 45:369–395.

Silverman, Helaine, and David B. Small, eds.
2002 The Space and Place of Death. Archeological Papers of the American Anthropological Association, 11. Arlington, VA: American Anthropological Association.

Sjögren, Karl-Göran
1986 Kinship, Labour and Land in Neolithic Southwest Sweden: Social Aspects of Megalith Graves. Journal of Anthropological Archaeology 5:229–265.

Steponaitis, Vincas P.
1978 Location Theory and Complex Chiefdoms: A Mississippian Example. *In* Mississippian Settlement Patterns. Bruce D. Smith, ed. Pp. 417–453. New York: Academic.
1991 Contrasting Patterns of Mississippian Development. *In* Chiefdoms: Power, Economy, and Ideology. Timothy K. Earle, ed. Pp. 417–454. Cambridge: Cambridge University Press.

Sullivan, Lynne P.
2001 Those Men in the Mounds: Gender, Politics, and Mortuary Practices in Late Prehistoric Eastern Tennessee. *In* Archaeological Studies of Gender in the Southeastern United States. Jane M. Eastman and Christopher B. Rodning, eds. Pp. 101–126. Gainesville: University Press of Florida.

Thomas, Julian
1999 Understanding the Neolithic. Rev. 2nd edition of Rethinking the Neolithic. London: Routledge.

Ucko, Peter J.
1969 Ethnography and Archaeological Interpretations of Funerary Remains. World Archaeology 1:262–280.

Van Dyke, Ruth M.
2003 Memory and the Construction of Chacoan Society. *In* Archaeologies of Memory. Ruth M. Van Dyke and Susan E. Alcock, eds. Pp. 180–200. Oxford: Blackwell.
2004 Memory, Meaning, and Masonry: The Late Bonito Chacoan Landscape. American Antiquity 69:413–431.

Van Dyke, Ruth M. and Susan E. Alcock
2003 Archaeologies of Memory: An Introduction. *In* Archaeologies of Memory. Ruth M. Van Dyke and Susan E. Alcock, eds. Pp. 1–13. Oxford: Blackwell.

Watkins, Joe
2004 Becoming American or Becoming Indian? NAGPRA, Kennewick, and Cultural Affiliation. Journal of Social Archaeology 4(1):60–80.

Wesson, Cameron B.
1998 Mississippian Sacred Landscapes: The View from Alabama. *In* Mississippian Towns and Sacred Spaces: Searching for an Architectural Grammar. R. Barry Lewis and Charles Stout, eds. Pp. 93–122. Tuscaloosa: University of Alabama Press.

Whittle, Alasdair, Alistair Barclay, Alex Bayliss, Lesley McFadyen, Rick Schulting, and Michael Wysocki
2007 Building for the Dead: Events, Processes and Changing Worldviews from the Thirty-eighth to the Thirty-fourth Centuries cal. BC in Southern Britain. Cambridge Archaeological Journal 17(1):123–147.

Williams, Howard
2004 Death Warmed Up: The Agency of Bodies and Bones in Early Anglo Saxon Cremation Rites. Journal of Material Culture 9:263–291.

2

The Social Life of Tombs in West Sumba, Indonesia

Ron L. Adams
Simon Fraser University
and
Ayu Kusumawati
Balai Arkeologi Denpasar

ABSTRACT

Ethnoarchaeological examination of the contemporary practice of erecting stone tombs within residential compounds in West Sumba, Indonesia provides important insights into active social processes that can be associated with residential burials. Residential tombs in West Sumba reach megalithic proportions and convey not only links to past ancestors but also social dynamics associated with power negotiation, achievement, and the continuity of living groups. This study of residential burial and tomb-building in West Sumba reveals actively changing and multifaceted social meanings linked to tombs as well as commonalities shared by both residential and monumental burials with intriguing implications for prehistoric mortuary practices. [burial, social memory, power, ethnoarchaeology, megaliths]

The analysis of burials in prehistoric residential contexts (i.e., residential burials) has the potential to illuminate a wide variety of social concerns. Archaeologists have often considered residential burials (particularly burials under the floors of houses) to be linked to the importance of social reproduction, land inheritance, and the long-term maintenance of social groups (e.g., Kenyon 1981; Kuijt 2001, 2008; Rollefson 1983, 1986). As social memory is an integral part of social reproduction, many researchers have considered its importance (Connerton 1989) in relation to prehistoric residential burials (e.g., Hodder and Cessford 2004; King, chapter 4, this volume) and mortuary practices in general (see Chesson 2001; Jonker 1995; Meskell 2003). The incorporation of social memory in archaeological discourse has broadened the interpretive frameworks associated with mortuary behavior, allowing for more insights into the lived experience associated with mortuary contexts and the importance of ritual and material culture in the construction and perpetuation of collective memories.

The study of residential burial in a living society has the potential to contribute significantly to this discussion of social memory in relation to mortuary behavior. The residential burial tradition of West Sumba, Indonesia, represents an ideal case in this regard since it is not only visible archaeologically but also has remained a common practice into the present day. The erection of tombs and associated funerary practices in West Sumba can offer insights into not only the meanings associated with burial placement (i.e., residential compounds versus cemeteries) but also the living processes that can be associated with their creation. In West Sumba, residential burial remains an integral part of the dynamics associated with power, relations, and the long-term perpetuation of clan groups. An examination of the living processes associated with this mortuary tradition shows how

ARCHEOLOGICAL PAPERS OF THE AMERICAN ANTHROPOLOGICAL ASSOCIATION, Vol. 20, Issue 1, pp. 17–32, ISSN 1551-823X, online ISSN 1551-8248. DOI: 10.1111/j.1551-8248.2011.01025.x.

residential burial and social memory can be entwined within a complex set of social concerns. In this case, the presence of the dead and their stone sarcophagi within the residential domains of the living is a reflection of not only the long-term maintenance of social groups but also the continued relevance of the traditional institutions tied to these groups.

Inquiry into the presence of tombs in residential contexts and the social entanglements tied to their creation can also illustrate how the issues associated with this type of mortuary behavior can change through time and vary depending upon the standpoint of the agents involved. The emblemic significance of tombs in West Sumba remains fluid and multifaceted from the time they are erected to long after they have become testimonials of the deceased. Because of this, tombs in West Sumba can be viewed from a diachronic or biographical standpoint, similar to that which has been applied to the analysis of objects and their exchange within societies (Kopytoff 1986). In this way, although they do not represent objects in circulation, West Sumbanese tombs can be considered to possess "social lives" (Appadurai 1986) with multifaceted implications for the individuals and groups associated with their erection and long-term maintenance.

West Sumba

The island of Sumba is located in the eastern part of the Indonesian archipelago, approximately 500 kilometers east of the island of Java (Figure 2.1). Due to its relative lack of highly valued trade commodities, low rice agricultural productivity in comparison to the wetter and more fertile areas of western Indonesia (e.g., Java, Sumatra, and Bali), and a location slightly off the major historical trade routes of the Indonesian archipelago, Sumba has traditionally been a relatively sparsely populated island lacking the kingdoms and states that emerged in other parts of Indonesia. West Sumba, in particular, remains one of the least "globalized" parts of Indonesia, where megalithic tomb-building, traditional clan social structures, and large feasts are vestiges of a pre-direct colonial period (in this case, pre-20th century as can be seen in the observations of Colfs [1888]) that are still important aspects of a society in which a significant portion of the population remains tied to the traditional economy based on rice agriculture and domesticated animals.

The ethnoarchaeological fieldwork for this study of stone tombs on Sumba was accomplished as a part of the Ethnoarchaeology of Southeast Asian Feasting Project directed by Brian Hayden. The bulk of these data on tombs was collected during a collaborative research project conducted in West Sumba by Ron Adams in collaboration with Ayu Kusumawati of Balai Arkeologi Denpasar (Indonesia) and Haris Sukendar of the Indonesian National Research Centre for Archaeology in 2003 (see also Adams 2005, 2007a, 2007b, 2009). Adams followed up this project with a trip to West Sumba in 2005. Prior to 2003, Adams conducted preliminary investigations in West Sumba as a part of field studies conducted in collaboration with Stanislaus Sandarupa of Universitas Hasanuddin (Indonesia) in 2001.

Sociopolitical Context

Traditional social organization in West Sumba is centered around exogamous clan groups. There are numerous

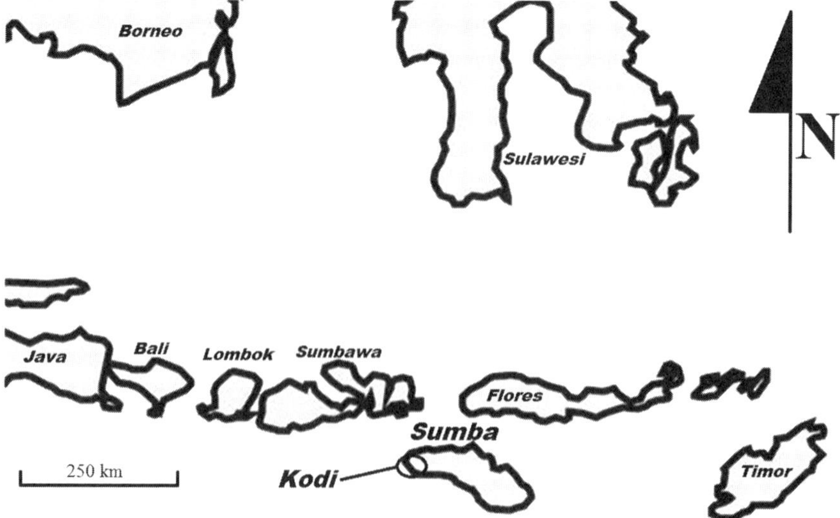

Figure 2.1. Location of West Sumba and Kodi in relation to other Indonesian islands.

clans found throughout West Sumba. In the Kodi area on the west coast of Sumba, where the bulk of the data for this study was collected, clans are referred to as *parona* and are made up of up to 200 households. Within each *parona* in Kodi, there are typically four ancestral houses (*uma*) that form subgroups within the clan that are comprised of up to 50 branch houses. All clan members are affiliated with both their clan and a particular *uma* within their clan. The founding *uma* of a clan, known as the *uma katakunata* (great house), is considered the spiritual, but not always political, center of the clan. All of the *uma* are located in the main clan ancestral village, which is comprised of the four *uma* as well as several branch houses affiliated with the *uma* and the large stone tombs that house deceased clan members. At the center of the ancestral village is the central ceremonial plaza of the clan, known as the *natara,* where the large feasts within a clan are held.

The majority of clan members in Kodi live in branch households located up to several kilometers outside of ancestral villages in small household clusters and hamlets adjacent to cultivated land where dry rice is grown along with maize and other more minor crops, such as coconuts, beans, and sweet potatoes. This land, along with a certain amount of uncultivated forest, is considered to be the collective property of a clan. However, each household holds usufruct rights to agricultural land that are passed along to successive generations. The various households are united by their affiliation to particular *uma* ancestral house groups and the larger clan and its collectively held property. As groups whose members are linked to their affiliated ancestral houses and ultimately the *uma katakunata* and collectively held resources of the larger clan, the *parona* clan groups fit the general parameters of what has been considered to characterize "house societies" in the anthropological literature (Adams 2007b; Gillespie 2000a; Lévi-Strauss 1983).

While there were loose confederations of *parona* traditionally, the *parona* was essentially the highest level of political authority prior to the Dutch colonial administration of West Sumba. Within the *parona,* leadership and decision-making authority concerning the larger clan group was vested in a small group of typically five to ten men who gained prominence through tomb-building and hosting large feasts. These men are traditionally known as *rato,* a title best translated as "big man" or "man of renown" in English in the context of achieved status but which also refers to ritual specialists in the traditional animistic *marapu* religion of Kodi. In Kodi, men achieve the status of *rato* by sponsoring the construction of tombs, hosting large feasts, and possessing oratory skills that enable them to attract followers. The title is testimony to the person's ability to attract supporters and amass livestock. The group of *rato* in a clan traditionally made the important decisions regarding dispute resolution, the use of corporately owned land, and the scheduling of large feasts, including those for tomb-building, within the clan. Today, feasting and tomb-building continue to be associated with power acquisition, although the Indonesian term *tokoh* (prominent individual) is often used in place of the traditional title of *rato* to describe the major power brokers in the social realm (Adams 2007a; Hoskins 1984).

In spite of the prominent role of these men in traditional clan structures, the designation of *rato,* as an achieved status, never led to the development of an entrenched hereditary ruling class in Kodi. Social class distinctions were present in Kodi, however, as there was traditionally a noble (*maramba*) class and slave (*hamba*) class. In this arrangement the vast majority of people were considered *maramba.* Informant estimates of the size of the *hamba* class indicate that approximately 20 percent of the population were slaves in the past. The slave class is said to have originated from nobles captured from enemy clans in war. Certain marriage proscriptions and inheritance rules related to social class standing led to the perpetuation of the slave class over time. Slaves were also prohibited from sponsoring tomb-building and other endeavors associated with achieving the status of *rato.* Slavery was officially outlawed in the early part of the 20th century, although the "former" noble classes of Sumba continued to dominate local administrative affairs well into the 20th century (Hoskins 1984:26; Keane 1997:42, 43).

Tombs and Ancestors

Stone tombs are found throughout the island of Sumba, although the current practice of building traditional stone tombs is primarily limited to the *kabupaten* (Indonesian regency administrative unit) of West Sumba. In comparison, stone tomb-building has become a much rarer occurrence in East Sumba. This is very likely attributable to the differing historical trajectories that the two halves of the island have experienced. East Sumba has a longer, more intense history of trade with external powers (with the Javanese and later the Portuguese and Dutch). The period of Dutch colonization was also much longer in East Sumba in comparison to West Sumba (Adams 2007a; Kapita 1976). Historically, this led to power consolidation on the part of local rulers in East Sumba related to access to trade with the Dutch East India Company beginning in the 18th century and the later establishment of local administrative heads as a part of Dutch attempts to gain indirect control of East Sumba in the 1840s (Hoskins 1984:14; Kapita 1976:21, 26). It was not until the early 20th century that the Dutch attempted to impose a colonial system of political hierarchies on societies in West Sumba. In spite of the colonial administration, real sociopolitical power in West Sumba continued to be characterized by competition, and an entrenched system of hereditary rulers never took hold in the same way as it occurred in East Sumba (Gunawan 1998:29–30; Hoskins 1984:17–19). These historical circumstances appear to have fostered a scenario in which tomb-building became reserved for a limited number of hereditary elites in East Sumba and was not as common as tomb-building in West Sumba, where tomb-building has traditionally been linked to achieved power and status.

As receptacles for the remains of the deceased, tombs in West Sumba are considered to be the "houses of the dead" (*alli mate* in the Kodi language of the western coast of Sumba) in contrast to *alli mopir,* or the "houses of the living." The most basic form of these tombs is a simple stone slab erected over a burial in the ground. However, it is much more common for tombs to consist of a stone-walled sarcophagus (Figure 2.2), with more elaborate versions made up of large stone table structures erected over the tombs and large freestanding stones erected in front of them. Oftentimes, designs are carved on the exterior of the stones comprising the tomb, and large tombs can be truly megalithic, being made of stones that can have a combined weight of 30 metric tons or more (Figure 2.3).

Spatially, West Sumbanese tombs were traditionally located in front of ancestral houses situated in the central ancestral villages of house-based clan groups (Figure 2.4). Because tombs have come to occupy nearly all of the space in front of houses, tombs are now found throughout the villages between and behind the major ancestral houses. While these tombs are not built within living residential structures, ancestral villages represent a domestic context similar to the way in which large houses represent residential contexts in other areas. In West Sumba, the traditional boundaries between one's place of private residence and one's affiliated clan ancestral village are blurred, with the ancestral village representing the residence of the group as a whole and a place where clan members gather for important events. Entering these villages can be akin to entering a home in a Western context, with the front verandas of the ancestral houses and clan ceremonial plaza representing a setting for daily domestic activities that can involve tombs as useful places for drying produce or clothing. Thus, while West Sumbanese tombs are not situated within the walls of a

Figure 2.2. Tombs in the village of Wainyapu, West Sumba. (Photo by R. Adams)

Figure 2.3. Large stone tomb in the Anakalang area of West Sumba. (Photo by R. Adams)

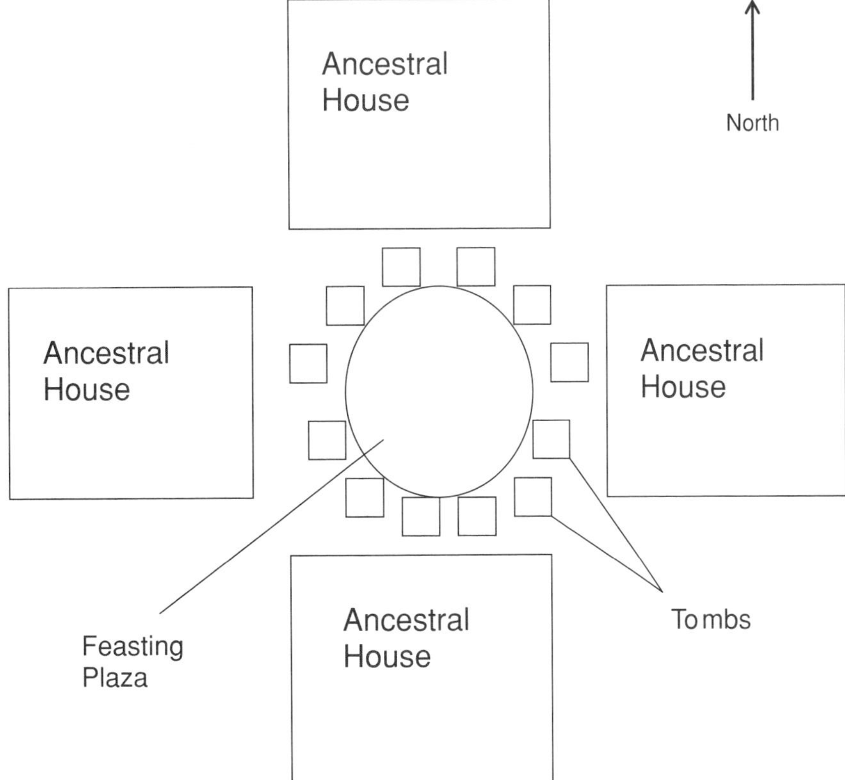

Figure 2.4. Idealized layout of a clan (parona) ancestral village in Kodi, West Sumba.

domestic structure, they are nevertheless residential in their spatial association with the domestic living areas of houses.

People in West Sumba consider the location of tombs in front of the ancestral houses of clan groups to be an important aspect of preserving the memory of ancestors interred in the tombs. It is said that tombs were originally placed in front of houses so that people would remember those who came before them. In fact, some clan members can recount the details regarding the identity and prominence of ancestors who have been interred in tombs for more than ten generations. Details concerning the size of the labor force and number of livestock slaughtered (the numbers of which may have been inflated over time) in the process of tomb-building are also remembered for large tombs built long ago.

As mnemonic devices for preserving the memory of past individuals and endeavors, tombs in West Sumba can be considered to represent what Maurice Halbwachs (1992[1950]; Connerton 1989:37) has referred to as "material spaces," which localize the collective memories of clan groups and give permanence to the "social spaces" occupied by these groups. The permanence of these stone tombs is of particular importance due to the impermanence of living structures made of bamboo and wood that can go into disrepair over time, especially when clan groups relocate their ancestral villages. In this way, West Sumbanese tombs become what could be considered long-lasting material manifestations of people's social link with their landscape through time (Basso 1996).

The social spaces within the ancestral villages and their associated tombs can serve to integrate clan members both literally and figuratively by their use as clan ritual feasting and ceremonial centers. In Kodi, tomb-building and other large feasts enhance the solidarity of clan groups, the members of which reside in spatially dispersed households (Adams 2007b). As noted above, the majority of clan members live in small household clusters and hamlets located up to several kilometers from the clan ancestral village. The feasts associated with tomb-building, as well as other large feasts, are traditionally held in the ceremonial area of clans. These feasts attract large numbers of clan members to the ancestral village for a specific event and enhance the cohesion of the group through participatory obligations and the collective pooling of resources (Adams 2007b:349–351).

Tomb placement within the ancestral village is also pertinent to the interaction between the living and the dead that is an important element of traditional Sumbanese beliefs. The importance of ancestors in West Sumbanese society is ultimately tied to the founders of ancestral houses and the larger clan groups of which they are a part. It is from these ancestors that land and livestock ultimately originate. These long-term links to the past are maintained through the continued rebuilding of ancestral houses in designated spaces within the ancestral clan village (Adams 2007b). The placement of tombs within the residential domain also exemplifies this continuity. While the souls of the deceased officially enter the realm of the ancestors when interred in tombs, they are still considered to be able to influence the events of the living and can be invoked in the major rituals that are performed in ancestral villages. The tombs, ancestral houses, and ancestral heirlooms within the ancestral villages all represent links to clan ancestors in a spatial domain where the dead are ever present and entwined with the living. In these respects, the dead in West Sumba are "actively" involved in structuring the lives of the living, a phenomenon implicated in some prehistoric mortuary contexts (e.g., Buikstra 1995; Parker Pearson 1999).

Tomb-building, along with the sponsorship of other large ritual feasts, represents an ancient practice, the continuation of which is considered important from the standpoint of maintaining links to ancestors. Informants in West Sumba spoke of a desire or pressure to "continue" the traditions of the past, including tomb-building. In this way, the event of erecting a tomb and hosting a large feast has the effect of promoting social reproduction and memory. The continuation of these traditions in West Sumba as a reverence for ancestors and, in a way, appeasing ancestors is important and akin to keeping a promise (Kuipers 1990). Kuipers (1990) describes these obligations to the ancestors as being similar to exchange obligations that, when unfulfilled, are considered to lead to hardships. In these cases, ancestors are considered to be able to negatively affect the lives of the living due to displeasure with the behavior of the living. In order to seek the forgiveness of ancestral spirits and other types of spirits for an infraction, such as neglecting to participate in feasting activities, people occasionally practice a ritual known as *yaigho* in Kodi and *zaizo* in nearby Weyewa, located to the immediate east of Kodi (Kuipers 1990:108). This rite tends to be performed after certain unfortunate incidents, such as when a person is struck by lightning or when a house is burned to the ground, which are believed to occur when spirits are displeased by the actions of the living.

In spite of the pressures to appease the ancestors through the continued performance of ritual feasts and building tombs, the costs involved in carrying out the most elaborate of these traditions are high, limiting them to the most prominent individuals in terms of wealth and their ability to attract supporters for the endeavor. The traditional methods of tomb-building have largely been abandoned in some parts of West Sumba due to high costs, the availability of trucks, which provide a lower-cost method of transporting large stones, and the gradual declining importance of tomb-building in relation to the political economy in some areas. This is particularly apparent in the more developed areas of West Sumba in and around the main administrative town of Waikabubak, where the correspondence between tomb-building and power acquisition is currently not as strong as it is in Kodi. Where tomb-building is still prevalent, it is its overriding relevance to daily existence that keeps it alive.

Tomb-Building

Tomb-building in West Sumba can entail a significant amount of time, labor, and resources (Figure 2.5). A combined labor of hundreds of individuals over a span of well over a month is necessary for building the largest tombs in West Sumba. People refer to those who sponsor tomb-building endeavors as *tuan batu* (tomb owners) in modern Indonesian terms. Tomb owners can build tombs for themselves while they are still living, and it is considered a goal for wealthy and socially prominent individuals to build their own tombs. However, if a person's deceased parents or grandparents were unable to build a tomb in their lifetime, that person must first build one on their behalf. In these cases, the remains of the deceased parents or grandparents are transferred from simple "temporary" in-ground burials to the large stone tomb. These rules concerning tomb-building create a situation in which persons can sponsor the construction of three tombs in their lifetime, no small undertaking considering the costs involved.

West Sumbanese tombs are usually fashioned from limestone. There are several limestone quarries located throughout West Sumba, where large stone slabs are mined by groups of stone quarriers. The quarriers use metal sticks with bamboo shafts to dig out the slabs, and it can take approximately two weeks to one month for a group of five to ten men to quarry all of the stone slabs used for building a tomb. The group of quarriers is led by a stone-working specialist (known as *tukango* in Kodi), who is contracted by the tomb owner (primary sponsor of tomb construction). The cost for hiring a quarry crew can range from one horse and one pig with a large piece of traditionally woven cloth (*kain*) to several buffaloes, several horses, and several pieces of woven cloth. In addition to the up-front costs in livestock and cloth, the tomb owner must provide the crew a meal each day they quarry the stone.

The distance from the quarry to the village of the tomb owner is typically between 500 meters and 5 kilometers,

Figure 2.5. Moving a large capstone for a tomb in the Anakalang area of West Sumba. (Photo by R. Adams)

although particularly desirable stones for tombs might be transported a distance up to more than 50 kilometers. The traditional method of transporting stones for tombs is to have them hauled by several hundred people who pull the slabs with vine ropes over wooden rollers obtained from forested clan-held lands. A group of 300 to more than 1,000 people is needed to pull the largest slab for a tomb, the capstone, from the quarry to the village. The time required to transport a capstone from the quarry to the village of the tomb owner can range from one day to one month, depending upon the size of the tomb and the distance from the quarry to the village. The process of hauling the stone can be intentionally delayed by the tomb owner in order to create an impressive display by feeding a large labor force several days in succession.

Before the tomb is complete, up to one additional month may be needed to construct the tomb and carve designs on the tomb's exterior. Assembling the capstone and leg stones of the tomb can take as little time as one day, although the carving of designs on the tomb's exterior, which necessitates the services of a specialized stone carver, can require several weeks to complete. Traditionally, the stone carver and his assistants are paid in livestock (e.g., a combination of water buffaloes and pigs) to complete the task of carving designs on a tomb. The designs can include motifs with water buffalo horns, human figures, gongs, or gold earrings (*mamoli*).

Throughout the entire process of tomb construction, pigs and sometimes water buffaloes are routinely slaughtered for feasts held to feed the labor associated with tomb-building. In some parts of West Sumba, large tomb consecration feasts are also held after the tombs are complete. These feasts can entail the slaughter of several water buffaloes and pigs to feed hundreds of guests. Overall, the largest tombs can require a total expense of over 100 pigs and more than ten water buffaloes for the feasts associated with tomb-building. It can take up to ten years of preparation for people to acquire the necessary livestock and assurances of livestock contributions from other households for these feasts.

Why Build Tombs?

Given the expenditures of time, labor, and resources for tomb-building, what prompts people to invest in and participate in these endeavors? Apart from concerns related to continuing with the traditional practices of the ancestors, there are practical considerations related to the sociopolitical dynamics of clan groups that encourage tomb-building. From the perspective of these practical considerations, people build tombs and invest in the construction of other people's tombs in order to (1) advance their own political standing within the clan by performing a key step in attainment of the title of *rato,* (2) maintain a voice in clan affairs and maintain relations of mutual support with fellow clan members, and (3) build alliances and support networks beyond their own clan.

Arguably, the primary driving motivation to build tombs in West Sumba is the connection that exists between tomb-building and power within clan groups. The clearest manifestation of the link between tombs and the social processes of the living is the power accrued by those who have built large stone tombs. As noted earlier, tomb-building is one of the necessary steps taken in order to be recognized as a *rato* or *tokoh.* In Kodi, sponsoring the construction of a large stone tomb in addition to sponsoring the erection of an ancestral house, and hosting the largest and most lavish of the feasts held in Kodi, the *woleka,* leads to the acquisition of this title. In daily power relations, the designation of tomb builder and feast giver is tied to the inner circle of clan authority. These positions achieved through feasting and tomb-building can also help individuals obtain modern administrative posts and attract prominent marriage alliances for themselves and their offspring.

From the perspective of the tomb owner's fellow clan members who choose to contribute livestock and/or labor for the erection of a tomb, the connection between tombs and clan power as a whole is important. In the broader scope of social organization, the connection between megalith building and living sociopolitical processes in West Sumba extends beyond individual power to the collective power of clan groups. As mentioned previously, tombs in West Sumba are intimately tied to clan structures, particularly in Kodi on the west coast of Sumba, where exogamous clans continue to represent important groups of sociopolitical action. The connection between tombs and clans is manifested not only in their placement within the clan ancestral village but also in the stones that make up the tombs. The stones that comprise a tomb are quarried from clan-owned land and in order for an individual to have tomb stones dug from the quarry site of another clan, a payment of livestock is required. This payment can mirror a bride-price payment (typically five water buffaloes and five horses), required when a man wishes to marry a woman in the context of patrilocal residence in Kodi. In the case of tomb-building, the stones themselves can be considered to be like a bride marrying into a different clan when they are quarried (Hoskins 1986).

In addition, while the sponsoring of tomb construction is associated with a single prominent individual who is considered to be the tomb owner, the stone tombs also fall under the collective ownership of the clan group as a whole. In fact, tombs typically lack any clear spatial association with the individual household of the tomb owner, although they are usually clearly associated with the person's affiliated ancestral house and always associated spatially with the person's clan group. This spatial orientation is in line with the emblemic significance of the tombs. When asked about what they thought when they saw a large tomb, informants indicated that (1) they believed the person who built it must be wealthy and socially prominent and (2) the person's clan must be prominent. In this way, tomb-building is linked not only to the individual power of the tomb owner but also to the collective power of the clan. Upon entering an ancestral clan village, one immediately can take stock of the number of tombs built by a clan. The presence of these tombs displays not only the ability of the tomb builders to garner large clan labor pools but also the willingness of clan members to participate in the endeavors with contributions of labor and livestock for associated feasts.

The traditional system of land tenure and the context of competition between clans attest to the importance of these displays of clan power and cohesiveness. As previously mentioned, all cultivated land within a clan's territory is theoretically the collective property of the clan as a whole, although individual households hold use-rights over specific parcels. As a result, land disputes between two households from separate clans often escalate into larger interclan disputes. In the past, these kinds of disputes were considered responsible for the warfare and feuding between clans that was endemic when Dutch colonial interests attempted to pacify the area in the early 20th century (Meijering et al. 1927:24). Such clan disputes remain common in Kodi and can still result in violence at times.

However, the importance of collectively held clan property does not necessarily implicate tombs and the power that they can convey for clan groups as territorial markers or as markers for land-use rights, signifiers attached to large stone tombs in past archaeological analyses in other contexts (e.g., Chapman 1981; Lidén 1995; Madsen 1982; Renfrew 1976). Disputes requiring the support of the larger clan group are linked not only to land but also to livestock, marriage arrangements, and, in the past, head-taking as well as slave raids. Thus, while there is indeed an indirect connection between resource control and tombs not unlike what Chapman (1981) envisioned for tombs in Neolithic Europe, the emblemic significance of tombs in West Sumba is not considered to be tied to land as much as it is to the ancestors, social memory, and the wealth and power of individuals and their affiliated clan groups, with their creation being part of a complex array of social issues that affect the living.

Beyond the collective power that can be embodied in large stone tombs, there are more directly relevant issues that prompt people to participate in the construction of a fellow clan member's tomb. Active participation in tomb-building and other large feasts held within one's clan, by providing either food (livestock and/or rice) or labor, is considered necessary for maintaining a voice in clan affairs and accessing clan support networks. These networks allow clan members to take part in cooperative labor arrangements within clans that are used for house building and agricultural work. In addition, clans are important for political support in cases of dispute with other clans and in accessing modern administrative posts. People can even be phased out of these support networks altogether when failing to participate in clan activities (Hoskins 1984:311, 312). Not surprisingly, informants in West Sumba spoke of an obligation to provide a water buffalo or pig for large feasts, including tomb-building feasts, held within their clan. Because of these obligations, the provisioning of food at these feasts can be largely a collective effort. At times, 50 percent or more of the livestock associated with tomb-building and other large feasts comes from fellow clan members who are not considered to be the primary sponsors of the events.

While the pressures and necessities associated with participation in tomb-building and other endeavors can make them a cooperative effort within the clan, individual concerns beyond mere existence within a group play a part in this collective action as well. Individuals can contribute livestock for a tomb-building feast in order to create a debt that would need to be repaid when the individuals build their own tomb at a later time. This is cited by informants as a major reason in people's choice to provide livestock for tomb-building. When contributions of livestock for tomb-building come from other clans, they are often part of debt relations associated with a larger network of supporters that also need to be repaid in kind. A significant portion of the labor force used to pull the capstone for a tomb can consist of individuals from allied clans making up this larger support network as well. Such contributions, especially livestock, are valuable in building alliances for future marriage consideration and sociopolitical support. In addition, a certain amount of social renown and credibility can be built up by being recognized as a major contributor of livestock for large feasts.

The Life Cycle of Tombs

The tradition of creating residentially based tombs in West Sumba is part of a larger system of competition and power within and between clan groups. The role of tomb-building in accessing individual power forms the most obvious factor encouraging the practice. At the heart of this power is the social structure of the larger clan group. It is from this standpoint that the importance of tombs in relation to social memory and the perpetuation of a social order is the clearest. This is perhaps best illustrated by examining the life cycles associated with these monuments, in which tombs can be viewed as having their own biographies similar to other kinds of objects (Kopytoff 1986).

Biographies in material culture studies are most typically associated with objects that circulate through traditional systems of exchange. In the context of West Sumba, Hoskins (1989) adopted a similar approach when analyzing a head taken in a head-hunting raid. Here, following the "life cycle" of the severed head as it circulated between households illuminated the differential meanings and values attached to objects as they are transferred over time. While such an approach is typically applied to transferable objects and their circulation through time, noncirculating objects can also be viewed as possessing biographies, as has been illustrated by Kopytoff (1986:67) in the case of central African huts. Waterson (2000) applied this perspective to the large *tongkonan* kindred houses of house societies in Tana Toraja, Indonesia. The genealogies, episodes of rebuilding, ceremonies, and heirlooms are all a part of the "life" of these houses, which symbolically anchor house members in a social landscape (Waterson 2000:182–184). A similar diachronic perspective is applicable to ancestral houses (*uma*) in West Sumba (Adams 2007b) and when extended to the tombs of these houses in West Sumba, the interplay of various social concerns related to mortuary structures is revealed.

At their beginning, tomb stones can be considered members of a clan either by virtue of being extracted from clan-owned land or as brides that have married into clans. This symbolic quality of the stone almost representing a person is also reflected in the way its journey from the quarry to the ancestral village is considered to mirror the journey the soul of the deceased (or yet to be deceased) will take to the realm of the ancestors (see also Hoskins 1986). During and after the tomb-building process, the tombs become objects of achievement, displaying the ability of prominent individuals to attract labor and garner the requisite resources for such an endeavor. The perpetuation of this activity is part of a larger set of social concerns surrounding the practical relevance of clan groups, including social memory. The emphasis on social memory is reflected in the traditional emphasis on continuing with tomb-building and other undertakings as a kind of debt owed to the ancestors (Kuipers 1990). The tombs are kept relevant to more mundane aspects of life within clan groups through their practical use as places to dry clothing or produce and even as steps to facilitate entering and exiting the verandas of ancestral houses. As time passes, the tombs become testimonials and memorials as houses of the dead, which retain their significance in expressing the long-term continuity of the group and the prominence of past clan ancestors, and in providing "material spaces" (Halbwachs 1992[1950]) that serve to create a locale for the collective memories of clan groups. They can even serve to preserve the importance of the past endeavors of clan ancestors through details of their age, tomb owner, and size of the labor force and numbers of heads of livestock required to build the tombs that can be passed through the generations in the oral tradition. The passing down of these details and the presence of these monuments within clans help preserve a collective sense of renown and power for the groups. Over the longer term and particularly when ancestral villages have been largely abandoned, the tombs become what may be considered a landscape of memory maintained by periodic visits on ritual occasions and in oral historical narrative (Basso 1996).

Broader Implications

As a megalithic burial tradition in a domestic context, the case of West Sumbanese tombs illustrates the congruence that can exist between residential and monumental forms of mortuary expression. Even in the more widely known examples of subfloor burial that typify discussions of prehistoric residential burial, connections have been made between residential burial and the perpetuation of descent groups as viable sociopolitical entities, concerns that foster the persistence of megalith building in West Sumba today. A similar relationship between residential burial and the unity and perpetuation of descent groups has been proposed for Mayan and Oaxacan mortuary practices (Gillespie 2000b; King, chapter 4, this volume; McAnany 1995). The emphasis on ritually invoking the ancestors among the Maya (Gillespie 2000b) is also akin to the interaction between the dead and living in West Sumba in ritual practice. In Southwest Asia as well, the link between residential burials and descent groups has been discussed in a context in which social memory and reproduction appear to have been bolstered through patterns of residential burial. At Çatalhöyük, the existence of what have been interpreted as house societies centered around symbolically elaborated residential structures is associated with a pattern of subfloor burials (Düring 2005; Hodder and Cessford 2004). These subfloor burials and the subsequent rebuilding of the houses in their particular location are considered to be reflective of the importance of social memory and social reproduction among the residents of the site (Hodder and Cessford 2004). The potential similarities between Çatalhöyük and house societies in eastern Indonesia, including West Sumba, have already been discussed (Adams 2005). In spite of some of the potential drawbacks of this analogy (see Hodder 2005), the general association between residential burials and the major ancestral houses in West Sumba is likely similar to the link between subfloor burials and the most elaborate residential structures at Çatalhöyük and could therefore strengthen claims of there being a link between residential burials and the long-term continuity of house societies in various archaeological settings.

What clearly sets the residentially based tombs in West Sumba apart from these prehistoric examples is their monumental nature. However, the connection between living groups and their deceased forebears that is invoked in subfloor burial practices is a theme that applies to prehistoric megalithic burials as well. Megalithic monuments of the European Neolithic appear to have been important mnemonic devices for referencing ancestors. According to Whittle et al. (2007), long barrow and long cairn burials of southern Britain in the fourth millennium B.C.E. were significant memorials that connected the living with deceased ancestors. Similarly, Hodder (1984, 1990) considered long barrows of the European Neolithic to have referenced a deep past when people centuries earlier lived in long houses similar in form to the long barrows. Archaeologists have also explored the links between megalithic monuments and prehistoric descent groups (e.g., Sjögren 1986). Powell (2005) has posited that Neolithic Irish Chamber tombs are a manifestation of the long-term continuity of lineage-based corporate descent groups in their design, which includes several interments arranged in a chamber with ends open to the world of the living, their proximity to settlements, and the domestic remains that have been found associated with the tombs.

While the evidence typically does not indicate that European megalithic monuments occurred within settlements, the active engagement of living groups with their deceased forebears through ritual practice is evident. Scarre (2001) has argued that the megalithic chamber tombs of Brittany were located in areas where important rituals took place during the Neolithic. Flemming (1973) argued long ago that large rituals were held in front of megalithic tombs throughout western Europe. Direct evidence for this ritual activity comes in the form of food remains found in association with megalithic tombs in various parts of western and northern Europe (Fischer 2002; Hayden 2003:232, 233; Hedges 1984:135; Sherratt 1991:56).

Closer geographically to West Sumba, prehistoric megalithic tombs within villages in the northern Massim of Papua New Guinea may represent a social phenomenon more clearly in line with that found currently in West Sumba. The tombs in the northern Massim date to a period between approximately 1500 B.P. and 600 B.P. and are associated with larger villages of the area. Blickler and Ivuyo (2002) have postulated that the monuments were focal areas for the communities and were indicative of center–periphery relations (Damon 1990; Irwin 1983, 1985; Wallerstein 1976) between large villages with stone monuments and the smaller outlying settlements that did not contain monuments. Alternatively, they may represent a pattern in which megalithic burials were centered within the major ancestral villages of descent groups similar to West Sumbanese clans. Indeed, elements of the ethnographically documented Trobriand chiefdoms in the northern Massim (where the tombs are found) bear resemblances to the structure of clans in Sumba in their being centered around small corporate groups known as *dala,* which appear to have been similar to West Sumbanese clans and were represented by a small-scale settlement hierarchy similar to the arrangement of ancestral villages and smaller outlying hamlets found in West Sumba (Johnson and Earle 1987). However, it is currently not clear how much continuity exists between the ethnographic Trobriand societies and the earlier megalithic monuments (Blickler 2006).

In other ethnographically documented societies within island Southeast Asia, patterns of residential burial similar to that in West Sumba do exist. Among the Batak of northern Sumatra (Indonesia), stone tombs situated in the villages of lineage-based groups were traditionally built in a context of competition between individuals and groups linked to the feasting economy (Barbier 1988). A similar pattern occurs on the island of Flores, where the placement of tombs in front of similar types of clan-based houses is considered to be linked to the remembrance of those interred in the tombs, and the spirits of the dead are considered to be ever present in the lives of the living (Kusumawati 2002). These tombs serve as the burial places for prominent clan ancestors (Arndt 1932:12, 40). On Nias, an island off the south coast of Sumatra, traditional competition for sociopolitical prominence within clan groups was expressed in large feasts of merit, the largest of which was associated with the erection of a stone monument in front of the house of the noble sponsor of the feast (Feldman 1988:37–39). The skulls of these individuals were often interred underneath these residential monuments (Beatty 1992:230).

In these ethnographic cases, there is a traditional emphasis on solidarity within extended family groups. All cultivated land among the central Nias is theoretically considered to be corporately owned by lineage groups. The houses and stone monuments of these groups are situated in distinct sections of villages designated for respective lineages. In this context, intergroup competition appears to have been expressed through large feasts and warfare traditionally (Beatty 1992). Cultivated land is also considered to be collectively owned by lineage and clan groups among the Batak (Sherman 1990). This cooperative, group-oriented social order is also reflected in the stone tombs, each of which can contain several prominent lineage ancestors (Barbier 1988). Corporate ownership of land on the part of clan groups is common among groups in central Flores as well (Forth 2001; Howell 1995; Schröter 1998). Warfare between groups appears to have been common among central Flores groups, usually stemming from land disputes (Forth 2001:76, 77; Howell 1989:423; Schröter 1998). In these cases, the indications suggest that the importance of group solidarity and social reproduction as well as competition both within and between groups may have been part of what drove these more elaborate examples of residential burial.

Bringing the discussion back to West Sumba, it is worth noting that the Sumbanese residential burial tradition has not always been associated with monumental displays. Within ancestral villages in Kodi, there are tombs represented by simple small slabs of stone that have been placed over burials below the ground. Informants claim that these tombs were erected during a time prior to the advent of the larger tombs that have dominated villages for hundreds of years. Interestingly, the simple, pre-monumental tombs in West Sumba are said to house the remains of many individuals, the identities of whom are not remembered by those who currently inhabit the villages. This contrasts with the continued memory of the names of those who built and are interred in the oldest (dating several hundred years based on genealogical depth) large tombs. The earlier burial tradition could represent a time when tombs were perhaps less associated with the accessing of individual power and more concerned with the social reproduction of the group as a whole. These are features that still can be found associated with tombs today, suggesting that the essence of this burial tradition is an emphasis on social memory, reproduction, and the constant interplay of the living and the dead. However, a more detailed archaeological exploration of these earlier burials is necessary before firm conclusions can be made concerning a deeper diachronic perspective on burial in West Sumba.

Conclusions

This case study of residential burial has shown how social memory and the burials that invoke these memories can be highly tied to the practical concerns of the living. This example of residential burial offers an expansion of the general interpretation of social reproduction in relation to house-based or lineage-based societies and provides a glimpse of how the maintenance of these social orders can be important in the context of everyday living. This approach brings the discussion of residential burial beyond a focus on how burial patterns serve to enhance reproduction of traditional social hierarchies to an understanding of why such conservation and maintenance of social orders occurs. In the case of West Sumba, we argue that the continued importance and social relevance of house society structures linked to relations of power, support, and competition are what drive the construction of social memory embodied in stone tombs.

This example of West Sumbanese tombs is not intended to be a "one size fits all" ethnoarchaeological analysis of residential burial. It is but one example of the variability that can be associated with residential burial traditions, a variability that is expressed throughout this volume. The relative lavishness associated with the tomb-building tradition in West Sumba clearly sets it apart from many prehistoric cases. The creation of these tombs appears to entail higher time, labor, and resource expenditures than would be the case with much simpler subfloor burials. These monuments are also clearly more display oriented in terms of their placement in front of houses as opposed to existing within houses. It is the ties between tomb creation and the systems of competition and power consolidation of individuals and groups that foster the megalithic proportions associated with the largest West Sumbanese tombs.

However, in spite of the apparent lack of wealth expenditures associated with prehistoric subfloor burials, social meanings similar to those associated with tombs in West Sumba may have been linked to these less extravagant burials. Indeed, the residential burial tradition in West Sumba illustrates the unifying themes that link monumental forms of burial with residential burials. Megalithic tombs in West Sumba and other areas both ethnographically and prehistorically exemplify connections between the living and the dead and are likely associated with similar concerns for social reproduction and the perpetuation of group structures that have been suggested for prehistoric subfloor burials, especially in the case of house societies and other large extended family groups.

In closing, we hope that this study can offer not only an illustration of how residential burial can be integrally tied to the social concerns of individuals and groups in West Sumba, but also an example of how the representational significance of these burials can be complex and is in no way static from a diachronic perspective. Following the life cycle of these monuments, as is the case with other material objects, can offer a fuller picture. As monuments built by those still living, West Sumbanese tombs represent the ability to garner resources and attract supporters and are a testimony to the achievement of a certain level of renown within and beyond one's clan, which is inexorably linked to political and economic power. Over time, they become testimony to the grandeur of clan ancestors, the collective power of the clan, the long-term perpetuation of the clan as a group, and part of a social landscape in which the ancestors are seen as actively affecting the lives of their living descendants. In some cases, they can be the last visible remnants of clan ancestral villages that have relocated and the physical remains of the tombs take on much more symbolic roles as a group's link to its past. As tomb-building becomes less frequent in some parts of West Sumba, the overall significance of these burials will likely be associated with the memory of groups' ancestors and a previous social context in which the power and solidarity within clan groups represented some of the most paramount social concerns.

Acknowledgments

We would first and foremost like to thank Joyce White for serving as the chair of the 2007 SAA session on which this volume was based and for initiating the concept of a residential burial volume. Many thanks also to Stacie M. King for agreeing to act as an editor for the volume and for providing very helpful comments on an earlier version of this chapter. The comments of Cathy Costin and anonymous reviewers on the submitted draft of this chapter were also very beneficial, leaving the shortcomings of this work the responsibility of the authors. The ethnoarchaeological data for this chapter were collected as a part of Ron Adams' Ph.D. thesis at Simon Fraser University. Brian Hayden acted as the senior supervisor for this thesis and his support has been essential to the completion of the project. Others who have played a role in this work include Piter Rehi, Thomas Tedawonda, Agusthinus Galugu, Pak Agustinus Sabarua, Pak Rehi Pyati, Pak Octavianus Ndari, Suzanne Villeneuve, Umbu Siwa Djurumana, Webb Keane, Janet Hoskins, and many informants in West Sumba, Indonesia. The fieldwork in Indonesia discussed above was funded by the Social Sciences and Humanities Research Council of Canada and was conducted in collaboration with Haris Sukendar (Pusat Penelitian Arkeologi Nasional, Jakarta), Ayu Kusumawati (Balai Arkeologi Denpasar), and Stanislaus Sandarupa (Universitas Hasanuddin). Field research in Indonesia was undertaken with permission from the Indonesian Academy of Sciences (LIPI).

References

Adams, Ron L.

2005 Ethnoarchaeology in Indonesia Illuminating the Ancient Past at Çatalhöyük? American Antiquity 70:181–188.

2007a The Megalithic Tradition of West Sumba, Indonesia: An Ethnoarchaeological Investigation of Megalith Construction. Ph.D. thesis, Department of Archaeology, Simon Fraser University.

2007b Maintaining Cohesion in House Societies of West Sumba, Indonesia. *In* The Durable House: House Society Models in Archaeology. Robin A. Beck Jr., ed. Pp. 344–362. Occasional Paper 35. Carbondale: Center for Archaeological Investigations, Southern Illinois University.

2009 Transforming Stone: Ethnoarchaeological Perspectives on Megalith Form in Eastern Indonesia. *In* Megalithic Quarrying: Extracting and Manipulating the Stones. Chris Scarre, ed. Pp. 83–92. Proceedings of the 15th World Congress of the International Union for Prehistoric and Protohistoric Sciences. BAR International Series 1923. Oxford: Archaeopress.

Appadurai, Arjun, ed.

1986 The Social Life of Things: Commodities in Cultural Perspective. Cambridge: Cambridge University Press.

Arndt, Paul

1932 Die Megalithenkultur der Nad'a (Flores). Anthropos 27:11–63.

Barbier, Jean Paul

1988 A Stone Rider of the Batak of Sumatra. *In* Islands and Ancestors: Indigenous Styles of Southeast Asia. Jean Paul Barbier and Douglas Newton, eds. Pp. 50–65. New York: te Neues.

Basso, Keith H.

1996 Wisdom Sits in Places: Landscape and Language among the Western Apache. Albuquerque: University of New Mexico Press.

Beatty, Andrew

1992 Society and Exchange in Nias. Oxford: Clarendon Press.

Blickler, Simon H.

2006 Prehistoric Stone Monuments in the Northern Region of the Kula Ring. Antiquity 80:38–51.

Blickler, Simon H., and Baiva Ivuyo

2002 Megaliths of Muyuw (Woodlark Island), Milne Bay Province, PNG. Archaeology in Oceania 37:22–36.

Buikstra, Jane E.
1995 Tombs for the Living . . . or . . . For the Dead: The Osmore Ancestors. *In* Tombs for the Living: Andean Mortuary Practices. T. D. Dillehay, ed. Pp. 229–280. Washington, DC: Dumbarton Oaks Research Library and Collection.

Chapman, Robert
1981 The Emergence of Formal Disposal Areas and the 'Problem' of Megalithic Tombs in Prehistoric Europe. *In* The Archaeology of Death. Robert Chapman, Ian Kinnes, and Klavs Randsborg, eds. Pp. 71–81. Cambridge: Cambridge University Press.

Chesson, Meredith, ed.
2001 Social Memory, Identity, and Death: Anthropological Perspectives on Mortuary Rituals. Archeological Papers of the American Anthropological Association, 10. Arlington, VA: American Anthropological Association.

Colfs, Albert
1888 Het journaal van Albert Colfs: eene bijdrage tot de kennis der kleine Soenda-Eilanden. A. G. Vorderman, ed. Batavia: Ernst.

Connerton, Paul
1989 How Societies Remember. Cambridge: Cambridge University Press.

Damon, Frederick H.
1990 From Muyuw to the Trobriands. Tucson: University of Arizona Press.

Düring, Bleda S.
2005 Building Continuity in the Central Anatolian Neolithic: Exploring the Meaning of Buildings at Aşikli Höyük and Çatalhöyük. Journal of Mediterranean Archaeology 18(1):3–29.

Feldman, Jerome
1988 The Seat of the Ancestors in the Homeland of the Nias People. *In* Islands and Ancestors: Indigenous Styles of Southeast Asia. Jean Paul Barbier and Douglas Newton, eds. Pp. 34–49. New York: te Neues.

Fischer, Anders
2002 Food for Feasting? An Evaluation of Explanations of the Neolithisation of Denmark and Southern Sweden. *In* The Neolithisation of Denmark: 150 Years of Debate. Anders Fischer and Kristian Kristiansen, eds. Pp. 341–394. Sheffield: J. R. Collis.

Flemming, Andrew
1973 Tombs for the Living. Man 8(2):178–193.

Forth, Gregory L.
2001 Dualism and Hierarchy: Process of Binary-Combination in Keo Society. Oxford: Oxford University Press.

Gillespie, Susan D.
2000a Beyond Kinship: An Introduction. *In* Beyond Kinship: Social and Material Reproduction in House Societies. Rosemary A. Joyce and Susan D. Gillespie, eds. Pp. 1–21. Philadelphia: University of Pennsylvania Press.
2000b Maya "Nested Houses": The Ritual Construction of Place. *In* Beyond Kinship: Social and Material Reproduction in House Societies. Rosemary A. Joyce and Susan D. Gillespie, eds. Pp. 135–160. Philadelphia: University of Pennsylvania Press.

Gunawan, Istutiah
1998 Hierarchy and Balance: A Study of Wanokaka Social Organization. Canberra: Australian National University.

Halbwachs, Maurice
1992 [1950] On Collective Memory. Lewis A. Coser, trans. Chicago: University of Chicago Press.

Hayden, Brian
2003 Shamans, Sorcerers and Saints: A Prehistory of Religion. Washington, DC: Smithsonian Books.

Hedges, John
1984 Tomb of the Eagles. London: Murray.

Hodder, Ian
1984 Burials, Houses, Women and Men in the European Neolithic. *In* Ideology, Power and Prehistory. Daniel Miller and Christopher Tilley, eds. Pp. 51–68. Cambridge: Cambridge University Press.
1990 The Domestication of Europe: Structure and Contingency in Neolithic Societies. Oxford: Basil Blackwell.

2005 Socialization and Feasting at Çatalhöyük: A Response to Adams. American Antiquity 70:189–191.

Hodder, Ian, and Craig Cessford
2004 Daily Practice and Social Memory at Çatalhöyük. American Antiquity 69:17–40.

Hoskins, Janet
1984 Spirit Worship and Feasting in Kodi, West Sumba: Paths to Riches and Renown. Ph.D. dissertation, Department of Anthropology, Harvard University.
1986 So My Name Shall Live: Stone-dragging and Grave-building in Kodi, West Sumba. Bijdragen to de Taal-, Land- en Volkenkunde 142(1):31–51.
1989 On Losing and Getting a Head: Warfare, Exchange, and Alliance in a Changing Sumba, 1888–1988. American Ethnologist 14(4):605–622.

Howell, Signe
1989 Of Persons and Things: Exchange and Valuables among the Lio of Eastern Indonesia. Man 24(3):419–438.
1995 The Lio House: Building, Category, Idea, Value. *In* About the House: Lévi-Strauss and Beyond. Janet Carsten and Stephen Hugh-Jones, eds. Pp. 149–169. New York: Cambridge University Press.

Irwin, Geoffrey J.
1983 Chieftainship, Kula, and Trade in Massim Prehistory. *In* The Kula: New Perspectives on Massim. J. Leach and E. Leach, eds. Pp. 29–72. Cambridge: Cambridge University Press.
1985 The Emergence of Mailu as a Central Place in Coastal Papuan Prehistory. Terra Australis 10, Department of Prehistory. Canberra: Research School of Pacific Studies, Australian National University.

Johnson, Allen W., and Timothy Earle
1987 The Evolution of Human Societies: From Foraging Group to Agrarian State. Stanford, CA: Stanford University Press.

Jonker, Gerdien
1995 The Topography of Remembrance: The Dead, Tradition and Collective Memory in Mesopotamia. Studies in the History of Religions, 68. Leiden: E. J. Brill.

Kapita, Oemboe Hina
1976 Sumba di dalam jangkauan jaman. Jakarta: BPK Gunung Mulia.

Keane, Webb
1997 Signs of Recognition: Powers and Hazards of Representation in an Indonesian Society. Berkeley: University of California Press.

Kenyon, Kathleen M.
1981 The Architecture and Stratigraphy of the Tell, vol. 3: Excavations at Jericho. T. Holland, ed. London: British School of Archaeology.

Kopytoff, Igor
1986 The Cultural Biography of Things: Commoditization as Process. *In* The Social Life of Things: Commodities in Cultural Perspective. Arjun Appadurai, ed. Pp. 64–91. Cambridge: Cambridge University Press.

Kuijt, Ian
2001 Place, Death, and the Transmission of Social Memory in Early Agricultural Communities of the Near Eastern Pre-Pottery Neolithic. *In* Social Memory, Identity, and Death: Anthropological Perspectives on Mortuary Rituals. Meredith S. Chesson, ed. Pp. 80–99. Archeological Papers of the American Anthropological Association, 10. Arlington, VA: American Anthropological Association.
2008 The Regeneration of Life: Neolithic Structures of Symbolic Remembering and Forgetting. Current Anthropology 49:171–197.

Kuipers, Joel
1990 Power in Performance: The Creation of Textual Authority in Weyewa Ritual Speech. Philadelphia: University of Pennsylvania Press.

Kusumawati, Ayu
2002 Megalitik dalam pola perkembangan masyarakat Ende (Flores) Nusa Tenggara Timur. Berita Penilitian Arkeologi, Pp. 34–52. Denpasar, Indonesia: Balai Arkeologi Denpasar.

Lévi-Strauss, Claude
1983 The Way of the Masks. London: Jonathan Cape.

Lidén, Kerstin
1995 Megaliths, Agriculture, and Social Complexity: A Diet Study of Two Swedish Megalith Populations. Journal of Anthropological Archaeology 14:404–417.

McAnany, Patricia
1995 Living with the Ancestors: Kinship and Kingship in Ancient Maya Society. Austin: University of Texas Press.

Madsen, Torsten
1982 Settlement Systems of Early Agricultural Societies of East Jutland, Denmark: A Regional Study of Change. Journal of Anthropological Archaeology 1:197–236.

Meijering, M., et al.
1927 Tot dankbarheid genoopt: Gedenkboek ter gelegenheid van den 25-jarigenzendingsarbeid op Soemba van wege de Gereformeerde Kerken in Groningen, Drente, en Overijssel. Kampen: J. H. Kok.

Meskell, Lynn
2003 Memory's Materiality: Ancestral Presence, Commemorative Practice and Disjunctive Locales. *In* Archaeologies of Memory. Ruth M. Van Dyke and Susan E. Alcock, eds. Pp. 34–55. Malden, MA: Blackwell.

Parker Pearson, Mike
1999 The Archaeology of Death and Burial. College Station: Texas A&M University Press.

Powell, Andrew B.
2005 The Language of Lineage: Reading Irish Court Tomb Design. European Journal of Archaeology 8(1):9–28.

Renfrew, Colin
1976 Megaliths, Territories and Populations. *In* Acculturation and Continuity in Atlantic Europe. Dissertationes Archaeologicae Gandenses 16:198–220.

Rollefson, Gary O.
1983 Ritual Ceremony at Neolithic Ain Ghazal (Jordan). Paléorient 9(2):29–37.
1986 Neolithic Ain Ghazal (Jordan): Ritual and Ceremony, II. Paléorient 12(1):45–52.

Scarre, Chris
2001 Modeling Prehistoric Populations: The Case of Neolithic Brittany. Journal of Anthropological Archaeology 20:285–313.

Schröter, Susanne
1998 Death Rituals of the Ngada in Central Flores, Indonesia. Anthropos 93:417–435.

Sherman, George D.
1990 Rice, Rupees, and Ritual: Economy and Society among the Samosir Batak of Sumatra. Stanford, CA: Stanford University Press.

Sherratt, Andrew
1991 Sacred and Profane Substances: The Ritual Use of Narcotics in Later Neolithic Europe. *In* Sacred and Profane. Paul Garwood, David Jennings, R. G. Skeates, and Judith Toms, eds. Pp. 50–64. Oxford: Institute of Archaeology.

Sjögren, Karl-Göran
1986 Kinship, Labour and Land in Neolithic Southwest Sweden: Social Aspects of Megalith Graves. Journal of Anthropological Archaeology 5:229–265.

Wallerstein, Immanue
1976 The Modern World-System, vol. 1. New York: Academic Press.

Waterson, Roxana
2000 House, Place, and Memory in Tana Toraja (Indonesia). *In* Beyond Kinship: Social and Material Reproduction in House Societies. Rosemary A. Joyce and Susan D. Gillespie, eds. Pp. 177–188. Philadelphia: University of Pennsylvania Press.

Whittle, Alasdair, Alistair Barclay, Alex Bayliss, Lesley McFadyen, Rick Schulting, and Michael Wysocki
2007 Building for the Dead: Events, Processes and Changing Worldviews from the Thirty-eighth to the Thirty-fourth Centuries cal. BC in Southern Britain. Cambridge Archaeological Journal 17(1):123–147.

3

In the Beginning: The Experience of Residential Burial in Prehispanic Honduras

Rosemary A. Joyce
University of California, Berkeley

ABSTRACT

This paper treats residential subfloor burial as a practice with a history. At Puerto Escondido, Honduras, this history includes placement of jewelry and pottery vessels in buildings under construction, and the disarticulation of figurines and monumental sculpture depicting human subjects and their burial in different places. Residential burial brings together already-existing practices of *incorporation* of materials into constructed spaces, *disjunction* or separation of parts of things and their deliberate placement in different locations, and *commemoration* or the creation of a place intended to evoke memory. The earlier histories of these practices motivated their coordination in residential burial. [memory, place, representation, history, burial]

Sophisticated analyses have demonstrated that residential burial in Mesoamerica contributed to the creation of localized, historically continuous group identities and to the reinforcement and naturalization of claims of differential social status. The question pursued in this chapter is how we might understand the *initial* development of practices we recognize retrospectively as "residential burial." We cannot assume that a practice was adopted in order to cause the effects that it eventually came to have. A similar question of cause and effect is the motivation for Vitelli's (1998) discussion of early pottery-making in Greece. She notes that assuming ceramics were adopted to facilitate storage or cooking ignores the fact that the earliest vessels are small, not uniform, and rare. Instead, she considers what knowledge people could have already had dealing with the use of clay and fire, and what goals they might have had for applying firing to small, diverse clay vessels. Her suggestion, that these earliest vessels were associated with medicinal practice, would not have ever arisen from trying to explain why people first decided to make cooking, serving, and storage vessels—ends to which the technology was applied after it was developed.

So we cannot assume that residential burial was from the beginning a self-conscious strategy *intended* to produce group identities or to naturalize claims of differential status. To do so risks generalizing the kind of hyperactive, self-aggrandizing agent that Clark (2000) has appropriately noted is central to much modern social theory, a product of particular political, social, and economic circumstances that cannot be naturalized. The origins of practices like residential subfloor burial need to be understood in terms of the society in which they developed, before they accumulated other meanings through their histories of repetition.

Such an analysis must build on long-term history in a single place to show how practices were organized before and after the development of what we recognize as subfloor residential burial. This essay uses data from excavations at Puerto Escondido, Honduras, a site with occupation extending from before 1600 B.C.E. to after C.E. 450, to provide just such a context. These data are used to explore the transition from other forms of disposal of the dead to residential burial. The central argument is that residential burial brings together already-existing practices of *incorporation* of materials into specific constructed spaces, *disjunction* or separation

ARCHEOLOGICAL PAPERS OF THE AMERICAN ANTHROPOLOGICAL ASSOCIATION, Vol. 20, Issue 1, pp. 33–43, ISSN 1551-823X, online ISSN 1551-8248. DOI: 10.1111/j.1551-8248.2011.01026.x.

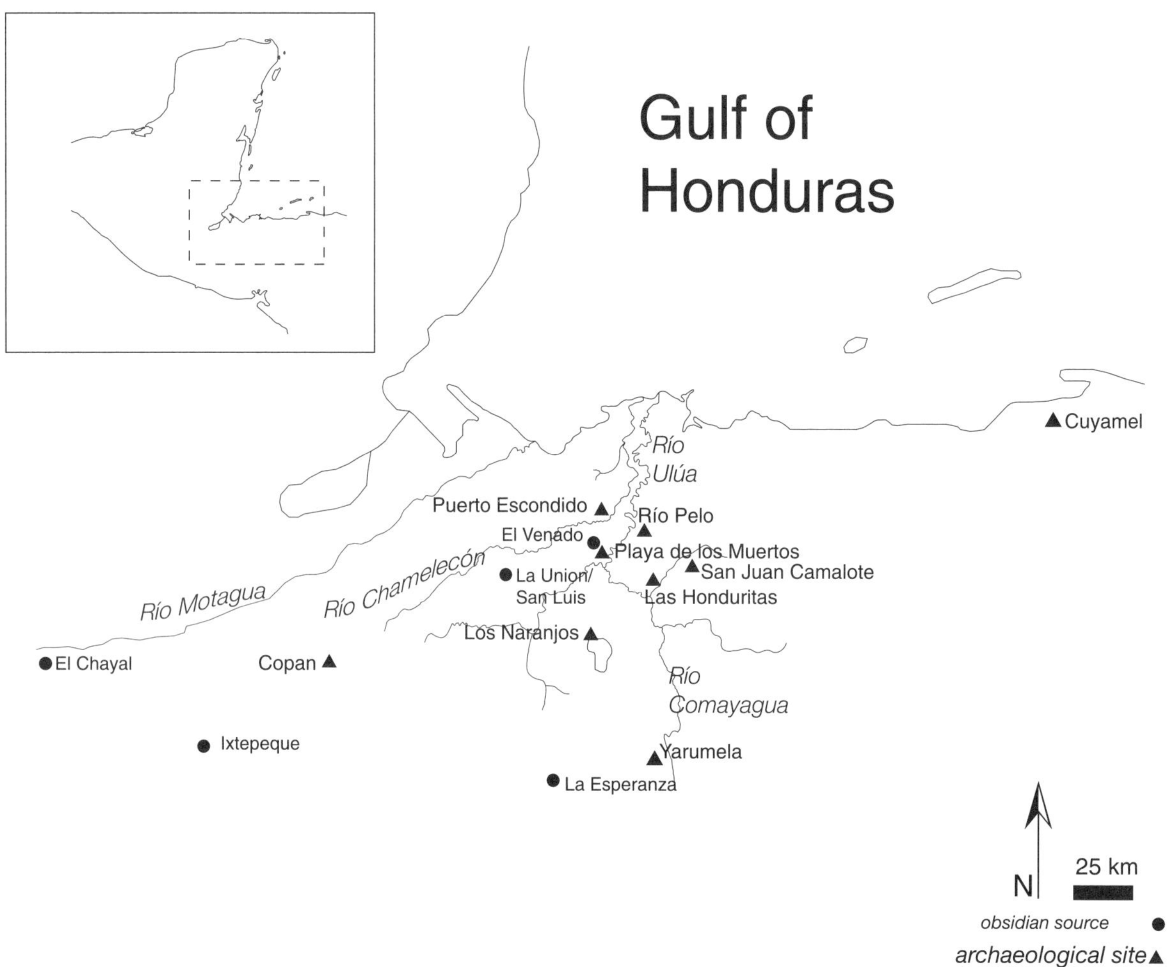

Figure 3.1. The location of Puerto Escondido.

of parts of unified things and their deliberate placement in different locations, and *commemoration* or the creation of a place intended to evoke memory. The earlier histories of these practices motivated their coordination in the complex set of practices that we recognize as residential burial.

Puerto Escondido: A History of Place

Puerto Escondido (CR-372) was initially recorded as a site represented by a number of large, relatively low, earthen mounds clustered along a tributary of the Chamelecón River in the floodplain formed by that river and the larger Ulúa River, which runs parallel to it today (Figure 3.1). At various times in the past the Chamelecón was a tributary of the Ulúa (Pope 1987). When first recorded, the site had already been extensively disturbed by modern construction activities, so that the total number of low earthen mounds that once existed cannot be stated with certainty. Two major, and at least three smaller, mounds were still intact when the site was first reported to the Honduran Institute of Anthropology and History and was tested by members of the staff of the Institute in 1993.

At the request of the Honduran Institute, in 1994 a joint Cornell–Berkeley project began investigations at the site under the direction of John S. Henderson and myself (Henderson and Joyce 1998). Our interest in the site was as an example of a category of very stable, long-occupied villages that developed in the fertile central floodplains of the lower Ulúa Valley, an area that in modern times has been a focus of intensive export agriculture primarily based on bananas and sugar cane.

In the Classic period (ca. C.E. 400–1000), these settlements formed what we characterize as a society of "wealthy farmers" among whom the development of social and economic inequality was limited more than in neighboring societies, producing a generally higher standard of living at the cost of a less exaggerated scale of economic differentiation. Our interest has been in understanding this social formation, to provide an alternative to more common models of societies in which pronounced social hierarchy developed in the presence of sufficient resources and time. The lower Ulúa Valley had an abundance of well-drained, fertile soils (Pope 1987); was historically a center of the production of cacao (Bergmann 1969; Henderson 1979), one of the major cash crops in prehispanic times; exported not only cacao but also other valuables to Maya cities in Yucatan in the sixteenth century (Henderson 1979); and in earlier prehispanic times produced a rich material culture, some of it exported, that required the support of a wide array of artisans (Lopiparo 2006; Luke and Tykot 2007).

We approached Puerto Escondido as an opportunity to employ broad-area excavations to understand the interrelationships of households and their development over time, to better understand the economic and power structures that developed from everyday domestic social relations in these villages. What we had not initially expected was to encounter superposition of the Classic period village that initially drew our attention over a stratified sequence of occupation whose earliest incidents we now know took place before 1600 B.C.E. (Joyce and Henderson 2001, 2007). Our subsequent research and continuing analyses have documented the histories of dwelling at Puerto Escondido, including changes in the use of imported goods. Obsidian was imported from both relatively nearby and distant sources (Joyce et al. 2004). The tradition of carving limited numbers of marble vases that culminates in the production of Classic Ulua Marble Vases between C.E. 500 and C.E. 1000 began as early as 1100 B.C.E. at this site (Luke et al. 2003). Our research has demonstrated that the people of Puerto Escondido were already using cacao beverages before 1100 B.C.E. (Henderson et al. 2007; Joyce and Henderson 2007). We have demonstrated that a variety of practices at the site show the residents were connected with a network of contemporary villages in Mesoamerica that used a complex symbolic system, exploited most notably by the Olmec of the Gulf Coast of Mexico to legitimize highly stratified societies, for example, producing locally made bowls and bottles with carved motifs identifiable with those of the Gulf Coast Olmec, and making and using stamps and seals with similar designs as those used in contemporary Highland Mexico (Joyce and Henderson 2001, 2002, 2003, 2010). We have traced the changing representations of human beings that first appear at the site by 1100 B.C.E. in the form of fired clay effigies, through the development of new forms of small ceramic figurines and larger stone sculptures, and the parallel creation of a rich array of costume elements in exotic shell and stone (Joyce 2003; Joyce and Henderson 2002). Our excavations have allowed us to demonstrate in detail how practices of architectural construction were developed in the construction and renovation of domestic buildings and were transformed as they were used to make larger special-purpose platforms (Joyce 2004a, 2004b, 2007).

The chronological relationships between excavated areas within the site are supported by 42 radiocarbon dates (Joyce and Henderson 2007). The latest preserved deposits we excavated date to the early Classic period. The upper levels of the site were bulldozed before our excavations, and diagnostic ceramics from mixed bulldozed deposits show occupation actually continued until circa C.E. 800–1000. Five radiocarbon dates for the latest intact deposits we documented provide a date span of C.E. 400–630 (calibrated two-sigma range).

In conjunction with these chronometric dates, excavations carried out in multiple areas of the site allow comparison of practices within the settlement at different points in time. Area excavations allow contextualization of features related to the practice of subfloor burial in relation to buildings and their remodeling. In counterpoint to the histories of development of practices related to the modification of the human body and its representation, evidence for the treatment of human skeletal remains at Puerto Escondido can be understood as part of a history through which residential burial emerged as a preferred way of disposing of the dead that incorporated the person in a delimited place or places linked through the disjunction of a formerly unified embodied person into a variety of parts. The heightened experience of the disjunction of the person and the incorporation of parts of the person in different locales was a critical way that mortuary ceremony produced social histories, literally through the commemoration of now-past persons shared by those who survived and carried on their identities (Joyce 1999, 2001).

Burying the Dead at Puerto Escondido

Residents at Puerto Escondido repeatedly remodeled dwellings and special-purpose buildings beginning before 1400 B.C.E. (Joyce 2007). The history of rebuilding culminated in the early Classic period (ca. C.E. 400–630) in houses arranged in groups around external yards containing burned features and associated with subsurface "bell-shaped" storage pits. Two dozen subfloor burials were documented in two extensively excavated house clusters of the early Classic village, placed under interior house floors, adjacent to house walls in the exterior yard space, and in reused storage pits.

The ubiquity of human remains in these late residential compounds contrasts vividly with earlier phases of occupation in the same areas, in which human remains were rare and the few encountered were placed deliberately in a special-purpose architectural feature, a low, broad earthen platform erected over and burying earlier houses. Rather than treat phases of occupation with burials as completely different from phases without these features, in the pages that follow I break down the practices that culminate in Classic period subfloor residential burial into a series of different actions that already existed in the historical community living at Puerto Escondido centuries earlier. The main body of the chapter consists of a narrative presentation of the sequence of development of such practices of incorporation, disjunction, and commemoration, showing how they were brought together in subfloor burial.

In the earliest phases of occupation (before 1400 B.C.E.), remodeling of buildings took place without any evidence of the placement of subfloor deposits or patterned breakage and disposal of artifacts. The very earliest deposits we excavated, the basis for our definition of the Sauce phase (dated before 1600 B.C.E. based on two radiocarbon dates from later levels with a calibrated two-sigma range of 1750–1310 B.C.E.), contained only nonarchitectural features probably representing exploitation of local plant and animal resources, perhaps by a transient population or by a small population residing elsewhere in the vicinity.

Once buildings were constructed, their remodeling, however, was remarkably conservative of placement and plan of architectural features (Figure 3.2). Rebuilding *in situ* is the first material practice that we can suggest created a localized memory trace (Joyce 2008), the ghostly presence of previous building walls, hearths, and pits that would have been known to residents, and even potentially visible. Rebuilding in place is consistent with other practices over the first few centuries of living at Puerto Escondido that increased the persistence of architecture, such as the adoption of plaster and stone as materials added to the basic pole and thatch construction techniques. In previous publications, I have proposed that the early cultivation of cacao trees, and the need for longer-term attention to groves that was required, may have been part of a shift in the way formerly mobile people related to place and history, promoting an increased interest in creating stable living sites for humans as well as for plants (Joyce 2007).

Around 1400–1100 B.C.E., we see the first evidence of the creation of deliberate subfloor deposits. While these do not contain any elements of human skeletons, they do include complete body ornaments (Figure 3.3). In previous work, I have proposed that what we today view as removable items of costume, badges of status or group affiliation, were tightly connected to and, indeed, constitutive of the identities of the persons who wore them (Joyce 1999, 2001, 2003). From that perspective, the incorporation of costume items in caches in buildings is significant in *the same way* that burial of skeletal elements would have been, commemorating social personae (compare Gillespie 2001).

It is worth noting that subfloor caches were deposited below the floors of the most durable architecture in use at this time (stone platforms), contrasting with the construction of more perishable structures in other parts of the village. Commemoration, incorporation, and disjunction were all practices of the occupants of the village at this early time, even though there is no indication that human bodies were subjected to these practices. Contemporary with this phase at Puerto Escondido, burials were placed in mountain caves across Honduras, where some show signs of cremation and all form parts of disarticulated group deposits (Brady et al. 2001; Gordon 1898; Healy 1974, 1984; Rue et al. 1989). While aspects of the human person represented by cultural symbols adopted during life were apparently subject to retention and commemoration in the living site, the corporeal body itself was in at least some cases destined to be incorporated in a mass burial site away from the locality of previous everyday life.

Between 1100 and 900 B.C.E., distinction in the permanency of architecture became even more significant in all areas of the village (Joyce 2007). The earliest examples of fired-clay figurines are attested at the same time (Joyce 2003). Disarticulated limbs of these durable representations of human subjects are the main items incorporated in architectural settings, while portions of the face are rare or absent, suggesting the possibility that figurines were disarticulated deliberately and their own "body parts" disposed of in different ways. Meanwhile, burial of costume ornaments in architectural contexts continued. At the beginning of this period of time, a pendant in the form of a bivalve shell (Figure 3.4) was deposited, along with an inverted bowl, on the floor of a building that was subsequently remodeled and expanded.

At circa 900 B.C.E., there were major episodes of remodeling in two areas of the site. These involved the conversion of what formerly were smaller buildings into large raised platforms, one faced with stone. Incorporated into the terraces of the second platform, a clay construction, were a series of intact pots, one containing costume ornaments, in this case two small jade pendants. Added to the existing repertoire of objects subject to incorporation in the new architectural form were the oldest human burials identified at Puerto Escondido, including what may have been

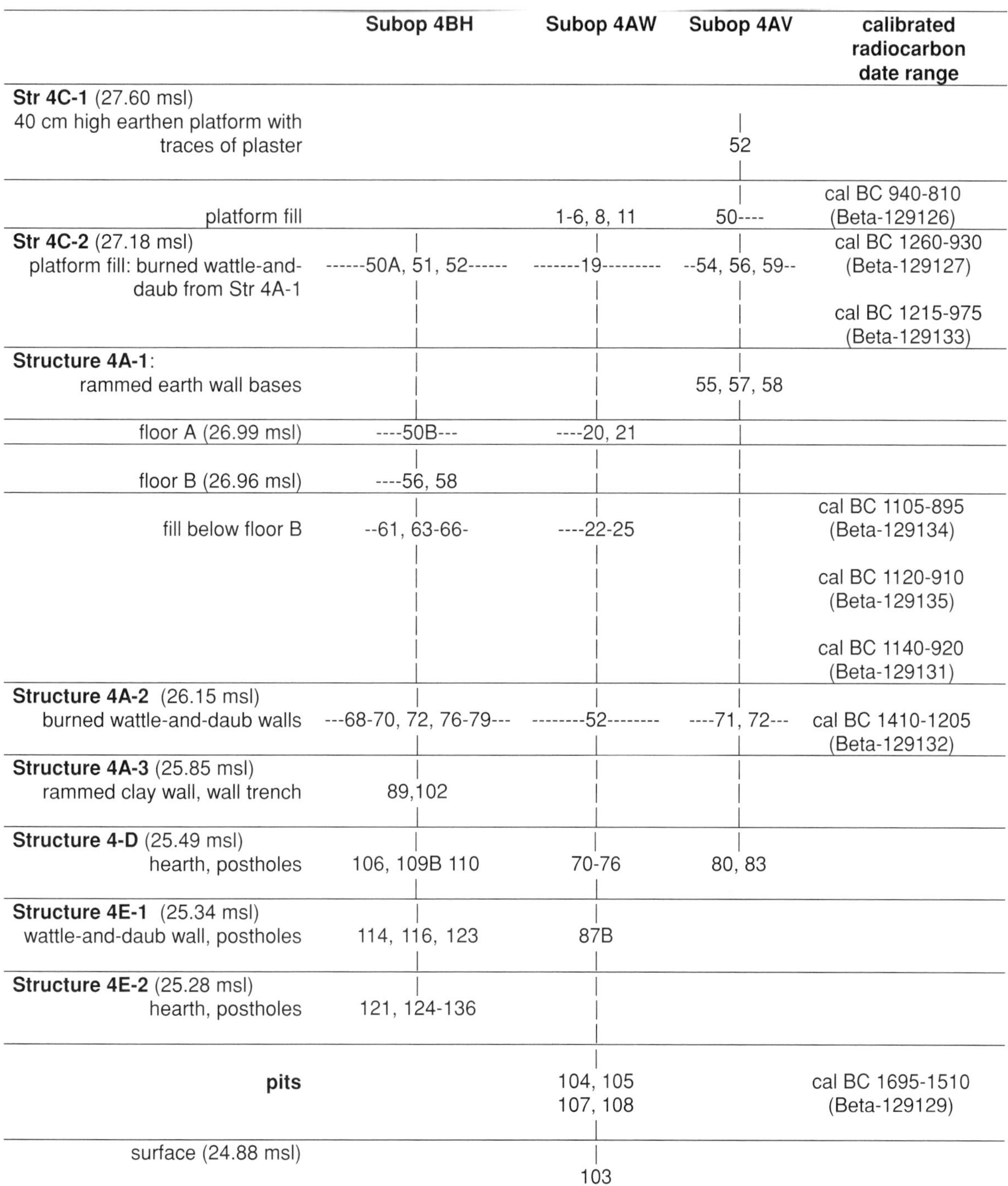

Figure 3.2. Modified Harris matrix showing the depositional history of rebuilding of structures in one area of Puerto Escondido over multiple centuries. Subop = suboperation; msl = meters above sea level.

arrangements of skeletal elements secondary to other treatment prior to this act of incorporation. The practices brought together at Puerto Escondido—the burial of costume ornaments and human skeletal elements in larger scale, more permanent architecture—are echoed at the contemporary site of Los Naranjos in the highlands at the south end of the lower Ulúa Valley (Baudez and Becquelin 1973). There, a burial in Structure IV, a six-meter-tall earthen platform,

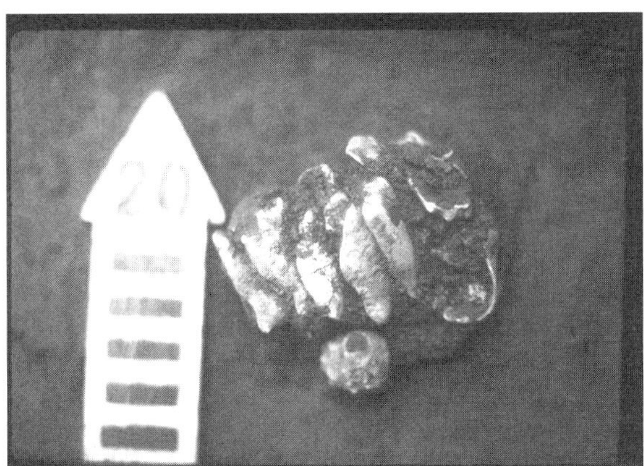

Figure 3.3. Subfloor deposit Op 7B-89 at Puerto Escondido: a marine shell belt coiled and deposited in a pit under a cobble platform.

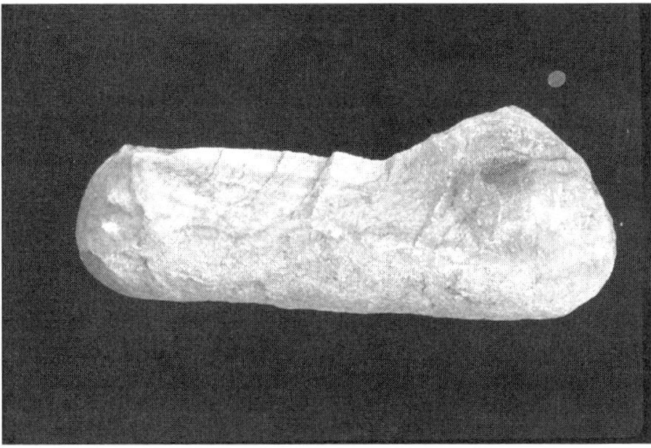

Figure 3.5. Puerto Escondido Monument 1: frontal view of crossed legs of seated figure, with "cup marks" on knees. Coin at upper right for scale (size equal to U.S. quarter).

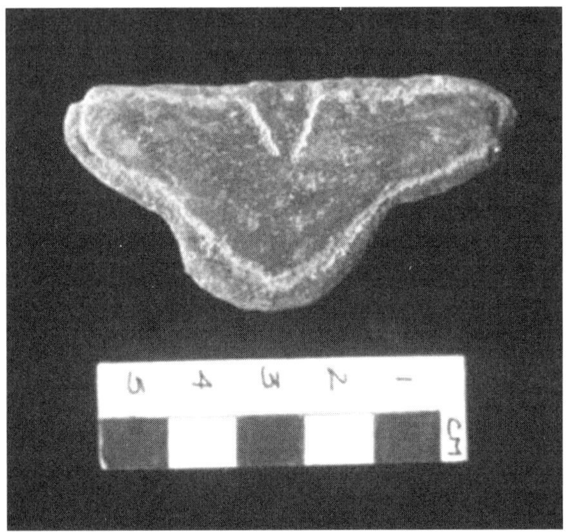

Figure 3.4. Fired clay pendant in the form of a bivalve shell, Puerto Escondido Op 4AM-42.

included a jade pendant hung from the center of a belt that is identical in shape and scale to the two cached at Puerto Escondido (Baudez and Becquelin 1973:49).

At this historical moment at Puerto Escondido, all the practices that constitute subfloor burial (disjunction, incorporation, commemoration) were finally focused on human remains. Yet the placement of human burials in residential groups that developed afterward must be seen as one part of a suite of practices whose more common foci were other things: complete pottery vessels, figurines, costume elements, and stone tools. In burials that become common in villages near Puerto Escondido after 900 B.C.E., such as Playa de los Muertos, such objects are commonly included in residential settings in the same deposits as human skeletal elements (Joyce et al. 2008). Rather than see these objects as mortuary offerings added to human burials that appear for the first time around 900 B.C.E., it is historically more consistent to regard the *human skeletal elements* as additions to existing practices of incorporation of objects in subfloor deposits. This encourages us to continue to examine the treatment of human remains in connection with the treatment of other objects subject to practices of incorporation, disjunction, and commemoration, even when there are no human skeletal elements associated.

At Puerto Escondido, the second area remodeled around 900 B.C.E. into a stepped platform differed from the earthen platform that yielded our earliest burials in the use of more durable stone in place of clay. This stepped terrace itself had a stone facing, a large stone hearth was placed in front of it, and several stone cists of a size appropriate to serve as tombs were part of this architectural assemblage. Isolated human teeth were found in one of these cists. A second completely excavated cist yielded no human skeletal remains but contained a fragment from a life-sized stone sculpture, depicting the crossed legs of a seated human figure, among the stones filling in the cist (Figure 3.5). A complete ceramic figurine, originally pierced for suspension as an ornament, showing a skeletalized human body, was set in the stones capping the cist (Figure 3.6). Rather than being "empty" simply because no human skeletal elements were incorporated, this deliberately constructed, durable chamber was the site of deposition of *two* products of disjunction of human subjects, one a figurine originally worn as a pendant, the other a durable bodily extension achieved by portraiture. The *personne* (after Mauss; see Gillespie 2001) whose life was commemorated by the people of this early village did not necessarily coincide with the physical body as we today understand it, and the presence of skeletal elements was not required for commemoration to be effective.

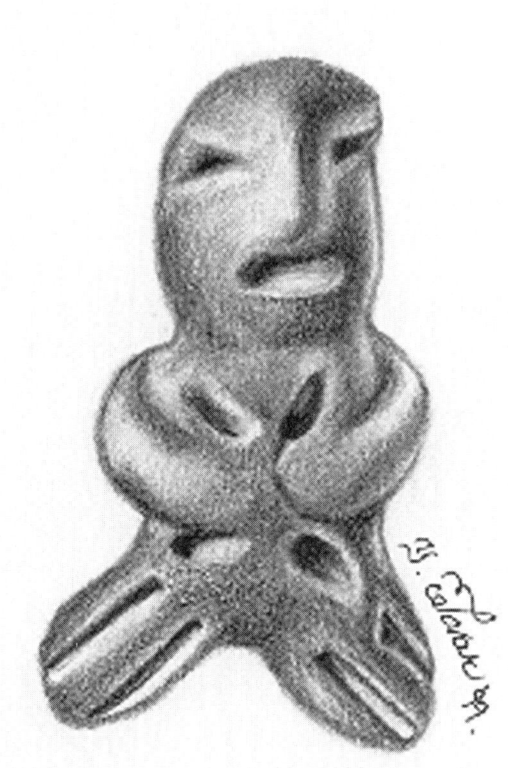

Figure 3.6. Small pendant figurine, Puerto Escondido Op 2BN-6. (Drawing by Yolanda Tovar)

At the End of a History: Residential Burial in Classic Period Puerto Escondido

A discontinuity in occupation in these two main areas of extensive area excavation appears to have lasted from circa 400 B.C.E. to C.E. 400. Occupation of the village itself continued elsewhere, as indicated by results from a program of test-pitting, so we can treat the people who built new features in the areas of earlier occupation as historically connected. In the area of our most extensive excavations, where around 900 B.C.E. we first saw evidence of placement of human skeletal remains in an earthen platform along with other buried objects, the final preserved component in the site (dated C.E. 400–630) took the form of groups of residential buildings and exterior features. This final preserved component shares the form of residential subfloor burial typical in many Mesoamerican sites: children and adults in extended burials below floors or in exterior patio spaces.

With the preexisting history of practices as a guide, we can see that the placement of skeletal remains below living floors should not be separated from other practices of incorporation, disjunction, and commemoration in this early Classic neighborhood of the village we today call Puerto Escondido. The use of subfloor storage pits, many found refilled with trash, but sometimes containing carefully prepared burials, is just one of a group of contemporary practices of subsurface caching in which buildings in the lower Ulúa Valley were layered with dense histories by the incorporation of objects, including the human objects that we recognize as the primary focus of burial practices (Joyce and Pollard 2010; Lopiparo 2006, 2007). Burials literally incorporate the bones of human deceased in the fabric of the residential compound.

At the same time, both figurines and items of personal adornment continue to form part of subfloor deposits incorporated in the local landscape. Figurines are now moldmade, but arguably reference human identities at the scale of the village or household that in earlier periods were secondary to stages of the personal life cycle (Joyce 2003; Lopiparo 2007). They simultaneously extend personhood beyond the locality of the corporeal body and beyond the temporal scope of the living actor and commemorate the existence of such actors at these particular places and times.

The example of body ornaments is particularly interesting. Where in earlier periods, marine shell and jade objects that were presumably valuable for the exotic origin of their rare materials were common objects in special deposits, in the early Classic village, these materials are never recovered from burials, even the most elaborate. Instead, the main items of personal adornment that continue to be incorporated in depositional histories of people in place are earspools, most made of fired clay, a few of shell or bone. There are clear instances where complete, delicate "napkin ring" earspools are recovered located on either side of the skull of the buried body, implying that these ornaments almost uniquely remained attached to the body at death. But even where there are very formalized burial facilities, it is relatively common to find fragmented earspools of different dimensions and even paste composition as part of the fill in or around burials. The association of earspool fragments with burials is statistically significant, with a Chi square statistic of 4.8416 with one degree of freedom, for a probability of less than 0.05 of this association being the result of chance. But the association of earspools with excavation units that yielded burials is also statistically significant, even when these objects were not directly associated with the human skeletal remains, implying they were broken and discarded separately as part of mortuary rituals. Apparently, earspools were particularly appropriate media for disjunction from living bodies in the early Classic, and for incorporation in household deposits that resulted from commemorative actions.

A total of 21 groups of human skeletal remains excavated in this area of the site can be assigned to the early Classic occupation (dating ca. C.E. 400–630 based on radiocarbon dates, consistent with ceramic cross-ties). At least three of these deposits consisted of isolated elements, long bones in two cases and a cranium without mandible along with an ulna in the third. The cranium and one of the sets of long bones showed the remains of red pigment applied to the bones, supporting the interpretation of these sets of elements as secondary burials or caches of previously processed human remains. Another 16 groups of skeletal remains were either complete extended burials or parts of extended burials that either extended into unexcavated deposits or were disturbed by recent construction digging. The final two contexts were too fragmentary to be certain but in general shared features with the extended burials. Physical anthropological assessment identified three juveniles among these burials, and while sex determination was in general difficult due to poor preservation, at least one burial was of an adult woman. Thus, the burial population included adults and children, women, and, presumably, men. In nine cases, skeletal elements were well enough preserved to be certain of burial orientation, including the position the head was facing. Four of these were oriented south of east, with the head to the east, facing north. The other five were oriented east of north, with the head north, facing east. The orientation resembles that documented in other settlements of the lower Ulúa Valley, where Lopiparo (2006, 2007) has suggested burial orientation responds to shared orientation to reference points on the surrounding horizon. In addition, at Puerto Escondido, it appears that many of these burials were parallel to house walls.

None of the burials from early Classic Puerto Escondido incorporated any complete ceramic vessels. Ten burials either contained intact earspools or had fragments of earspools in close proximity. Yet only in one case was a pair of identical size and color found located near the skull of the buried individual, as if the person were buried wearing earspools. Most other burials were accompanied by a single fragment of an earspool.

The exception to the general simplicity of burial treatment is a burial with exceptional characteristics, including the use of a special burial facility, inclusion of broken ceramic vessels, and other evidence of elaborate mortuary rituals. This individual was buried with fragments from at least five distinct earspools (including two complete earspools from different pairs, and seven other fragments), disjoined from their original persons and incorporated in one single burial. This individual also was accompanied by the only evidence for deposition of ceramic vessels, all broken as part of the closing of the grave.

The person accorded this burial would normally be viewed as the top of a social hierarchy, and indeed, he or she must have been a person of some importance. But with the long-term perspective provided by considering practices of incorporation, disjunction, and commemoration throughout the history of inhabitation here, we can consider this more unusual burial from a much different perspective, as epitomizing the practices united to give residential subfloor burial its historical meaning and social impact, rather than as merely the reflection of a preexisting rank based on some other attributes of the deceased person.

In the residential compound explored, where we exposed parts of at least two groups of buildings arranged around small courtyards, this unique burial was associated with an otherwise undistinguished building. He or she was placed in a reused subterranean pit with a narrow neck, of the kind referred to in Mesoamerica as a "bottle-shaped" pit. It is believed these pits served for domestic storage before, in most cases, being reused for other purposes such as trash disposal (as was another in this area). We originally identified the neck of the pit on the basis of a concentration of large potsherds, including the pieces of a three-dimensional effigy of a feline. This is a kind of ceramic sculpture that, perched on a lid, crowned vessels in which plant materials were burned as incense (Joyce and Pollard 2010). Other fragments of the same clay mixture recovered here suggest a second vessel, a human effigy holding a bag in its hand, may have been broken and incorporated in the deposit as well. In addition to these indications of the ritual burning of resins, fragments of five small cylindrical vessels called "candaleros," understood as used for burning resin as well, were included in this deposit.

Continued excavation here showed that the neck of the subterranean pit had been blocked entirely by large ceramic sherds and fragments of ceramic figurines. In all, fragments of up to 20 figurines, including one complete figurine of a seated woman holding a vessel, and one complete whistle in the shape of a bird head, were recovered here. The themes of figurine fragments included animals (a feline) and at least five depictions of humans, both women and men. While in general there was no statistically significant association of figurines with burials, this probably reflects the fact that figurines were used in a range of household-based rituals, including those relating to death, rather than that they were unrelated to mortuary commemoration. Of the 18 burials included in the Chi square analysis, 14 did have associated fragments of figurines. In contrast, in 36 excavation units without burials, half had fragments of figurines, and half did not.

After clearing the neck of the pit, we encountered a series of lenses of carbon-rich soil alternating with clay, in which were mixed a variety of pottery fragments, some from very unusual vessels, and obsidian flakes and blades. The broken pottery deposited here included examples of local polychrome serving vessels (dated roughly to the period C.E. 650–700), as well as imported pottery from the Belize River valley across the Caribbean, and sherds from a spectacular imported vase covered with thin stucco painted with red specular hematite and dark blue pigments. Two local mold-made vessels represented by fragments in this deposit were an effigy of the rare carved Ulua Marble Vase, and a second vessel similar in paste depicting a frontal skull.

The body incorporated in this commemorative deposit was laid out on its back, with the head north, facing east, at the extreme southwest edge of the pit, away from the pit neck. The body rested above alternating layers of carbon and ash and clay. The arms of the buried individual were extended along the sides of the body, while the lower legs were crossed. Rarer objects included in the deposit were a single feline incisor; a shell pendant "tinkler" made from a marine shell (*Oliva* species); the interior spiral from a conch shell; a fragment of a ceramic stamp; a single tubular grey ceramic bead; and a single ceramic sphere 14 millimeters in diameter. While many of these items are parts of body ornaments, and the rectangular stamp was arguably used to mark patterns on the body or on bark cloth, in no case were all pieces of an item of costume recovered.

In fact, the only object clearly associated directly with the body was a unique rectangular plaque of black obsidian, made from a very large blade (30 by 32 millimeters). Abraded on all edges, this compares most closely to mirrors that, made of a variety of materials, were part of Mesoamerican costume by 1000 B.C.E. and were still in use in the sixteenth century C.E. Objects like this are widely understood as emblems of authority or badges of office, especially due to their use in ritual divination.

Neither the earliest person buried in this household compound, nor separated definitively from others by placement in a tomb or other special facility, even this most distinguished person was only one part of a practice of commemoration of the dead through their bodily incorporation in the local place, along with disjoined fragments of the extended persons of a multiplicity of other actors.

Implications

For reasons that are perhaps obvious, archaeologists tend to come to analysis of burials with a human-centered bias. We ask questions about what social statuses led to different treatment of the people whose deaths are commemorated by their incorporation in planned deposits. We may be led at times to wonder whether some human skeletal remains were incorporated as objectified things rather than persons, as with the inclusion in multi-person burials of additional individuals considered possible "sacrifices." But we normally understand this as a special exception to a general rule in which burial of human remains is meaningfully oriented to the recognition and remembering of a distinct person.

Because burial of human remains in ways that suggest such deliberate commemoration of a dead person can be recognized already in the earliest stages of the history of our species, we tend to avoid the historical question of just how specific practices of disposal of the dead were developed at the scale of a local, historically connected, population. This essay has attempted to rigorously attend to fully developed burial practices evident in the early Classic period at Puerto Escondido as a culmination of a history of practices that did not originate specifically for the purpose of commemorating a human person by incorporating his or her body in the dwelling site.

This historical examination leads me to recognize human remains as one of a series of things that were incorporated in dwelling sites at Puerto Escondido over a period of more than 1,500 years. The things incorporated within these localized places may well have helped perpetuate the memory of persons, through reference to their corporeal bodies, to their most distinctive body ornaments, and to their iconic or indexical representations in figural sculptures. But the human bodies incorporated in these history-filled places never entirely dominate the scene. They contribute to a series of actions through which the dwelling itself was made more solid over time and was historicized by association with the events whose traces we see today as distinctive deposits: refilling of storage pits, whether with the debris of a feast (as in two cases examined in detail at Puerto Escondido) or that of a mortuary ceremony (in the case described here); placement of individual objects or groups of objects as "caches," or burials of person-like things; and burial of human skeletal remains, subject at times to continuing treatment as things, by selection, reconfiguration, pigmentation, and placement in a secondary location.

So in the end, my understanding of the treatment of the durable parts of the human body, both those that grow organically (bones) and those that are manufactured (fired clay earspools), comes about because of the social interests of actors at Puerto Escondido in enhancing the dwelling and its history. Incorporating the durable bodily remains of human beings is an extension of the incorporation of durable remains of human persons, such as the shell belt, ceramic pendant, or jade belt pendants that were earlier objects of burial practices. The incorporation of these indices of human beings or persons makes more specific the inherent reference of the continually rebuilt dwelling to all of its human inhabitants, whose labor is indexed in the walls, floors, hearths, and other built features. To understand why human burials are part of the house requires us to understand why houses themselves are the subject of work intended to reproduce them and give them ongoing histories. People are part of that story, but only part.

References

Baudez, Claude, and Pierre Becquelin
1973 Archéologie de los Naranjos, Honduras. Etudes Mesoaméricaines 2. Mexico, D.F.: Mission Archeologique et Ethnologique Française au Mexique.

Bergmann, John
1969 The Distribution of Cacao Cultivation in Pre-Columbian America. Annals of the Association of American Geographers 59:85–96.

Brady, James E., Christopher Begley, John Fogarty, Donald J. Stierman, Barbara Luke, and Ann Scott
2001 Talgua Archaeological Project: A Technical Assessment. http://www.calstatela.edu/academic/anthro/Talgua_pre.htm, accessed December 7, 2008.

Clark, John E.
2000 Towards a Better Explanation of Hereditary Inequality: A Critical Assessment of Natural and Historic Agents. *In* Agency in Archaeology. Marcia-Anne Dobres and John Robb, eds. Pp. 92–112. London: Routledge.

Gillespie, Susan D.
2001 Personhood, Agency, and Mortuary Ritual: A Case Study from the Ancient Maya. Journal of Anthropological Archaeology 20:73–112.

Gordon, George Byron
1898 Caverns of Copan, Honduras. Memoirs of the Peabody Museum of Archaeology and Ethnology, vol. 1, no. 5. Cambridge, MA: Harvard University.

Healy, Paul
1974 Cuyamel Caves: Preclassic Sites in Northeast Honduras. American Antiquity 39:433–437.
1984 Northeast Honduras: A Pre-Columbian Frontier Zone. *In* Recent Developments in Isthmian Archaeology: Advances in the Prehistory of Lower Central America. Fred Lange, ed. Pp. 227–242. Proceedings of the 44th International Congress of Americanists, Manchester. BAR International Series 212. Oxford: Archaeopress.

Henderson, John S.
1979 The Valle de Naco: Ethnohistory and Archaeology in Northwestern Honduras. Ethnohistory 24:363–377.

Henderson, John S., and Rosemary A. Joyce
1998 Investigaciones arqueológicas en Puerto Escondido: Definición del Formativo Temprano en el Valle Inferior del Río Ulúa. Yaxkin 17:5–35. Tegucigalpa.

Henderson, John S., Rosemary A. Joyce, Gretchen R. Hall, W. Jeffrey Hurst, and Patrick E. McGovern
2007 Chemical and Archaeological Evidence for the Earliest Cacao Beverages. Proceedings of the National Academy of Sciences 104:18937–18940.

Joyce, Rosemary A.
1999 Social Dimensions of Pre-Classic Burials. *In* Social Patterns in Pre-Classic Mesoamerica. David C. Grove and Rosemary A. Joyce, eds. Pp. 15–47. Washington, DC: Dumbarton Oaks.
2001 Burying the Dead at Tlatilco: Social Memory and Social Identities. *In* Social Memory, Identity, and Death: Anthropological Perspectives on Mortuary Rituals. Meredith S. Chesson, ed. Pp. 12–26. Archeological Papers of the American Anthropological Association, 10. Arlington, VA: American Anthropological Association.
2003 Making Something of Herself: Embodiment in Life and Death at Playa de los Muertos, Honduras. Cambridge Archaeological Journal 13:248–261.
2004a Unintended Consequences? Monumentality as a Novel Experience in Formative Mesoamerica. Journal of Archaeological Method and Theory 11:5–29.
2004b Unprecedented Projects: The Birth of Mesoamerican Pyramids. Expedition 46(2):7–11.
2007 Building Houses: The Materialization of Lasting Identity in Formative Mesoamerica. *In* The Durable House: House Society Models in Archaeology. Robin A. Beck Jr., ed. Pp. 53–72. Occasional Paper 35. Carbondale: Center for Archaeological Investigations, Southern Illinois University.
2008 Practice in and as Deposition. *In* Memory Work: Archaeologies of Material Practices.

Barbara J. Mills and William H. Walker, eds. Pp. 25–40. Santa Fe, NM: School for Advanced Research Press.

Joyce, Rosemary A., and John S. Henderson

2001 Beginnings of Village Life in Eastern Mesoamerica. Latin American Antiquity 12:5–24.

2002 La arqueología del periodo Formativo en Honduras: Nuevos datos sobre el "estilo olmeca" en la zona maya. Mayab 15:5–18.

2003 Investigaciones recientes de la arqueología del periodo Formativo en Honduras: Nuevos datos según el intercambio y cerámica Pan-mesoamericana (o estilo "olmeca"). *In* XVI Simposio de Investigaciones Arqueológicas en Guatemala, 2002. Juan Pedro Laporte, Bárbara Arroyo, Héctor L. Escobedo, and Héctor E. Mejía, eds. Pp. 819–832. Guatemala: Museo Nacional de Arqueología y Etnología and Asociación Tikal.

2007 From Feasting to Cuisine: Implications of Archaeological Research in an Early Honduran Village. American Anthropologist 109:642–653.

2010 Being "Olmec" in Formative Honduras. Ancient Mesoamerica 21:187–200.

Joyce, Rosemary A., Julia A. Hendon, and Russell N. Sheptak

2008 Una nueva evaluación de Playa de los Muertos: Exploraciones en el periodo Formativo Medio en Honduras. *In* Ideología Politica y Sociedad en el Periodo Formativo: Ensayos en Homenaje al Doctor David C. Grove. Ann Cyphers and Kenneth G. Hirth, eds. Pp. 283–310. Mexico, D.F.: Instituto de Investigaciones Antropológicas, Universidad Nacional Autonoma de Mexico.

Joyce, Rosemary A., and Joshua Pollard

2010 Archaeological Assemblages and Practices of Deposition. *In* The Oxford Handbook of Material Culture Studies. Dan Hicks and Mary Beaudry, eds. Pp. 289–304. Oxford: Oxford University Press.

Joyce, Rosemary A., M. Steven Shackley, Kenneth McCandless, and Rus Sheptak

2004 Resultados preliminares de una investigación con EDXRF de obsidiana de Puerto Escondido. *In* Memoria del VII Seminario de Antropología de Honduras "Dr. George Hasemann." Pp. 115–129. Tegucigalpa: Instituto Hondureño de Antropología e Historia.

Lopiparo, Jeanne

2006 Crafting Children: Materiality, Social Memory, and the Reproduction of Terminal Classic House Societies in the Ulua Valley, Honduras. *In* The Social Experience of Childhood in Ancient Mesoamerica. Traci Ardren and Scott Hutson, eds. Pp. 133–168. Boulder: University Press of Colorado.

2007 House Societies and Heterarchy in the Terminal Classic Ulúa Valley, Honduras. *In* The Durable House: House Society Models in Archaeology. Robin A. Beck Jr., ed. Pp. 73–96. Occasional Paper 35. Carbondale: Center for Archaeological Investigations, Southern Illinois University.

Luke, Christina, Rosemary A. Joyce, John S. Henderson, and Robert H. Tykot

2003 Marble Carving Traditions in Honduras: Formative through Terminal Classic. *In* ASMOSIA 6, Interdisciplinary Studies on Ancient Stone—Proceedings of the Sixth International Conference of the Association for the Study of Marble and Other Stones in Antiquity, Venice, June 15–18, 2000. L. Lazzarini, ed. Pp. 485–496. Padova: Bottega d'Erasmo.

Luke, Christina, and Robert H. Tykot

2007 Celebrating Place through Luxury Craft Production: Travesia and Ulua Style Marble Vases. Ancient Mesoamerica 18:315–328.

Pope, Kevin

1987 The Ecology and Economy of the Formative-Classic Transition along the Ulua River, Honduras. *In* Interaction on the Southeast Mesoamerican Frontier: Prehistoric and Historic Honduras and El Salvador. Eugenia J. Robinson, ed. Pp. 95–128. BAR International Series 327(i). Oxford: Archaeopress.

Rue, David J., AnnCorinne Freter, and Diane A. Ballinger

1989 The Caverns of Copan Revisited: Preclassic Sites in the Sesesmil River Valley, Copan, Honduras. Journal of Field Archaeology 16:395–404.

Vitelli, Karen D.

1998 "Looking Up" at Early Ceramics in Greece. *In* Pottery and People. James Skibo and Gary Feinman, eds. Pp. 184–198. Salt Lake City: University of Utah Press.

4

Remembering One and All: Early Postclassic Residential Burial in Coastal Oaxaca, Mexico

Stacie M. King
Indiana University

ABSTRACT

Residential burial at Río Viejo marked deceased adults as members of particular houses and as witnesses and actors within the world of the living after their physical deaths. The standardization in burial locations, positions, and offerings emphasized the group identity of Río Viejo adults and their shared house histories. The simultaneous commitment to keeping individual bodies separate and intact, however, indicates that this group identity was not achieved through the subjugation of individual identities. Instead, at Río Viejo, the deceased were celebrated as a cohort of ancestors made up of unique individuals, rather than as a single-minded collective group. [residential burial, Mesoamerica, ancestors, social identities, age]

Two important, seemingly antithetical, interpretations emerge in archaeological study of mortuary practices. One is that burial practices say something unique about a deceased person's social position or individual identity in life. This perspective is most closely linked to the Saxe-Binford approach (see Adams and King, chapter 1, this volume), whereby burials and grave offerings provide important data for understanding individual identity and social hierarchies in past societies (Binford 1971; Saxe 1970). However, another common interpretation is that mortuary rituals make statements about collective membership in particular social groups or communities in part by de-emphasizing social ranking (e.g., Parker Pearson 2000). According to this interpretation, burial practices largely reflect (and help to construct) widely shared community norms, and mortuary rituals emphasize group identities by focusing on the similarities between people in death. In cases where burial occurs in shared living space, such as within residential areas and below house floors, it is tempting to lean toward the latter interpretation and argue that mortuary practices say something about group membership and group identity. In this chapter, I explore mortuary practices at the site of Río Viejo, in coastal Oaxaca, Mexico (Figure 4.1), to show how both interpretations apply. At Río Viejo, residential burial became an intrinsic part of the creation of strong group identities associated with house membership, yet it did so while still preserving the opportunity to celebrate individual identity. Schiller (2001), in an ethnographic study of mortuary monuments and identity in Indonesian Borneo, argues a similar point about the *tiwah* ritual. During *tiwah*, bones of the dead are exhumed and redeposited inside a mausoleum along with much fanfare and celebration. She argues that the communal celebration of *tiwah* helps to "create and foster sentiments of affinity, on the one hand, and of estrangement on the other" and is an important space in which notions of Ngaju identity are negotiated (Schiller 2001:78). The mortuary practices at Río Viejo allowed for similar kinds of identity negotiations. Burial within residential structures conceptually harnessed the social, economic, and political power of deceased house members in service of the collective group, while at the same time the firm adherence to maintaining nonoverlapping grave spaces created a simple, yet elegant means of acknowledging individual identity. Residential burial at Río Viejo communicated the identities of both individuals (*one*) and the group (*all*) by simultaneously emphasizing difference and sameness.

ARCHEOLOGICAL PAPERS OF THE AMERICAN ANTHROPOLOGICAL ASSOCIATION, Vol. 20, Issue 1, pp. 44–58, ISSN 1551-823X, online ISSN 1551-8248. DOI: 10.1111/j.1551-8248.2011.01027.x.

In ancient Mesoamerica, ancestors played important roles in the everyday lives of living peoples and residential burial was a common practice (Hendon 1999; Joyce 1999; McAnany 1995; Ruz Lhullier 1968). In Mesoamerican cosmology, the cultural, natural, and spiritual worlds were not sharply divided and a deceased person's ties to the living did not end with death (Houston et al. 2006; Léon-Portilla 1963; McAnany 1995). Burial within the house expressed the connections between the deceased and the living both figuratively and physically. Mortuary practices at the site of Río Viejo are no exception. Although Río Viejo was once a political capital and regional headquarters with sharply delineated social hierarchies (Joyce 2008), circumstances had changed by the Early Postclassic. Dating to between C.E. 975 and C.E. 1220, the Early Postclassic occupation of the site was much smaller, restricted to a few residential neighborhoods without any evidence for hierarchical social ranking (King 2003). In one neighborhood at the site, deceased adults were interred beneath the floors of houses, a practice that incorporated the deceased as witnesses and actors within the world of the living after their physical deaths. Here, burial within the confines of separate house structures marked specific people as the deceased ancestors of particular houses. Yet at the same time, the similarity in burial treatment across the site reinforced a common, shared community history incorporating both the living and the dead and tying the members of separate households to one another.

Evidence for residential burial in coastal Oaxaca extends back to the Late to Terminal Formative periods (100 B.C.E.) (Barber 2005; Joyce 1994). In highland Oaxaca, residential burial was a practice in use from the Middle Formative to the Classic period (500 B.C.E.–C.E.800) (Barber 2005; Drennan 1976:129; Lind and Urcid 2010:100; Winter 1995). The manner in which subfloor residential burial was executed at Río Viejo, however, is unique and compelling for two reasons. First, the mortuary sample at Early Postclassic Río Viejo shows that only adults (or people above the age of 17 or so) were buried beneath house floors. The two child burials that were found were both placed outside the confines of house walls, showing that children and adults were treated in distinct manners. Residents seem to have made a conceptual distinction between intramural space and outside space, with children buried *outside* of the confines of specific house structures, separated from at least some adults in death. I have explored this distinction between child and adult burial in a separate publication, but will summarize it again here since it is important for understanding the meaning and significance of residential burial at Río Viejo (King 2006).

Second, residential burial at Río Viejo is unique because the subfloor burials were precisely planned and standardized, such that no burial impacts another. All individuals are buried in similar positions with similar offerings, and the burial ritual depended on the knowledge and remembrance of previous grave locations. While the inclusion of only adults in residential burials signals something important about membership in households, the planning within particular houses and standardization across the site suggests both individual and generalized ancestors were subjects of commemoration. In this chapter, I focus primarily on this latter aspect of coastal Oaxacan residential burial and argue that both individual and group identities were celebrated and commemorated simultaneously. The precise and enduring memory of grave locations of specific deceased adults shows that it was important for the living to honor and maintain the integrity of each particular deceased relative's individual identity, while the striking standardization reveals strong community burial standards and recognition of shared group identity. Burial in similar ways serves to reference and celebrate collective house memories by transforming deceased house members into generalized house ancestors. The statement that is being made through separate burial locations and the shared mortuary rites is that each deceased house member stood on his or her own and as part of the group simultaneously. Burial within residential boundaries shows that both individual and collective social action were most appropriately mediated through the house.

The Early Postclassic Mortuary Sample

The Early Postclassic occupation of Río Viejo consists of clusters of houses distributed in multiple residential neighborhoods. The houses were built directly on top of the monumental remains of the abandoned Late Classic period acropolis associated with the former regional urban capital, dating to roughly C.E. 500–800 (Figure 4.2). The new houses that Early Postclassic residents constructed were modest wattle-and-daub, single-room structures with stone foundations on top of the Classic period ruins, which at times incorporated stone construction material, including a broken carved stone stela fragment and groundstone tools, from earlier occupations. In these clustered neighborhoods, residents established a stable and enduring community based in part on the success of household social relationships, community-wide religious rituals, and craft production focused on cloth, figurines, jewelry, musical instruments, and costume ornaments. Early Postclassic residents participated in interregional exchange networks that supplied coastal

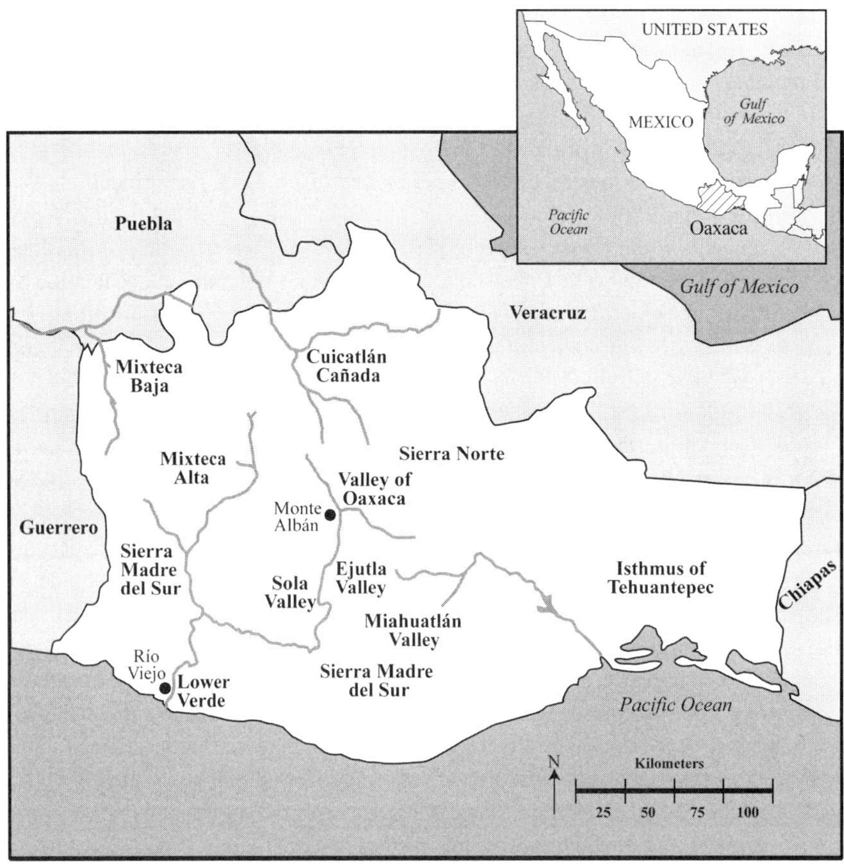

Figure 4.1. Map of Oaxaca showing the location of Rio Viejo.

cotton thread to highland Oaxaca (King in press). In return, Río Viejo residents received obsidian from several different highland sources, which was manufactured into blade tools and used by every household in the community. These exchange routes probably extended through the highland Mixteca Alta region, connecting Río Viejo both economically and socially to the large Early Postclassic centers of Cholula and Tula and the greater Postclassic Mesoamerican world (King 2008a).

In 2000, I directed the excavation of one of these neighborhoods, which included portions of six house structures dating to the Early Postclassic, along with a full suite of domestic artifacts and the mortuary remains of 16 individuals (Figure 4.3). Arthur Joyce directed the excavation of a second contemporaneous neighborhood, uncovering portions of five additional house structures and four burials (Joyce et al. 2001; Joyce and King 2001). The burial patterns in the two neighborhoods were quite different. The Operation A sample excavated by Joyce included two child burials, both of which were interred outside of buildings in flexed positions, an adult male buried outside a structure with no offerings, and two adults interred underneath a patio (one of which may have been part of a sacrificial ritual). By contrast, all 16 Early Postclassic burials found in the Operation B neighborhood were the result of primary burial events and included only one individual (Table 4.1). Each body was placed in the ground in a similar way, extended on the back, head to the south, with arms resting either alongside the torso or crossed on the abdomen. The presence of diagnostic Early Postclassic ceramic vessel offerings interred with most of the deceased confirms the association of this burial pattern and these burials with the Early Postclassic. Large fragments of broken ceramic vessels similar to those placed in the burials were found in a midden in Operation B that yielded a calibrated radiocarbon date between C.E. 1035 and C.E. 1187 (two-sigma variation, AA40040, reported in King 2006).

Most of the Early Postclassic burials in Operation B were interred beneath the floor of a single house, Structure 8–8b (Figure 4.4). The structure measures 5 by 11 meters, and is rectangular with the long axis running east to west. Within this structure, bodies were laid out side by side across nearly the entire subfloor area of the building, paralleling the north–south–running structure walls. All individuals were

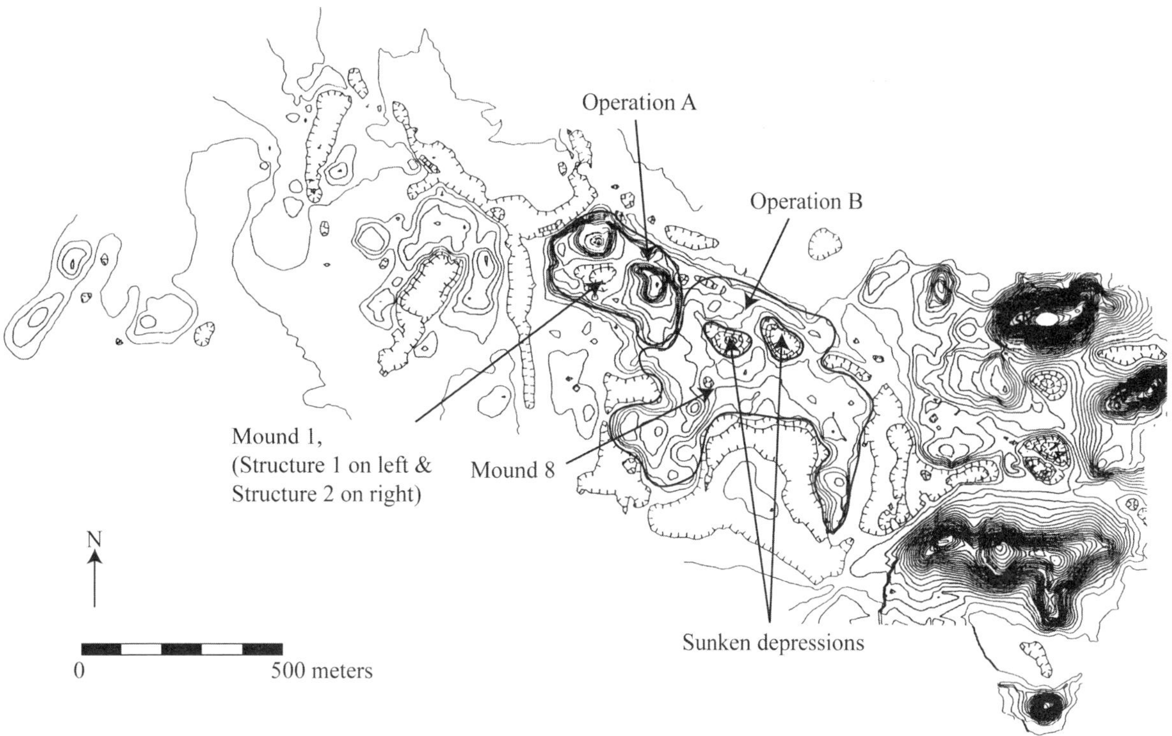

Figure 4.2. Plan view of Río Viejo, showing the location of the Operation A and Operation B neighborhoods.

oriented similarly with their heads to the south. This placement is seemingly purposeful so as to fit more burials in the space, forming a rough row of bodies across the length of the structure, as shown in Figure 4.4.

The remaining five burials were uncovered beneath the floor of Structure 8–7, in nearly identical positions, although in this case the long axis of the 5-by-11-meter structure runs north–south rather than east–west (Figure 4.5). This created a slightly different burial plan whereby multiple rows were possible. Only in a few locations within the excavation limits did we clear to the level where the burials are found (below the house floor). Additional rows of burials may exist in the northern half of the structure, which is outside the excavation limits, and in the southernmost section of the structure, where we did not excavate below the house floor. Had we excavated the entire house to the levels below the floor surface, we may have located additional burials.

The Early Postclassic burial patterns are quite distinct from burial practices in earlier time periods in the lower Río Verde valley. Among the 102 burials from Late and Terminal Formative period residential zones at the site of Cerro de la Cruz (Joyce 1991b, 1994), subfloor and subpatio burial was common, but there the burials included primary and secondary burials and single- and multiple-individual burials of people of all ages and sexes. Burial positions were either flexed or extended, and burial orientations varied, most often running parallel to structure walls. The Classic period sample includes 30 individuals recovered from test pits at the site of Río Viejo, or intrusive deposits at Cerro de la Cruz (Christensen 1999; Joyce 1991a, 1994), and again exhibits great variation in number, context, and orientation. The Early Postclassic pattern of placing the dead in single, primary burials in highly standardized, similarly oriented, nonoverlapping graves is highly distinct.

Residential Burial and House Membership

As mentioned earlier, burial beneath house floors and within residential zones is a common practice across Mesoamerica. Most recently, scholars have linked the practice of subfloor burial to ancestor worship or ancestor veneration, which is connected to the belief in a fluid boundary between life and death in Mesoamerican cosmology (Geller 2006; Gillespie 2002; McAnany 1995; Manzanilla 2002; Miller 1995; see also Smith 2002:112, in which the lack of burials beneath house floors at Aztec sites is used to argue that Aztecs did not practice ancestor veneration). Subfloor burials provided living people with daily access to the ancestors and gave them spiritual support. At the same time, the

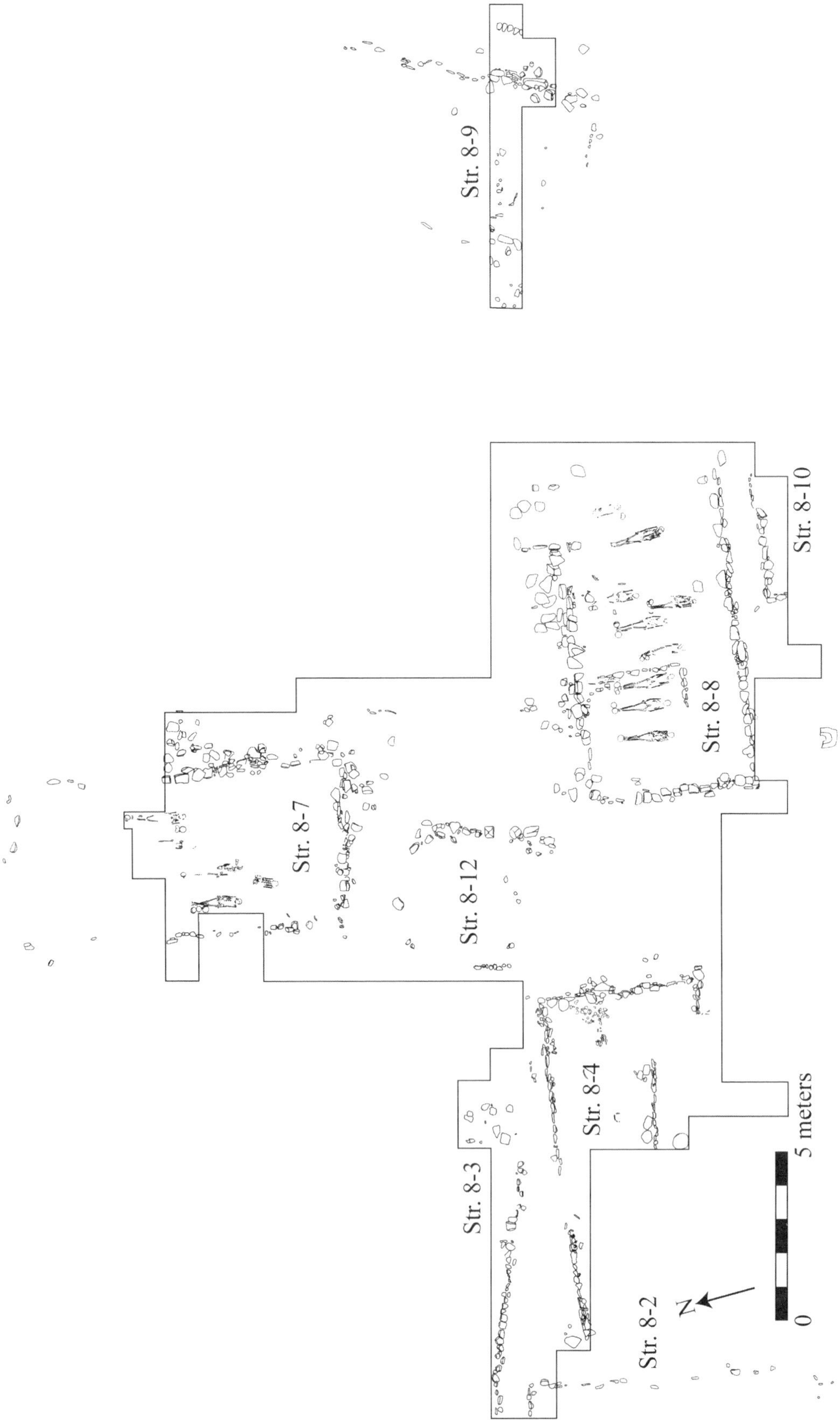

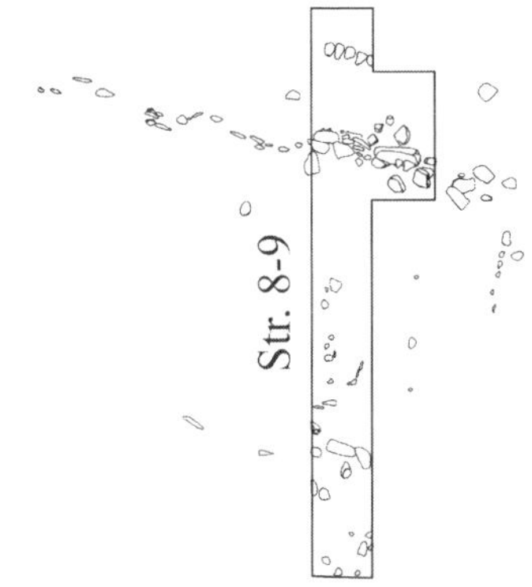

Figure 4.3. Plan view of the Operation B neighborhood, Río Viejo.

Table 4.1. Mortuary Data for the Early Postclassic Burials Found in Operation B, Río Viejo

Burial	Indv	Location	Sex*	Age**	Orientation	Vessels	Other Offerings
26	34	Str. 8–8	x	a	8° W of N	2	
27	35	Str. 8–8	x	a	4° E of N	0	3 obsidian blades and 1 quartz burnisher
28	36	Str. 8–8	m	a	4° W of N	3	
29	37	Str. 8–8	x	sa	7° E of N	2	
30	38	Str. 8–8	x	a	4° E of N	2	1 quartz burnisher
31	39	Str. 8–8	f?	a	4° E of N	2	
32	40	Str. 8–8	m	a	6° E of N	2	
33	41	Str. 8–8	x	a	7° E of N	2	
34	42	Str. 8–8	x	a	6° E of N	1?	
35	43	Str. 8–8	m	a	2° E of N	0	
37	45	Str. 8–8	unexc.			1	
43	52	Str. 8–7	f	a	17° E of N	3	
45	54	Str. 8–7	x	a	22° E of N	0	
46	55	Str. 8–7	m	a	9° E of N	1	5 shell pendants
50	59	Str. 8–7	x	a	12° E of N	1	
53	62	Str. 8–7	unexc.	a		2	

*Sex categories: x = indeterminate, m = male, f = female, unexc. = unexcavated.
**Age categories: a = adult, sa = subadult.

emotional and physical proximity of ancestors also served as a constant reminder of proper behavior—and, as Gillespie (2001, 2002) has argued, gave those still living access and rights to the material (and nonmaterial) property of their ancestors. Keeping the deceased buried within the house not only kept close the physical remains of ancestors, but also encapsulated and controlled the intangibles of wealth, status, and privilege that formed important parts of each ancestor's individual and group identities. In this way, the architectural space of the house structure was linked closely to the social landscape of the house (Kuijt 2001:89, 2008). The standardization in mortuary ritual present at Río Viejo can be interpreted as both reinforcing and reflecting community and generational continuity (Kuijt 2001; McAnany 1995), and especially pertinent to this case, the spatial location of residential burials within *separate* house buildings differentiates one house from another. What this creates is a sense of separation ("estrangement" in the words of Schiller 2001:78) at the same time that it creates connections between the houses and house ancestors ("affinity" in the words of Schiller 2001:78).

Residential burial is linked to both house membership and house identity (Hendon 1999). Here, I am adopting a house-centered approach (see Gillespie 2007:27) for talking about social organization at Río Viejo that draws on archaeological applications of Claude Lévi-Strauss' house societies model (notably Gillespie 2000a, 2000b, 2000c; Joyce 2000; and essays in Beck 2007). Rather than a strict adoption of the specific model of house societies that Lévi-Strauss developed (Lévi-Strauss 1982:176–187), what I think is most useful for this case study is how the framework connects physical (material) traces of houses, a flexibly defined, yet meaningful and ethnographically grounded social group, and the everyday practices or activities that help to maintain house continuity. In house societies, all members of a house have rights and access to the tangible and intangible property, wealth, status, and privilege that is passed down through the house. This property is often communicated through a physical house structure (architecture), heirlooms, and the material remains of small-scale social relations (Joyce 2007:54). Although Río Viejo houses were not especially wealthy, the emphasis on house membership is most evident in distinctive burial practices and the distribution of activities relative to architecture. Most people in the neighborhood participated in similar kinds of everyday economic activities, but some activities, including the highly symbolic task of food preparation, were completed within specific house structures. Activities, food production, burial, and residence are all connected to the construction of a shared corporate house identity.

In the lower Río Verde valley, residential burial was common throughout the entire sequence of occupation (Joyce 1991b, 1994; King 2006). Unlike in earlier time periods, at Early Postclassic Río Viejo, residential burial specifically targeted adult members of the community (King 2006). Remains of children (or of anybody under the age of 17) were notably absent from subfloor burial and from burial within the limits of house structures. In the Operation A neighborhood, two children were found buried outside of residential space, and we have not yet located any children buried in

Figure 4.4. Plan view of Structure 8–8b, Operation B, Rio Viejo.

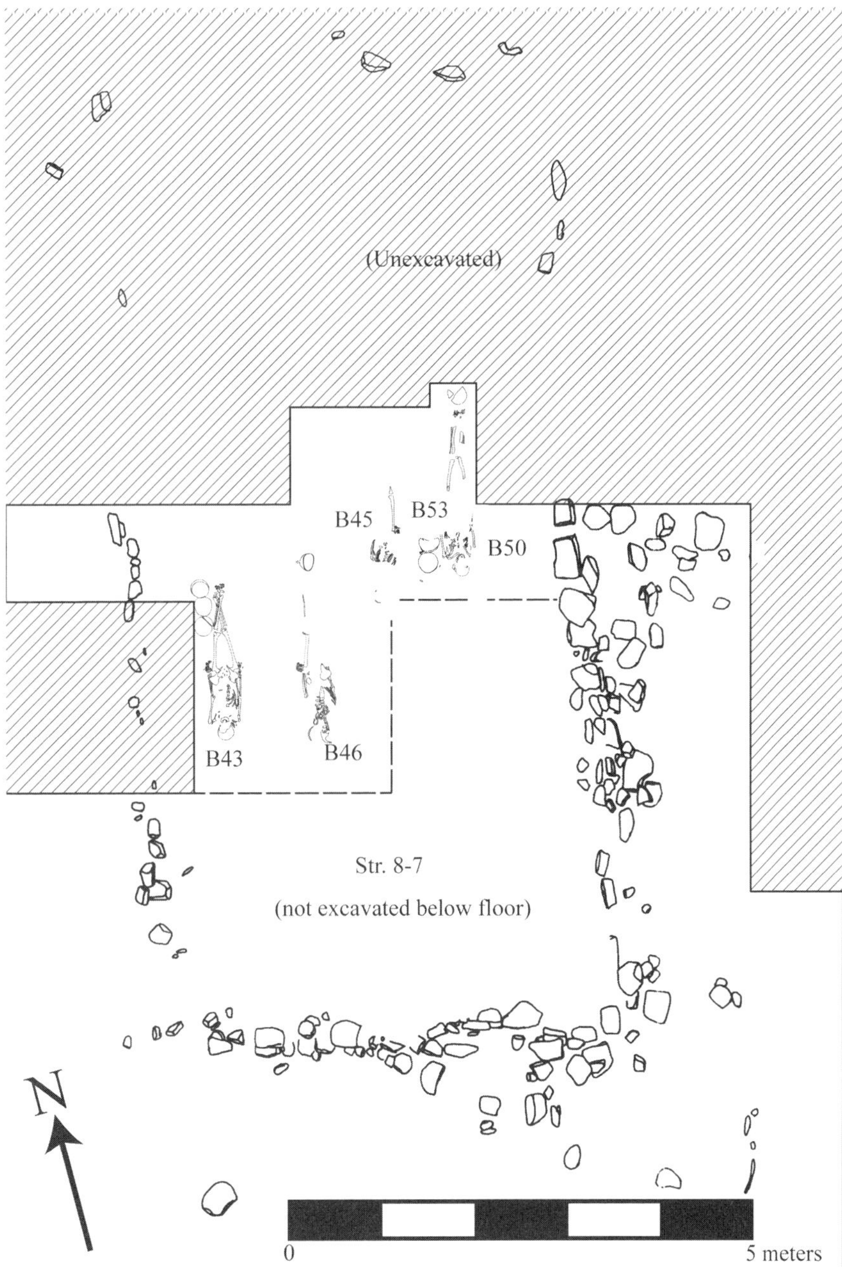

Figure 4.5. Plan view of Structure 8–7, Operation B, Río Viejo.

the Operation B neighborhood. I have argued elsewhere that the absence of children in subfloor burial within the limits of house space is indicative of the place of children in Early Postclassic Río Viejo and their membership in houses (King 2006). It may have been the case that in order to attain membership in a house or serve as a legitimate house ancestor, one needed to reach a certain age or age grade. In this way, only adults (as defined by Early Postclassic house residents) could appropriately serve as house ancestors. This separation between children and adults in residential burial shows that only adults could provide certain kinds of services to the group and only adults had access to certain kinds of property, rights, and privileges or deserved a particular kind of commemorative practice. Regardless of what the distinction means, that the distinction exists marks a conceptual separation between child and adult burials and mortuary ritual. Uruñuela and Plunket (2002:29) note a similar division between adult and child burial locations at Formative period

Tetimpa, Puebla, and cite Ravesloot (1988:18) in suggesting that children may have required different burial treatment because they had not yet participated in initiation rites that would have allowed them to enter the adult social sphere.

I have also argued the possibility that children occupied a more flexible and tenuous position in the community, whereby they were perhaps considered members of multiple houses until they reached a particular age-status (King 2006). If Río Viejo residents practiced the bilateral kinship system widely suggested for peoples of Oaxaca (Nader 1969:347–348; Spores 1967:10; Whitecotton 1977:153), parents would have come from different houses of origin, and a child's position and identification with a specific house might not have been predetermined. If a child died prematurely before ties were established to a particular house, this could have foreclosed their opportunity to belong to a particular house and be buried within house space. I argued that, for this reason, it might have been more common for children to be buried in open, non-house spaces, as evidenced in the Operation A neighborhood (King 2006). Because a child's position within one house might not yet have been determined, the death of that child could have brought together a larger and more diverse group of mourners from multiple houses and could have required a more public, open-access venue for mortuary ritual. At the same time, the death of children could have been viewed as particularly dangerous, suspicious, or auspicious, such that it required a different set of mortuary practices in a spatially distinct, outside-of-house location. This would have limited the amount of contact or changed the form of contact between the spirits of these children and living kin, and would have kept deceased children from interacting regularly with living house residents in the same way as those persons buried beneath the floor.

Adult burials were highly standardized, with adult male and female individuals placed in nearly identical positions, extended on their backs, oriented with their heads to the south, feet to the north, and with their arms either at their sides or crossed. Most individuals were interred with between one and three ceramic vessels placed around their feet, some of which were obviously used prior to interment, as evidenced by their broken supports or well-worn *molcajete* (grinding) surfaces (King 2003). Maize phytoliths were present in at least one of these vessels, demonstrating that a maize-based food was either presented to the dead or shared among participants in funerary rites, or that well-used and/or unwashed vessels were selected as offerings (see also Joyce 1999:20; King 2008b). Grave goods other than ceramic vessels were much less common, but do occur. One individual wore jewelry (shell pendants), one had obsidian blades placed inside the mouth, and two others had well-worn, heirloom quartz burnishers used in ceramic production placed beneath their heads. Rather than marking wealth, I suspect that these offerings subtly and less visibly referenced individual identities. These grave goods occur too infrequently to reveal a particular meaning-bearing pattern, such as patterning with respect to sex of the individual. In fact, a comparison of these burials with burials from earlier periods in coastal Oaxaca reveals that sex-specific differences in grave goods have never been statistically significant in coastal Oaxacan assemblages throughout all time periods (King 2006).

Individuals buried within structures tend to be buried with offerings across all time periods, while extramural burials often lack grave goods; however, this relationship is not statistically significant. This pattern is most clear for the Early Postclassic, when deceased individuals buried beneath house floors were nearly always buried with grave goods (14 of 16, or 81.3 percent), while burials found outside structures (those in Operation A) were buried with none. The possible correlation between grave location and grave offerings in the Early Postclassic could support the interpretation that people buried beneath house floors might have had unique access to wealth, status, property, and privilege associated with being a house member or an important house ancestor, even though the offerings are admittedly quite meager. The dead buried outside house floors were exempt from such status, which affected both where they could be buried and what kinds of objects could be included as offerings (King 2006). Alternatively, since the burials found in the Operation A neighborhood did not follow the same pattern of under-floor burial, one could argue that the spatial separation and differences in mortuary ritual between the two neighborhoods mark some sort of qualitative difference between the residents of each—perhaps different ancestors, origins, traditions—that is masked by the similarity in house architecture and spatial configuration, economic practices, and material culture (Joyce and King 2001; King 2003).

The houses at Río Viejo were not static and unchanging throughout the Early Postclassic. Multiple people lived in the houses and people moved around between houses through time—such that residential burial was a common and repeated part of the life cycles of houses. Houses were occupied before, during, and probably after burial events, and were not constructed solely for the purpose of "housing" the deceased. They were multipurpose structures that encapsulated and encoded different forms of social behavior and traditions. In the Operation B neighborhood, the separation of the subfloor burials among two distinct house structures might suggest a social division into two different houses, each with its own set of members and important, remembered ancestors. At the same time, the overall similarity in the mortuary ritual across the neighborhood shows that strong community standards and traditions governed the treatment of the dead and connected each house to one another.

Individual and Collective Identity among House Ancestors

Burial practices in the Operation B neighborhood of Río Viejo show that one of the important references being made in residential burial was membership in the house. These practices foreground a deceased adult's collective group identity as a house member and house ancestor over his or her individual identity in life or death. While some aspects of individuality are maintained (as evidenced by the unique shell pendant and quartz burnisher grave offerings), the overall statement being made in death rites is about the similarity between adult male and female house members, group membership, and one's role as a house ancestor.

However, if we consider the locations of the burials more closely, we see at the same time the extreme precision and standardization in body position and the placement of each burial side by side one another, so that no body or burial event impacts or intrudes upon a previously interred individual. This precision is the complete opposite of the characteristic mortuary practices from earlier time periods in coastal Oaxaca. Here, as in other parts of Oaxaca, tombs and graves were often frequently reused, scattering or otherwise pushing aside the bones of earlier interments (Martínez López et al. 1995:236; Middleton et al. 1998; Miller 1995; Whalen 1981, 1988). The subfloor burials from Late and Terminal Formative period contexts in coastal Oaxaca often impacted and disturbed the remains of previously deceased individuals, creating noticeable palimpsests (Joyce 1991a, 1994). With reference to Valley of Oaxaca tombs, Miller (1995:241) argues that this kind of spatial reconfiguration of human skeletal elements and offerings in tombs was purposeful, so that the connections between the newly deceased individuals, "heads of household," and those still living could be (strategically and spiritually) rewritten and redefined. In coastal Oaxaca, the burial contexts were less formal earthen pits (not tombs), and so probably did not warrant or require restructuring of burial space to accommodate a newly deceased person. Instead, surviving family members chose to avoid already occupied space rather than to reconfigure old space. This means that living members of Early Postclassic houses who were burying deceased house members specifically avoided disturbing the remains of previously deceased individuals when interring newly deceased adults and likely knew and remembered the precise locations of those previously interred. This precision calls into question the interpretation that the only important reference being made through residential mortuary practice was to collective identity and membership in a house (see King 2006).

The first issue that must be raised about this patterned spacing and separation of burials is whether the burial events were simultaneous or sequential—that is, did all of the individuals buried in these subfloor graves die around the same time, so that burial side by side would not have been a difficult pattern to create, or were they buried at different points in time? While I wish that the stratigraphy clearly demonstrated a sequence and separation in time between burial events, the lack of clear stratigraphic distinctions between burial fill, burial pit cuts, and the surrounding platform fill does not easily allow us to detect the timing of the different burial events. Grave pits were not distinguishable during excavation owing to both the fine texture of the deposits and the extreme heat, sun, and dry weather conditions that quickly baked the walls into hard clay. Thus, for the most part, we cannot order the burial events through time. In addition, unlike other places in Mesoamerica and across the globe, formal earthen burial chambers or plastered floor surfaces were not present to help distinguish one burial event from another. Combined with the lack of superimposition of the actual bodies, the lack of visible floor cuts makes reconstruction of the exact sequence and timing of interment difficult.

Pathological indicators and the age-at-death profile of the individuals buried beneath the floor surfaces give no indication that the burials were the result of a single traumatic mass-death event, such as a violent massacre or an epidemic. Instead, the skeletons exhibit normal signs of aging and degenerative bony afflictions such as osteoarthritis in the spinal column and in one case the hand, osteoporosis, wear on the teeth, and antemortem tooth loss. They also include individuals in both early and later adulthood.

At the same time, each burial was not exactly the same. Some bodies lie lower than others, and some appear wedged between two previously interred bodies. For example, Burial 28 is almost resting on its side to fit into the space between a stone wall from an earlier structure and Burial 31, suggesting that there is some time delay between each burial event (Figure 4.6). We also have evidence for architectural renovation and stratigraphic changes through time in the neighborhood that indicate that the Early Postclassic occupation of the site spanned multiple generations, equaling roughly 200 years. Therefore, it is most reasonable to argue that these burial events span the entire Early Postclassic occupation of particular houses and of the site in general. Given the lack of positive evidence for simultaneous burial,

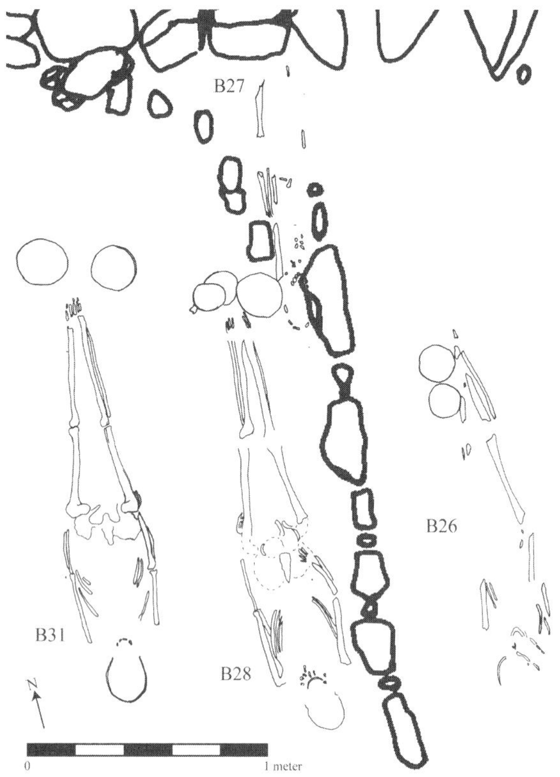

Figure 4.6. Close-up of burials in Structure 8–8b showing wedging of burial space, Operation B, Rio Viejo.

I feel most comfortable concluding that the burials are sequential. This would accord with the scenario of gradual death events over multiple generations in a residential setting and the extant accumulation of living debris on interior and exterior occupation surfaces.

Each burial chamber was a remembered location and the bodies of the deceased, or ancestors, occupied specific places beneath the floor and retained certain rights over that space. People avoided impacting or disturbing the remains of previously deceased ancestors when burying the newly deceased. This might perhaps indicate that people would have had reason to mark grave locations in some manner, perhaps with a semipermanent above-ground marker. Alternatively, the cuts and disturbed sediment of used graves might have remained visible in the floor surface for some time and thus the locations of graves were detectable and easy to remember. We found no evidence of archaeologically preserved above-ground grave markers, in the form of either portable or nonportable artifacts—that is, there is no evidence of constructed altars or markers made of nonperishable material such as stone—and filled grave cuts are no longer visible on floor surfaces.

Another possibility is that Río Viejo residents marked these locations with some sort of semipermanent or perishable marker that may not leave visible traces. To answer this question I refer to the results of the analysis of soil chemical residues from house floors and occupation surfaces at the site (King 2008b). In this study, I tested floor surfaces at one-meter intervals across the entire excavated area for 12 elements commonly associated with human settlements and human products such as perishable plants, animals, wood, food, and excreta, accumulating 435 archaeological samples. The method was chosen to examine the distribution, locations, and social implications of food processing and food sharing activities in Early Postclassic households (King 2008b). Although the sampling strategy and sampling interval, with samples taken at one-meter intervals on all interior and exterior occupation surfaces, might not have been fine enough to catch perishable burial markers, the soil chemistry results demonstrate no clear evidence of specific, repeated perishable grave markers placed above each grave. Further, a burn feature located in one of the houses containing burials, which I have interpreted as evidence of a small-scale, repeated food processing activity (King 2008b), was specifically positioned so that it did not directly overlie burials. The location of this feature suggests an avoidance of certain areas for specific non-burial activities.

These purposeful arrangements of burials and features leave open the possibility that a burial plan existed *before* people died—such that specific zones of the house were chosen as resting areas for specific adult members of the house, and specific areas were deemed appropriate burial areas for specific people. From the soil chemistry, we should be able to detect whether people were buried under patterned, meaningful locations within the house. For example, if people were buried beneath the floor area where they slept while alive, the residues of sleeping mats or evidence of a clean surface should be detectable. The chemical and phytolith results, however, do not support this conclusion (King 2003, 2008b). A preordained burial plan would explain not only the regular spacing but also larger, seemingly purposeful gaps between bodies in some parts of the houses. It seems that some locations were saved for later use and were never filled, perhaps because the families moved prior to the death of the individuals who would have been buried in those locations or because for some other reason the bodies of those deceased never made it back for burial.

The mortuary sample from Early Postclassic Río Viejo is far too small to identify distributional patterns in burial location based on the sex of the buried individual, especially since sex in most cases was difficult to determine due to poor preservation of the skeleton. Also, since there is little internal architectural differentiation within houses and most structures were single-roomed rectangular structures, there is no way to determine whether the positions of particular kinds of burials (male, female, older adult, younger adult, etc.) are associated with burial beneath or next to specific kinds of architectural features (for example, the east wall, altar, center line). The lack of patterned differentiation in grave offerings also suggests that wealth or status was not a predictable determinant of burial in a certain location.

Regardless, residents of Río Viejo maintained the integrity of specific burials and remembered where to bury (or where not to bury) the next person who passed. From an interpretive standpoint, the commitment to keeping individual bodies complete and the protection of specific resting places for specific ancestors perhaps show that the effort to treat adult male and female burials similarly and thus create generic adult house ancestors was not achieved through the *subjugation* of individual identity. Instead of forced sameness, the sense of community and corporate identity was achieved through the celebration of specific individuals, which kept individuals distinct and separate from one another and yet treated them all in the same manner.

Ancestors were important at Río Viejo—not as a generic collective group referencing house identity, but as individual people who together formed a cohort. In this sense, the actions of living house members were monitored and witnessed not by a group of generalized ancestors who acted as one on behalf of their shared house identity, but by the musings, influence, and penetration of numerous, separate, specific ancestors. People lived under the watchful eye of multiple adult ancestors, whose individual identities were explicitly maintained, emphasized, remembered, memorialized, and protected within the context of and with reference to the group. The celebration of group identity in light of such difference and distinction makes the decision of living survivors to mark each body in a similar way upon death, de-emphasizing individual identity, even more powerful and meaningful. To be sure, residential burial at Río Viejo provided an intense link between living peoples and their remembered ancestors. Individual grave sites were acknowledged and commemorated in a way that linked all living house members and their ancestors together as a unified group, even though each group, the living and the dead, was composed of separate, uniquely celebrated individuals.

Conclusion

Both individual and group identity is implicated in residential burial at Río Viejo. Residential burial is not just a statement about who was considered a house member and who was not, but indicates that mortuary ritual was an appropriate social means through which individual and group identities could be expressed, celebrated, and differentiated (Hendon 1999). The differences in burial practice and mortuary rites for people of different ages reinforced and perhaps celebrated a meaningful social distinction between children and adults. It also may indicate variation in the definition of residential burial, such that for some places, the distinction between intramural and extramural residential burial may indeed be important.

Houses were the social conduits for both group action and individual social practice. For the dead, residential burial placed deceased adult house members among a group of peers, and bestowed upon them the social recognition as important individual ancestors within a community of house ancestors. Owing to distinct burial locations away from or outside of houses, deceased children were both physically and conceptually separated from their adult counterparts. This might indicate that they were restricted from active participation as house ancestors or were different kinds of actors. The membership of children in specific houses may not yet have been solidified, to the degree that a different form of burial was required. Instead, residential burial recognized the positions of adults specifically as social individuals who witnessed, constrained, and celebrated the actions of those in the world of the living and celebrated their roles as preservers of collective house memory. For the living, residential burial was a way to remember *one* (specific persons) and *all* (the group of adult ancestors) at the same time, and to enact the claim that, in perpetuity, in life and in death, self, house, and community were important and interwoven expressions of identity.

Acknowledgements

I would like to first and foremost thank Ron L. Adams and Joyce White for their invitation to participate in the 2007 Society for American Archaeology symposium on which this volume is based, and later for Ron's invitation to participate in the volume both as contributor and co-editor. The Río Viejo Residence Project excavations were generously supported by the Foundation for the Advancement of Mesoamerican Studies, Inc., with Arthur Joyce; the Stahl Endowment of the Archaeological Research Facility, University of California Berkeley; the Lowie-Olson Fund of the Department of Anthropology, University of California Berkeley; and the National Science Foundation (in a grant to Arthur Joyce). In particular, I would like to thank Ron L. Adams, Rosemary Joyce, Patricia McAnany, Cathy Costin, and outside reviewers for insightful comments on this and earlier drafts of this chapter.

References

Barber, Sarah B.
2005 Heterogeneity, Identity, and Complexity: Negotiating Status and Authority in Terminal Formative Coastal Oaxaca. Ph.D. dissertation, Department of Anthropology, University of Colorado, Boulder.

Beck, Robin A., Jr., ed.
2007 The Durable House: House Society Models in Archaeology. Occasional Paper 35. Carbondale: Center for Archaeological Investigations, Southern Illinois University.

Binford, Lewis R.
1971 Mortuary Practices: Their Study and Their Potential. *In* Approaches to the Social Dimensions of Mortuary Practices. J. A. Brown, ed. Pp. 6–29. Memoirs of the Society for American Archaeology, 25. Washington, DC.

Christensen, Alexander F.
1999 Apéndice 3: Los restos humanos. *In* El Proyecto Patrones de Asentamiento del Río Verde. A. A. Joyce, ed. Pp. 487–494. Informe entregado al Consejo de Arqueología y el Centro INAH Oaxaca.

Drennan, Robert D.
1976 Fabrica San Jose and Middle Formative Society in the Valley of Oaxaca. Ann Arbor: University of Michigan Museum of Anthropology.

Geller, Pamela L.
2006 Maya Mortuary Spaces as Cosmological Metaphors. *In* Space and Spatial Analysis in Archaeology. E. C. Robertson, J. D. Seibert, D. C. Fernandez, and M. U. Zender, eds. Pp. 37–45. Calgary: University of Calgary Press.

Gillespie, Susan D.
2000a Lévi-Strauss: *Maison* and *Société à Maisons*. *In* Beyond Kinship: Social and Material Reproduction in House Societies. R. A. Joyce and S. D. Gillespie, eds. Pp. 22–52. Philadelphia: University of Pennsylvania Press.
2000b Maya "Nested Houses": The Ritual Construction of Place. *In* Beyond Kinship: Social and Material Reproduction in House Societies. R. A. Joyce and S. D. Gillespie, eds. Pp. 135–160. Philadelphia: University of Pennsylvania Press.
2000c Rethinking Ancient Maya Social Organization: Replacing "Lineage" with "House." American Anthropologist 102:467–484.
2001 Personhood, Agency, and Mortuary Ritual: A Case Study from the Ancient Maya. Journal of Anthropological Archaeology 20:73–112.
2002 Body and Soul among the Maya: Keeping the Spirits in Place. *In* The Space and Place of Death. H. Silverman and D. B. Small, eds. Pp. 67–78. Archeological Papers of the American Anthropological Association, 11. Arlington, VA: American Anthropological Association.
2007 When Is a House? *In* The Durable House: House Society Models in Archaeology. R. A. Beck Jr., ed. Pp. 25–50. Occasional Paper 35. Carbondale: Center for Archaeological Investigations, Southern Illinois University.

Hendon, Julia A.
1999 The Pre-Classic Maya Compound as the Focus of Social Identity. *In* Social Patterns in Pre-Classic Mesoamerica. D. C. Grove and R. A. Joyce, eds. Pp. 97–125. Washington, DC: Dumbarton Oaks.

Houston, Stephen D., David Stuart, and Karl A. Taube
2006 The Memory of Bones: Body, Being, and Experience among the Classic Maya. Austin: University of Texas Press.

Joyce, Arthur A.
1991a Formative Period Occupation in the Lower Río Verde Valley, Oaxaca, México. Ph.D. dissertation, Department of Anthropology, Rutgers University.
1991b Formative Period Social Change in the Lower Río Verde Valley, Oaxaca, México. Latin American Antiquity 2:126–150.
1994 Late Formative Community Organization and Social Complexity on the Oaxaca Coast. Journal of Field Archaeology 21:147–168.
2008 Changing Power Relations and Interaction in the Lower Río Verde Valley. *In* After Monte Albán: Transformation and Negotiation in Oaxaca, Mexico. J. P. Blomster, ed. Pp. 219–254. Boulder: University Press of Colorado.

Joyce, Arthur A., Laura Arnaud Bustamante, and Marc N. Levine

2001 Commoner Power: A Case Study from the Classic Period Collapse on the Oaxaca Coast. Journal of Archaeological Method and Theory 8:343–385.

Joyce, Arthur A., and Stacie M. King
2001 Household Archaeology in Coastal Oaxaca, México. Foundation for the Advancement of Mesoamerican Studies, Inc. http://www.famsi.org/reports/99012/index.html, accessed January 11, 2011.

Joyce, Rosemary A.
1999 Social Dimensions of Pre-Classic Burials. *In* Social Patterns in Pre-Classic Mesoamerica. D. C. Grove and R. A. Joyce, eds. Pp. 15–47. Washington, DC: Dumbarton Oaks.
2000 Heirlooms and Houses: Materiality and Social Memory. *In* Beyond Kinship: Social and Material Reproduction in House Societies. R. A. Joyce and S. D. Gillespie, eds. Pp. 189–212. Philadelphia: University of Pennsylvania Press.
2007 Building Houses: The Materialization of Lasting Identity in Formative Mesoamerica. *In* The Durable House: House Society Models in Archaeology. R. A. Beck, Jr., ed. Pp. 53–72. Occasional Paper 35. Carbondale: Center for Archaeological Investigations, Southern Illinois University.

King, Stacie M.
2003 Social Practices and Social Organization in Ancient Coastal Oaxacan Households. Ph.D. dissertation, Department of Anthropology, University of California, Berkeley.
2006 The Marking of Age in Ancient Coastal Oaxaca. *In* The Social Experience of Childhood in Ancient Mesoamerica. T. Ardren and S. R. Hutson, eds. Pp. 169–200. Boulder: University Press of Colorado.
2008a Interregional Networks of the Oaxacan Early Postclassic: Connecting the Coast and the Highlands. *In* After Monte Albán: Transformation and Negotiation in Oaxaca, Mexico. J. P. Blomster, ed. Pp. 225–291. Boulder: University Press of Colorado.
2008b The Spatial Organization of Food Sharing in Early Postclassic Households: An Application of Soil Chemistry in Ancient Oaxaca, Mexico. Journal of Archaeological Science 35:1224–1239.
In press Thread Production in Early Postclassic Coastal Oaxaca, Mexico: Technology, Intensity, and Gender. Ancient Mesoamerica.

Kuijt, Ian
2001 Place, Death, and the Transmission of Social Memory in Early Agricultural Communities of the Near Eastern Pre-Pottery Neolithic. *In* Social Memory, Identity, and Death: Anthropological Perspectives on Mortuary Rituals. M. S. Chesson, ed. Pp. 80–99. Archeological Papers of the American Anthropological Association, 10. Arlington, VA: American Anthropological Association.
2008 The Regeneration of Life: Neolithic Structures of Symbolic Remembering and Forgetting. Current Anthropology 49:171–197.

Léon-Portilla, Miguel
1963 Aztec Thought and Culture: A Study of the Ancient Nahuatl Mind. Norman: University of Oklahoma Press.

Lévi-Strauss, Claude
1982 The Way of the Masks. Sylvia Modelski, trans. Seattle: University of Washington Press.

Lind, Michael, and Javier Urcid
2010 The Lords of Lambityeco: Political Evolution in the Valley of Oaxaca during the Xoo Phase. Boulder: University Press of Colorado.

McAnany, Patricia A.
1995 Living with the Ancestors: Kinship and Kingship in Ancient Maya Society. Austin: University of Texas Press.

Manzanilla, Linda
2002 Houses and Ancestors, Altars and Relics: Mortuary Patterns at Teotihuacan, Central Mexico. *In* The Space and Place of Death. H. Silverman and D. B. Small, eds. Pp. 55–66. Archeological Papers of the American Anthropological Association, 11. Arlington, VA: American Anthropological Association.

Martínez López, Cira, Marcus Winter, and Pedro Antonio Juárez
1995 Entierros humanos del Proyecto Especial Monte Albán. *In* Entierros Humanos de Monte Albán: Dos Estudios. M. Winter, ed. Pp. 79–247. Contribución No. 7 del Proyecto Especial

Monte Albán 1992–1994. Oaxaca: Centro INAH Oaxaca.

Middleton, William D., Gary M. Feinman, and Guillermo Molina Villegas
1998 Tomb Use and Reuse in Oaxaca, Mexico. Ancient Mesoamerica 9:297–307.

Miller, Arthur G.
1995 The Painted Tombs of Oaxaca, Mexico: Living with the Dead. Cambridge: Cambridge University Press.

Nader, Laura
1969 The Zapotec of Oaxaca. *In* Handbook of Middle American Indians, vol. 7: Ethnology, part 1. E. Z. Vogt, ed. Pp. 329–357. Austin: University of Texas Press.

Parker Pearson, Mike
2000 Mortuary Practices, Society, and Ideology: An Ethnoarchaeological Study. *In* Interpretive Archaeology: A Reader. J. Thomas, ed. Pp. 246–265. London: Leicester University Press.

Ravesloot, John C.
1988 Mortuary Practices and Social Differentiation at Casas Grandes, Chihuahua, Mexico. Tucson: University of Arizona Press.

Ruz Lhullier, A. R.
1968 Costumbres funerarias de los antiguos Mayas. México: UNAM.

Saxe, Arthur A.
1970 Social Dimensions of Mortuary Practices. Ph.D. dissertation, Department of Anthropology, University of Michigan.

Schiller, Anne
2001 Mortuary Monuments and Social Change among the Ngaju. *In* Social Memory, Identity, and Death: Anthropological Perspectives on Mortuary Rituals. M. S. Chesson, ed. Pp. 70–79. Archeological Papers of the American Anthropological Association, 10. Arlington, VA: American Anthropological Association.

Smith, Michael E.
2002 Domestic Ritual at Aztec Provincial Sites in Morelos. *In* Domestic Ritual in Ancient Mesoamerica. P. Plunket, ed. Pp. 93–114. Cotsen Institute of Archaeology, Monograph 46. Los Angeles: University of California.

Spores, Ronald
1967 The Mixtec Kings and Their People. Norman: University of Oklahoma Press.

Uruñuela, Gabriela, and Patricia Plunket
2002 Lineages and Ancestors: The Formative Mortuary Assemblages of Tetimpa, Puebla. *In* Domestic Ritual in Ancient Mesoamerica. P. Plunket, ed. Pp. 20–30. Cotsen Institute of Archaeology, Monograph 46. Los Angeles: University of California.

Whalen, Michael E.
1981 Excavations at Santo Domingo Tomaltepec: Evolution of a Formative Community in the Valley of Oaxaca, Mexico. Ann Arbor: University of Michigan Museum of Anthropology.
1988 House and Household in Formative Oaxaca. *In* Household and Community in the Mesoamerican Past. R. R. Wilk and W. Ashmore, eds. Pp. 249–272. Albuquerque: University of New Mexico Press.

Whitecotton, Joseph W.
1977 The Zapotecs: Princes, Priests and Peasants. Norman: University of Oklahoma Press.

Winter, Marcus, ed.
1995 Entierros Humanos de Monte Albán: Dos Estudios. Contribución No. 7 del Proyecto Especial Monte Albán 1992–1994. Oaxaca: Centro INAH Oaxaca.

5

Residential Burial and the Metal Age of Thailand

Joyce C. White
University of Pennsylvania Museum
and
Chureekamol Onsuwan Eyre
University of Pennsylvania Museum

ABSTRACT

Mortuary programs have great potential to provide insights into ritually-integrated social systems of house societies. Metal age house societies of prehistoric Thailand, such as the Ban Chiang Cultural Tradition, are argued to have practiced residential burial, with interment of corpses in close physical proximity to spaces occupied by the living in daily life. It is suggested that this mortuary practice contributed to sustaining long-lived socio-settlement systems that were characterized by low levels of inter-community conflict. The mortuary ceramics interred in metal age burials reveal sub-regional stylistic and technological groupings that appear to imply territorial subdivisions in these apparently acephalous and decentralized societies. [Ban Chiang, burials, Southeast Asia, house society, heterarchy]

Societies differ greatly as to the actual physical separation of the living and the dead. (Silverman 2002:4)

Where a society places its deceased individuals is an important variable for archaeologists studying mortuary remains to determine, as spatial location of mortuary behaviors has important implications for reconstructing past social systems (Goldstein 2002). Characterization of the social organization of metal age Thailand (ca. 2000 B.C.E.–C.E. 500) has long been rooted in interpretation of metal age mortuary remains as interments in cemeteries (e.g., Higham 2008; Sørensen 1967).[1] We argue that this taphonomic interpretation is in most cases incorrect and that the prevalent mortuary program in metal age Thailand was residential burial, that is, burial in, under, and/or around houses. Some implications for this revised view of mortuary taphonomy for interpreting the metal age societies of Thailand are reviewed in this chapter. We propose that the practice of residential burial was one means by which metal age societies of Thailand sustained flexible social hierarchies (i.e., heterarchy) and decentralized settlement systems throughout the time period.

Following a background section, this essay reviews how and why burial taphonomy has been misinterpreted by regional archaeologists. The essay proceeds to outline the regional context for the practice of residential burial, particularly the tendencies for site occupations to be long term and for mortuary ceramics to show marked subregional variation. Several implications of residential burial for understanding the pre-state period are then noted, as well as what theoretical concepts, such as house societies and landscape approaches, hold particular promise for elucidating prehistoric middle range societies and their mortuary practices in this region.

In general, we hypothesize that the practice of residential burial in ceramic subregions reflects enduring supravillage affiliative social groupings that used stylistic and technological practices and ritual behaviors to signal,

ARCHEOLOGICAL PAPERS OF THE AMERICAN ANTHROPOLOGICAL ASSOCIATION, Vol. 20, Issue 1, pp. 59–78, ISSN 1551-823X, online ISSN 1551-8248. DOI: 10.1111/j.1551-8248.2011.01028.x.

demarcate, and maintain group identities in a regional system of dynamically counterpoised and geographically situated "middle range societies" (Rousseau 2006). The practice of residential burial at enduring settlements may have fostered societal differentiation, integration, and hence "complexification" (Rousseau 2006) at the local and regional levels in a variety of ways. The particular example of residential burial during metal age Thailand may contribute to social theory of how past societies developed sustained systems of flexible social integration.

Background

The search for evidence of social, political, and economic hierarchies in mortuary evidence as part of an overarching investigation of the origins of states has stimulated much archaeological research in Thailand as it has elsewhere in the world (e.g., Bayard 1984, 1996–97; Higham 1996, 2007). Since the 1960s, several open-air, low mound sites have been excavated whose remains suggest occupation by societies that would fall into the general category of middle range societies (more complex than simple hunter-gatherers and less complex than states [vide Rousseau 2006; Saitta 1999; Scarry 1999; Spielmann 1998; Upham 1987, 1990]).

The low mound sites, generally only a few meters in height, have evidence of both occupation and mortuary activities from sedentary societies that were agricultural or maritime oriented. Excavations of these mixed mortuary/occupation sites reveal use of such sites spanning hundreds to more than 2,000 years. Occupations fall within the time range of just before 2000 B.C.E. (following chronology in White 2008) to about C.E. 500. Site surveys indicate that metal age low mound sites are found widely in northeast and central Thailand on flat and sloped arable lands (see Eyre 2006, 2010 for review of archaeological surveys in Thailand). Current evidence suggests that the settlement system emerged shortly before the appearance of bronze metallurgy, probably in the late third millennium B.C.E., and continued after the appearance of iron metallurgy, up to the point of the appearance of state-like entities in the mid-first millennium C.E. The origin of this settlement system is not precisely known due to the dearth of archaeological evidence in Thailand from the preceding time period (middle Holocene) (White et al. 2004:127). Some archaeologists, though, have suggested that the settlement system originated with migration to Thailand of rice-cultivating societies from southern China (Higham 2006; Rispoli 2008). However, this idea does not satisfactorily explain the occupation of non-rice-growing lands in some parts of Thailand at the beginning of the settlement system.

Although the origins of the metal age settlement system still require much research, once established by the early second millennium B.C.E. in northeast and central Thailand the settlement system shows considerable continuity to roughly C.E. 500. Some scholars have argued that the appearance of iron technology in Thailand by circa 500 B.C.E. rapidly resulted in marked overall regional trends towards hierarchical forms of social integration, such as centralization, intensified wet rice agriculture, social hierarchy, warfare, the appearance of public works, and other "chiefdom" attributes (Higham 1989, 2002; O'Reilly 2007b, 2008; Pigott et al. 1997:119). This argument for a rapid "package" of change has been undermined as more evidence has accrued, and a more protracted process playing out over a millennium is now seen (Eyre 2010). In particular, it is now recognized that the development of what had been termed "moats" (channels encircling many sites in northeast Thailand) had more to do with efficiently managing water resources in a drying environment during the latter part of the iron age than defense (Boyd 2008). Although during the iron age settlement expanded into northern Thailand (Pautreau et al. 2001) and other upland areas (Welch and McNeill 1991), overall greater continuity between the bronze age and iron age occupation of many parts of Thailand is now recognized (Higham 2009a:256). A more multifaceted, more regionally variable, more contextually specific picture is emerging for iron age social complexity in Thailand (Boyd 2008; Eyre 2006; Källén 2004; McGrath and Boyd 2001; Talbot 2007). However, around C.E. 500, 1,000 or more years after the appearance of iron, abrupt changes in the settlement system do coincide with the appearance of clear site hierarchies and state-like manifestations in major river basins (Eyre 2006; Mudar 1993; Stark 2006). At least in parts of northeast Thailand, these first millennium C.E. settlement shifts and abandonment of late iron age sites appear to be related to both changes in hydrology and human degradation of the vegetation cover (Boyd 2007).

Much of the post-excavation analysis and publication of the low mound sites of Thailand has focused on the mortuary evidence. The mortuary remains from most of these low mound sites (Figure 5.1), including Ban Kao (Sørensen 1967), Non Nok Tha (Bayard 1984, 1996–97), Ban Na Di (Higham and Kijngam 1984a, 1984b, 1984c), Khok Phanom Di (Higham and Thosarat 1994:23), Nong Nor (Higham and Thosarat 1998), Ban Wang Hai (Pautreau et al. 2001), Ban Lum Khao (Higham and O'Reilly 2004:301), Noen U-Loke (Talbot 2007:305), and Ban Non Wat (Higham 2008, 2009a; Higham and Thosarat 2006), have all been discussed explicitly in terms of being "cemeteries"—implying that the ancient societies designated spatially discrete, formal areas for disposal of corpses separate from living areas. Although

Figure 5.1. Location of sites mentioned in the text.

aspects of the non-mortuary evidence of these sites, especially fauna and artifacts, have been addressed sometimes in detail (e.g., Higham 1993), the overall site formation processes that relate and integrate the occupation and mortuary deposits tend to be glossed over and described as "fugitive" (Higham n.d.:18).

Framing the mortuary remains in cemetery terms has facilitated discussion of social differentiation among graves via the Saxe-Binford approach and other neo-evolutionary models, which in turn has facilitated the use of Thailand's metal age sites primarily as vehicles to investigate the origins of states in Southeast Asia (Higham 2007:608). Drawing from the Saxe-Binford approach and Goldstein's (1980) modifications, clustered burials in such cemeteries are inferred to be lineages with corporate rights in scarce resources such as land and prestige goods (e.g., Higham 2007:607; see review of theory in Rakita and Buikstra 2005). Differences in energy expenditure in grave interments, particularly variation in numbers of grave goods, are used to infer the socially, economically, or politically more powerful from less powerful groups and individuals (e.g., Higham n.d.).

Assessment of variation in grave wealth in mortuary remains recovered from the low mound sites has revealed undoubted social differentiation. Graves range from "poor" (no grave objects) to "rich" (dozens of pots, hundreds of ornaments). Outstandingly rich graves include males and females, and children's interments can be extremely well furnished. While variation in grave wealth shows that these societies were not egalitarian, unequivocal evidence for a discrete, apical, and enduring elite class or politically dominant lineage has not emerged. With a few exceptions, wealth at individual sites tends to be arrayed on a continuum. Unusual wealth is episodic and short lived; phases with very wealthy graves at maritime-oriented Khok Phanom Di, bronze age Ban Non Wat, and iron age Noen U-Loke are superseded by poorer graves (e.g., Talbot 2007).

Are wealthy burials evidence for lineages of aristocrats (Higham 2009b)? Individual aggrandizers (Higham n.d.)? A starburst of "hierarchical state-forming activity" (Higham and Higham 2008:1)? While this variation in grave wealth is noteworthy, interpretation of the larger social, economic, and political meaning of the wealth variation among burials from these sites is not straightforward, once the data are reviewed in detail (e.g., Bacus 2006; Higham n.d.; Talbot 2007; Theunissen 2003). Study of the distribution of special artifacts like agate and carnelian has found these do not cluster in simple ways to suggest elite control over exotic trade goods (Theunissen 2003). Wealthy burials were spatially distributed among less well-to-do ones and waxed and waned in frequency. There is no evidence that production of special artifacts was controlled by elites or occurred in attached contexts. Rather, household and community specialization appears to have been the common production context (White and Pigott 1996). In short, the expectations of "top down" models for the development of social stratification have not been met in the mortuary assemblages of the low mound sites of Thailand. Evidence for sustained exclusionary and centralizing trends has not emerged in the mortuary data. Variation in relative wealth and variation in individual grave treatments suggestive of individual identities have been observed in metal age burials, indicating considerable flexibility in social structure in both bronze (Bacus 2006; O'Reilly 2003; White 1995a) and iron (Talbot 2007) ages.

Scholars are at the early stages of exploring alternative interpretations involving bottom-up, flexible, and networking metaphors for pre-state social development in Thailand. Heterarchy has been applied by several (Eyre 2006, 2010; O'Reilly 2003; Talbot 2007; Theunissen 2003; White 1995a) and transegalitarian concepts have seen recent attention (Higham n.d.). These concepts bring agency and alliance perspectives to the data (Higham n.d.) that are more compatible with the fluctuating and contextual hierarchies strongly suggested in the data.

Mortuary and Occupation Taphonomy: A Revised Assessment

We propose a revised taphonomic interpretation for mixed mortuary/occupation sites of metal age Thailand, namely that corpses were interred in domestic contexts. Furthermore, we propose that understanding this practice of residential burial in prehistoric Thailand is critical to understanding the development of social complexity in this region.

The possibility of residential burial practice has not been widely appreciated by prehistorians working in Southeast Asia for several reasons, but most importantly because of the nature of domestic architecture in the region. The predominant practice of living in dwellings made of perishable organic materials raised above ground level on wooden posts has left behind for the archaeologist little besides postholes and unstructured debris. Definable living surfaces are rare, as is clear evidence for perimeters of buildings. Occupation features have been identified that were deposited between superimposed burials during usage of a locale as a purported "cemetery." One example comes from Ban Na Di, where a small bronze-working facility was positioned stratigraphically between two burials interred during mortuary phase 1 (Higham and Kijngam 1984a:27).

In contrast to the confusing occupation deposits, burials from many excavations of metal age sites in Thailand provide archaeologists with abundant well-preserved evidence from virtual time capsules with unassailably contemporaneous contents. Human biology, ritual behaviors, and relatively intact material remains all contribute to rich, accessible, and visually compelling evidence of the sociocultural past. Small wonder that the mortuary remains from metal age sites in Thailand receive the initial focus and bulk of the attention from archaeologists (e.g., Higham and Thosarat, eds. 2004; Sørensen 1967:15), even when laborious studies of fauna (e.g., McCaw 2007), the paleoenvironment (e.g., Boyd 2008), and material culture from occupation contexts (e.g., Higham 1993) have been undertaken.

However, research designs focused on locating and excavating burial sites have distorted regional understandings of site taphonomy and settlement systems. Relatively little methodological attention has been paid to fundamental questions such as site formation processes and relating mortuary data to occupation evidence in cultural and taphonomic terms. The larger taphonomic relationship between occupation and mortuary deposition at individual sites has been avoided, presumably because at prehistoric sites in Thailand the taphonomic relationship between the two kinds of deposits is not obvious. Gravecuts may or may not have been identified by excavators, and determining from what "level" or surface interments derive is often based on deduction and guesswork. Many burials appear to "float" in deposits of occupation debris, which are essentially large middens. Layouts of graves are often illustrated without including the features from the surrounding occupation deposits (e.g., Higham and Thosarat 2004a). The fact that such plans show that the burials are often densely spaced, aligned, superimposed, clustered, and otherwise indicative of

Figure 5.2. Lower Early Period Ban Chiang square D5 showing intercutting of occupation and mortuary depositions.

deliberate placement with respect to each other has fostered the view over the past four decades that they were interred in "cemeteries," that is, formal bounded areas used exclusively for the disposal of the dead (e.g., Bayard 1984; Higham 2008; Higham and Kijngam 1984a:28; Higham and Thosarat 1994; Sørensen 1967:15).

An "Ah Ha" Moment

An "Ah Ha" moment occurred to the senior author some years ago while analyzing the stratigraphy of Ban Chiang when she recognized that the Ban Chiang burial deposition made more taphonomic and stratigraphic sense if the corpses were deposited not in a cemetery segregated from the living but rather under and/or around houses in an ongoing occupation. Ban Chiang's excavation records carefully document mortuary and occupation features at two separate excavation locales each deposited over the course of more than two millennia and each spanning the bronze and iron ages (White 1986, 1997, 2008). Occupation features such as small dumps and postholes were among and around the graves (Figures 5.2 and 5.3). Separating out periods of mortuary deposition that were stratigraphically discrete from periods of occupation deposition proved to be impossible. It became clear that occupation features with the same ceramics as the burials were found at levels above, at, and below the burials themselves. In addition, comparing the two Ban Chiang excavation locales, called "BC" and "BCES," showed that while both were used over the bronze and iron ages, intensity of usage shifted at the two locales, which were about 100 meters apart. For example, both sites have Middle Period Phase VII burials, but whereas the BC locale has evidence for interment of two individuals in that phase, the BCES locale has evidence for interment of 19 individuals. Interments from other phases may only be present in one

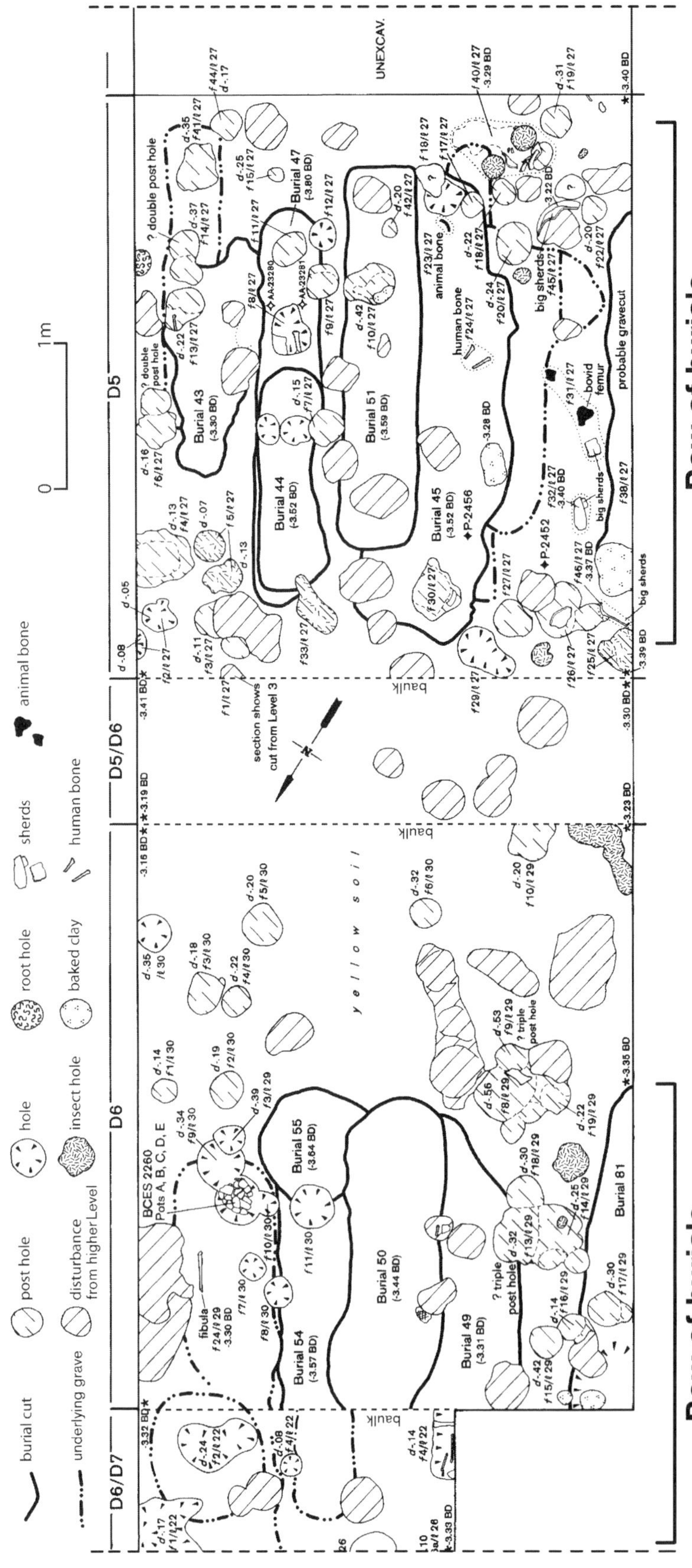

Figure 5.3. Plan of lower Early Period Ban Chiang (Level 2b squares D5 and D6) illustrating two rows of burials and their tight intercutting with occupation deposits.

locale and not the other, demonstrating intra-site shifting of settlement use.

Review of the stratigraphic descriptions for other excavated low mound sites in northeast and central Thailand indicates that residential burial was the likely scenario in most sites with prominent mortuary remains such as Khok Phanom Di (Higham and Bannanurag 1990), Ban Na Di (Higham and Kijngam 1984a), and Ban Non Wat (Higham 2008, 2009a). The clusters and rows of graves recognized at many metal age sites (e.g., Ban Chiang, Figures 5.2, 5.3) would in the case of residential burial taphonomy reflect spatial relationships to occupation localities such as dwelling structures made from organic materials. Only at a few low mound sites such as Ban Don Ta Phet (Glover et al. 1984) do contemporaneous occupation materials seem to be absent.

The inference that many metal age mortuary deposits represent burial under or next to houses in villages or other occupation contexts in prehistoric Thailand is not a new idea. Over the years others have occasionally proposed that burials were interred in domestic and production contexts at prehistoric sites in Thailand and elsewhere in Southeast Asia. MacDonald (1980a, 1980b) in particular advocated that the burials at Non Nok Tha and Ban Kao were interred in residential contexts and not cemeteries, although his view was never widely adopted (Bayard 1984). Källén (2004:194) argues that burials at Lao Pako, especially infants buried in jars, are part of a larger ritual space that incorporated metal artifact production. At other sites, interment close to domestic contexts was noted as a possibility but rejected as the basis for interpretation. For example, the middens and remains of structures surrounding the burials at Khok Phanom Di were interpreted as evidence of feasting and mortuary structures for the deceased rather than occupation evidence (Higham 2002:56–78; Higham and Thosarat 1994:107).

A few taphonomically less ambiguous examples of prehistoric burials interred within occupation contexts have been identified in Thailand. Henriksen (1982) excavated the remains of a single well-defined pile-built house within the bounds of which he recovered two skeletons. A group of ceramics also located under the house had forms similar to those from the Ban Kao site, indicating a second millennium B.C.E. date. At the other end of the metal age, the large (50 hectare) terminal iron age site of Non Muang Kao has evidence for burials interred through clay floors that could have been domestic or production spaces (O'Reilly 2007a:559, 2007b:585).

These few proposals for burial deposition in occupation and production contexts have not impacted the general interpretations of mortuary data from prehistoric Thailand, which generally reflect the Saxe-Binford approach (e.g., Higham and Thosarat 2004b, 2006; Talbot 2007). However, we note that archaeologists working in other parts of the world are revisiting taphonomic interpretation of interments originally published as cemeteries and finding that the interments instead occurred within villages of perishable houses (e.g., Joyce 2001:13). The taphonomic reinterpretations greatly broaden the theoretical perspectives that can be brought to bear on the archaeological remains, and the contribution mortuary evidence can have to understanding past societies. This revised taphonomic interpretation may help explain a variety of social puzzles with which archaeologists of Southeast Asia have long dealt.

Regional Context for Residential Burial in Thailand

Long-Term Mortuary/Occupation Sites

In addition to recognizing that corpses likely were interred within domestic contexts, the apparent longevity of this practice at individual sites is a noteworthy characteristic of metal age settlements in Thailand. At Ban Chiang, the practice seems to have begun by 2100 B.C.E. and continued into the early centuries C.E. Other sites, such as Khok Phanom Di and Ban Na Di, demonstrate the practice over at least hundreds of years. Over the sequences recovered from individual sites, there appear to have been *intra*-site shifts in intensity of usage of particular localities for mortuary and non-mortuary activities, resulting in localized hiatuses or intensification of depositional events within sites, as can be demonstrated for example at Ban Chiang, Ban Mai Chaimongkol (Onsuwan 2000:64), Ban Non Wat (Higham 2008), and other sites. These shifts are best interpreted as palimpsest or horizontal stratigraphy that formed as usually small intra-site adjustments were made by the occupants.

That long-term occupations practicing residential burial may have been the norm in metal age Thailand is strongly suggested by the intensive survey recently conducted by Eyre (2006, 2010) in central Thailand. Of the 25 open-air sites Eyre found, ranging in size from less than 1 to 91.5 hectares, 19 sites had evidence of occupation spanning most of the bronze and iron ages. Among the many intriguing findings of the survey was the absence of any site used only for mortuary deposition; mortuary evidence always co-occurred with habitation evidence although not necessarily the reverse. The 12 sites that had evidence for mortuary deposition were all multiphase, multicomponent bronze and iron age sites. Ceramic evidence showed that most were established during the early second millennium B.C.E. and most lasted until about C.E. 400. The lack of discrete mortuary sites found by Eyre's intensive pedestrian survey helps to undermine the prevalent interpretation that cemeteries, formal bounded burial grounds separated from domestic space, characterized the mortuary program for metal age Thailand.

Eyre's data furthermore suggest that the longevity of sites like Ban Chiang or Ban Non Wat occupied for over 2,000 years was not anomalous in metal age Thailand. Her data suggest, rather, that an extraordinary societal commitment to specific localities on the landscape over hundreds of years may have been the norm in this time period.

In addition, Eyre's data show that enduring mixed mortuary/occupation sites were situated on land with obviously differing agricultural potential, including both lowland flat alluvial areas conducive to wet rice cultivation and upland areas with slope and soil porosity not conducive to wet rice cultivation that must have been cropped by dry-land, probably swidden, techniques. Including Khok Phanom Di with its maritime orientation as among the examples of mixed mortuary/occupation sites likely practicing residential burial, this practice does not appear to simply have been a byproduct or correlate of one particular subsistence strategy, such as wet rice agriculture. Instead, residential burial may have been the common mortuary program for sedentary societies with varying subsistence bases in Thailand during the time period circa 2000 B.C.E.–C.E. 500.

Conclusive demonstration that residential burial was the normative burial program in metal age Thailand may require additional decades of excavations of mixed mortuary/occupation sites and will likely require methodological changes in excavating, analyzing, and reporting these sites to better understand the non-mortuary deposits. However, for the purposes of this essay, we postulate that residential burial was the predominant metal age mortuary program in Thailand in order to begin to explore its potential meaning for mortuary analyses as they go forward.

Ceramic Subregions

The burials that we argue were interred in residential areas at the low mound sites commonly contain grave goods, including ceramic vessels. As more of these mixed mortuary/occupation sites have been excavated, the accumulating mortuary ceramic evidence is revealing intriguing and distinctive subregional variation in ceramic morphology and style suggesting supravillage groupings of some sort (Eyre 2006; Ho 1992; McNeill 1997; White 1995a). At the time of writing this essay, at least 13 ceramic subregions have been recognized and more are likely to be defined (Figure 5.4).

White (1995a) has proposed ceramic subregions and possible co-occurring variation in mortuary ritual as a reflection of heterarchical social dynamics—flexible lateral differentiation—in metal age Thailand. The pottery was locally made, probably in all or most villages in a subregion, for much of the metal age. Within the Ban Mai Chaimongkol subregion, subtle site-to-site variability in stylistic motifs within a single ceramic form and manufacturing tradition argues against one or two pot-making villages supplying the subregion as a whole (Eyre 2006:258–259, 316). Voelker (2007) has provided evidence for some consolidation of pottery production in the Upper Mun subregion during the late iron age, but continued variability in vessel fabric supports an overall continuation of decentralized pottery production. Limited technical analyses of metal age ceramics indicate that subregional distinctiveness is found not only in morphology and style but also in technological attributes such as vessel formation techniques and clay fabric (Glanzman and Fleming 1985; White 1986:235–236; White et al. 1991).

Variations in mortuary ritual may co-occur with the ceramic subregions (White 1986:236–237) and this topic needs much more research. As one example, White (1986:236) pointed out that not only did Ban Chiang and Ban Na Di, only 20 kilometers apart, have distinctly different ceramics at contemporaneous time periods, but also they had distinct grave treatments in terms of what fauna and which body parts of fauna were interred with corpses, what range of vessels comprised a grave assemblage, and how those vessels were placed in graves (i.e., deliberately broken at Ban Chiang but not at contemporaneous phases at Ban Na Di). Yet, there is ample evidence that metal age communities in different subregions traded with each other, exchanging metals, metal technology, and other craft items such as shell and stone bangles, as well as the occasional pot, showing that subregions were not isolated from each other technologically, economically, or socially.

The stylistic and ritual distinctiveness that is shared among groups of sites but is differentiated from the styles and rituals of sets of neighboring sites suggests the presence of social group "signaling" at the regional level (Wobst 1977, 1999), much as jewelry and fabric signal ethnic groups in uplands of Southeast Asia in the ethnographic present (Lewis and Lewis 1998). Regional archaeologists are at the earliest stages of defining these localized ceramic technological traditions, but the subregionally distinct vessel fabrication practices already evident suggest the presence of supravillage communities of potting practitioners who shared potting technologies. One example of a highly localized ceramic tradition is the "Elephant hide" pottery made by pressing clay into a large coarse basket. This pot-forming tradition appears at the earliest stage of the Khao Wong Prachan Valley subregion (Rispoli 1997).

The marked stylistic distinctions between contemporaneous Ban Chiang and Ban Na Di pottery are mirrored

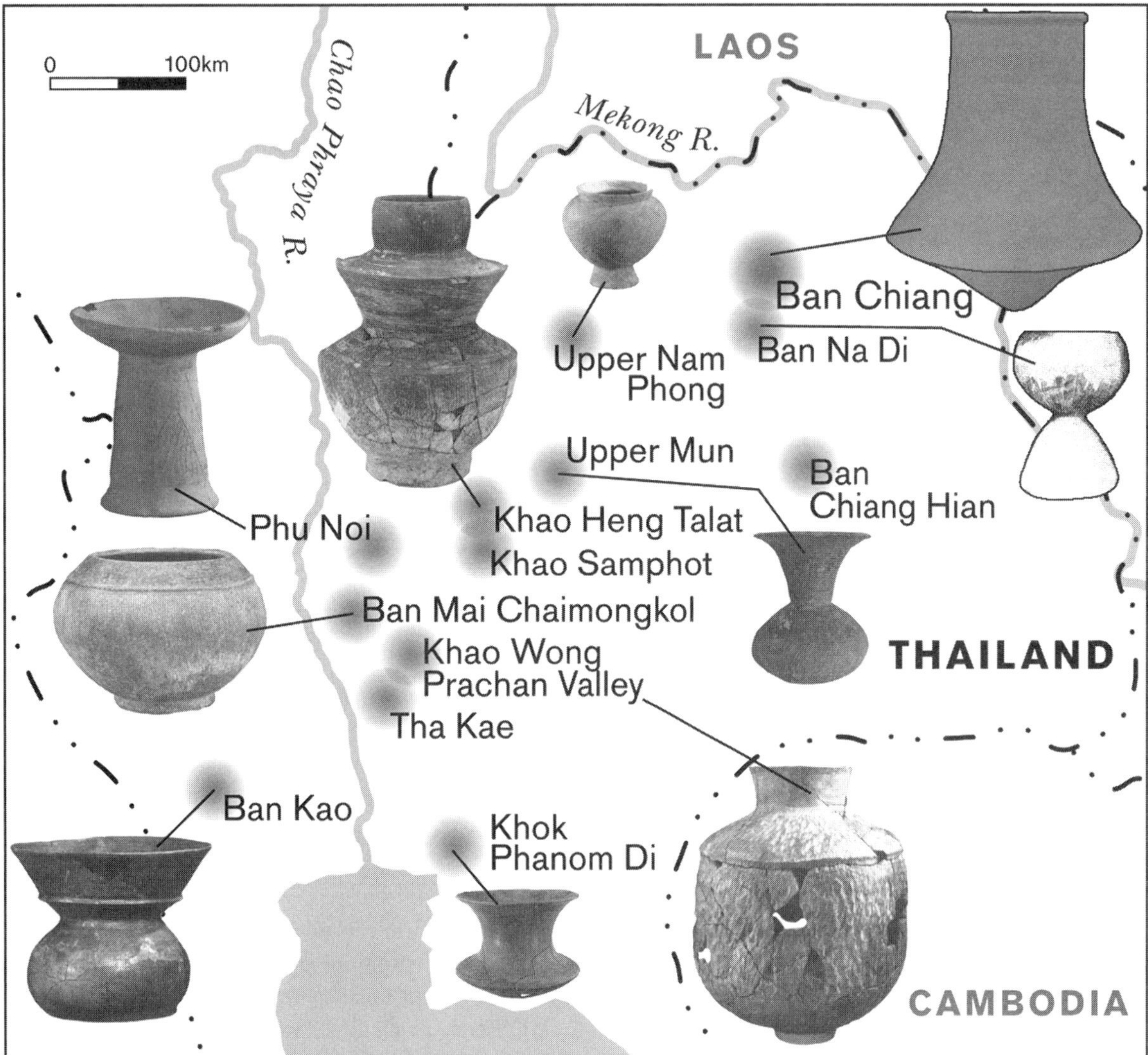

Figure 5.4. Locations and names of the 13 ceramic subregions thus far recognized for metal age Thailand. Selected examples of distinctive mortuary pottery vessels illustrate regionality of stylistic variation. Note that the example vessels are not all contemporaneous, because detailed ceramic sequences of Thailand are mostly unpublished. However, each vessel depicted is distinctive to the area from which it comes. As ceramic data are published in the future, new versions of this map can be constructed for specific time periods.

in distinct vessel fabrication techniques, even though the sites are only 20 kilometers apart. Ban Na Di potters used lump and mold fabrication and nonorganic temper (Vincent 1984), while contemporaneous Ban Chiang dwellers used lump and slab with plant temper (McGovern et al. 1985; White 1986:235–236). This subregional variability is clearly evident in mortuary ceramics beginning at least in the second millennium B.C.E., suggesting the ceramic "signaling" of subregional group identity and/or their technological tradition occurred from the bronze age and was an important part of the residential burial program.

Subregions Over Time

Generally, the ceramic subregion phenomenon with its associated residential burial program appears to continue from the bronze through the iron age in both central and northeast Thailand. Much research is needed to investigate how individual ceramic subregions changed spatially, technologically, ritually, and economically over the course of the metal age. Current evidence suggests that many subregions maintained their distinctive ceramics over time, but shifts in their socio-settlement systems did not mirror one another.

One of the subregions, the Upper Mun valley, begins to have evidence for developing large-scale water management and increased range in burial wealth during the latter part of the iron age. In central Thailand, Mudar's (1993) intensive settlement research provides broad measures of increasing integration during the iron age, and Eyre's (2006, 2010) settlement data show the presence of variable site size and site use within one ceramic subregion. Most importantly, though, Eyre's data show continuity of settlement location (Eyre 2006:484–489) from the bronze age until the end of the iron age, including in the uplands. Development of water management systems is not attested in central Thailand at the same time period as these systems appear in the northeast. While additional supportive data are needed, provisionally Eyre's data show that variability in metal age site size probably began in the bronze age, but no evidence that the larger sites were centralized or dominant nodes in an economically or politically hierarchical landscape. Alternatively, we might consider that the large mixed mortuary/occupation sites dating from the bronze age may have been core affiliative settlements in a differentiated ritual landscape. The larger, long-lived mortuary/occupation settlements may have been founder or origin settlements (Waterson 2000) that served as ritual or group identity "attractors" (vide Kirch 2000). However, many questions remain, for example, whether there was fissioning and/or fusing of ceramic subregions over time and what such settlement collectivities might mean regarding societal dynamics.

New Perspectives for the Pre-State Period from Residential Burial

How might residential burial, long-term occupations, and ceramic subregions together shed new light on pre-state social dynamics in Thailand? Some may argue that there is no substantial difference for social interpretation if kin groups are interring family members in clusters in formal disposal areas like cemeteries, separate from settlements, or in clusters under and around houses in a village; assessment of presence of social hierarchy through assessment of differential effort in interments is sufficient for their objectives.

We propose that residential burial in villages should have important implications, not only for stratigraphic interpretation of Thailand's metal age sites but also for interpreting the societies that undertook this mortuary practice. The other chapters in this volume and the large body of literature from the past 20 years of mortuary studies around the world (e.g., Beck 1995; Chesson 2001; Rakita et al. 2005; Silverman and Small 2002) show that a much greater richness of understanding the past is available if archaeologists reassess their assumptions based on older cultural evolutionary stage models (e.g., O'Reilly 2008) and expand and fine tune their methodological and theoretical approaches to mortuary data. Spatial positioning of the dead relative to the living is highly variable and has significant consequences for the descendant communities (Silverman 2002). Alternative perspectives may help assuage the frustrated search in Southeast Asia for unambiguous evidence for top-down social, economic, or political structures (elite lineages in centers controlling access to scarce resources) and guide archaeologists in looking for other kinds of evidence that might inform on decentralized mechanisms (sodalities, distributed knowledge and power, and oscillating networks) characteristic of bottom-up corporate modes of complexity. We explore a few new perspectives below.

House Societies

The proposal that corpses were commonly interred in physical relationship to long-lived family dwellings or at least intravillage "family ritual loci" is perhaps best interpreted using the concept of "house societies" (Gillespie 2000a, 2000b, 2001; Joyce and Gillespie 2000; Lévi-Strauss 1982; see also Adams and King, chapter 1, this volume). Levi-Strauss developed the house society concept in part to describe social subgroupings in societies that are *not* based on unilineal descent groups (Gillespie 2000a) but nonetheless have enduring corporate collectivities.

Many of the ethnographic studies upon which the house society concept was developed are located in island Southeast Asia, a region long known for its ambilaterality, bilaterality, and cognatic forms of social organization. The house society concept may help archaeologists detach from the expectations implied in using the word *lineage* when discussing evidence of social units (such as grave clusters) for metal age sites. "Lineage" connotes that *descent* prescribed group membership, often implying that lineage relations were the primary factor in collective action and power relations. In house societies, household membership includes many blood relations but also fictive and distant kin who have elected, negotiated, or manipulated their affiliation with a house, perhaps only for a period of time. House societies are noted for their flexibility in group membership.

Not all house societies practice residential burial, but many do (Kirch 2000; Waterson 2000). The physical proximity and continuity of residence with the physical remains of ancestors suggests that an ongoing intimacy of the living with the dead was central to a residential mortuary program, whether that practice related to fear of or comfort from the spirit world—both are attested in the historical and ethnographic literature (Adams 2007; Barber 1988:140–141). The house society concept has proved useful in examining archaeological cultures from many parts of the Old and New Worlds at many "stages" of complexity, from iron age Iberia (González-Ruibal 2006), to markedly stratified state societies such as the Maya (Gillespie 2000c, 2000d), to "neolithic" societies like Çatalhöyük (Hodder and Cessford 2004).

Burials, Houses, and Landscapes

One repeated theme in house society literature is that of "place-making," the imbuing of enduring meaning and cultural identity to specific locations on landscapes. Gillespie's statement that "a key function of houses is to anchor people in space and to link them to time" (Gillespie 2000a:3) is remarkably congruent with the picture emerging from the enduring metal age settlement system in Thailand. While burial within villages is found in many house societies, and the village is one key sociopolitical unit within such societies, the frame of reference for house societies is really the region.

House societies commonly have territorial dimensions (Adams 2007; González-Ruibal 2006). Supralocal organizations, flexible confederations of villages, and cross-cutting alliances among various subunits of the society provide flexible and overlapping integrative structures beyond individual villages. Noncentralized cross-cutting sodalities serve a variety of societal needs and are particularly important for the preservation of social memory or tradition in nonliterate societies (Kuijt 2001).

The existence of the ceramic subregions in metal age Thailand strongly suggests that supravillage territorial dimensions existed and endured over the time period, and the striking variability in ceramic style likely was one marker for recognized territories. Given the territorial dimension to house societies, "landscape" approaches to archaeology that seek to move beyond a site focus to understand past societies in their larger social and natural environments may assist in better understanding them (e.g., Anschuetz et al. 2001; Ashmore and Knapp 1999).

The commitment to place suggested by permanent occupation of sites and residential burial over hundreds and in many cases thousands of years at sites of metal age Thailand may at first seem unimaginable to an archaeologist born in the West. In addition to cultural discomfort with living in close proximity to decaying bodies, even of loved ones, Western scholars may question the likelihood of such a burial practice in long-lived permanent settlements, especially on lands that cannot sustain wet rice cultivation. However, ethnography of swiddening societies in southwest China (Yin 2001) demonstrates that they too can have deep commitment to ancestral village location, irrespective of shifting field systems.

The continuity of burial clusters, individual settlements, and ceramic subregions over hundreds of years, however, argues for importance placed on bottom-up affiliation with societal collectivities rather than top-down coercion by/control by/exclusion from dominant subgroups as the social "glue" (vide Salganik et al. 2006).

Ritual Integration

In house societies, rituals centered on house units are important integrative activities crafting identity and social memory over space and time (Chesson 2001; Kuijt 2001). There is as yet in metal age societies in Thailand no evidence for centralized ritual spaces or hierarchically managed ritual activities for a village or subregion as a whole. On the other hand, investment in mortuary ritual is clearly evident, whatever its taphonomic context. Burials may thus provide the main source of archaeological evidence for ritual integration in metal age societies in Thailand, as they have for many other middle range societies (e.g., Holliman 2001).

Situating mortuary activities including interment with residential units within villages, or at least primary or focal residential units, provides evidence that conduct of key integrating social rituals, in this case death rituals, occurred in a decentralized framework. A sustained mortuary program of interment in close association with ancestrally defined domestic/mortuary places suggests that family identification with place was an enduring and prioritized organizing principle for metal age societies in Thailand. Family claim to and preservation of place in the social and natural landscape in contradistinction to other residential/family units would be reiterated with each interment irrespective of numbers and kinds of grave goods placed with the deceased. Funerary activities can be viewed as integrative performance rituals for the descendants of the deceased, blood related or not, as well as for local residents generally even if primarily in counter-distinction. Mortuary activities provide periodic occasions when social structure and core values are restated in word and action. The variable grave accoutrements within clusters at sites like Ban Non Wat suggest that individualized identities were also important and recognized, but not necessarily cross-generationally enduring. Such outliers and cluster shifting are consistent with theories of collective social dynamics (Salganik et al. 2006).

Sustainability and Cycles

We suggest that societal investment in permanent settlements, and *houses* therein, could be ritually sustained at least in part through the practice of residential burial, which supported the success of this settlement system at the regional scale over more than two millennia. Houses practicing residential burial were likely one key element among several ongoing, counter-poised segmental integrative structures of the village societies, along with various co-existing nested and overlapping segments including the villages themselves and the ceramic subregions. However, the waxing and waning of burial clusters, and to a lesser extent sites, also suggests that at a local scale, such as individual houses or neighborhoods, cyclic phenomena occurred.

It is likely that sustainability of an enduring house society system is based on relative predictability in the subsistence, environmental, and social realms. Sustainable subsistence systems need to be able to respond to the degree and type of perturbations that occur in the environment at least within living memory. There are a variety of factors that promoted decentralized and hence flexibly adaptive subsistence strategies in Southeast Asia. Primary among these was the likelihood that numerous subsistence strategies, from variant dryland and wetland cropping techniques to hunting and gathering, were known and practiced within each village (White 1995b). As Yin (2001) documents for groups in Yunnan, the great range of known cultivation practices and resources can be contextually attuned to annual changes in rainfall and niche environments. Overall system sustainability may have been related to the low interannual variability in rainfall in Thailand in comparison to some other parts of monsoon Asia (Dewar 2003). Low interannual variability in rainfall is particularly important for rain-fed rice agriculture.

The late development of intercommunity conflict within Thailand also speaks to predictability in intervillage relations over most of the metal age until the late iron age about C.E. 400, when arrow points become more common in the Upper Mun valley. Other parts of Southeast Asia may have developed regular societal conflict earlier than Thailand, including northern Vietnam and Cambodia (Phum Snay; O'Reilly and Sytha 2001). This intra-regional variation is interesting in and of itself, but the earlier development of social conflict in some parts of Southeast Asia does not negate the significance of sustained low levels of conflict in metal age Thailand.

The relationship of variation in wealth to mortuary treatment in ritually integrated societies may differ from that in societies structured as entrenched hierarchies. Parker Pearson (1999:86–87) and others have noted that ostentatious mortuary displays may be a "cyclic phenomenon" related to shifting claims to legitimation. Such displays may occur during relatively unstable periods and alternate with phases of simpler mortuary treatments, as material manifestations of leadership shift over time. A cyclic patterning for the presence of unusually wealthy graves has been observed in metal age Thailand (e.g., Bacus 2006; Higham 2008). Periodicity of increases (and decreases) in material investment in the mortuary domain may be more significant for understanding variation in local and regional social dynamics than documenting individual wealthy burials as evidence for entrenched elites (vide Beck 2006).

Variation in the intensity of clustering of graves over time also has been noted at some sites in Thailand (Talbot 2007). This is an important area of investigation, and our data may be particularly rich for examination of oscillating and cyclic cultural phenomena. We may hypothesize, for example, that the clustering of graves relates to periods or situations in which individual identification to village subgroups was prioritized. Talbot (2007) suggests that intensification of clustering at Noen U-Loke in the late iron age was due to "stress," possibly drought and/or intercommunity conflict. But variation in clustering over time is noted at many sites from other time periods without association of conflict or food shortages (e.g., lower Early Period Ban Chiang; White 2008), raising the point that "stress" is likely a locally contingent variable, and possibly only one of many reasons to closely space interments. Social stress may take many forms from local changes in everything from demography to river courses, to region-wide changes in precipitation from El Niño years.

Moreover, extrapolating from Eyre's data, not every metal age site has evidence of mortuary usage, although larger sites generally do. This observation suggests that corpses were not buried merely in whatever house in which the individual happened to die, but that there was preferential interment in relationship to particular parts of the landscape, particular buildings, or particular family ancestors, perhaps along the lines of the "family homestead" or "family compound."

Over time and depending on circumstances ranging from drought to appearance of charismatic leaders, the segments at various scales (sodalities, villages) could ally or fission, much as Leach (1954) has described in the *gumsa/gumlao* oscillation of the Kachin in Burma or Yin (2001) describes for the Wa. The archaeological evidence indicates that rather than hierarchical relationships among lineages or sites becoming entrenched as predicted by origins of states models, entrenchment was situated in other, more spatial, landscape-based components of the social system (such as houses and settlements). This investment in multi-scalar place-making resisted structural change and apparently resisted entrenched hierarchization and centralization for over 2,000 years.

Conclusions

Among the various factors that promoted and sustained the ritually integrated socio-settlement system in metal age Thailand, we argue, was the practice of residential burial. The physical and ritual anchoring of descendants to ancestors at specific locations on the landscape via direct spatial association with interred remains of deceased forebears appears to be a primary key to understanding the social continuity of metal age Thailand.

Taphonomic reassessment of mortuary deposition in metal age Thailand supports this re-evaluation of the region's metal age societal dynamics. Recognition of the practice of residential burial opens the door to perceiving the integration of mortuary actions and deposits as part of sustaining living communities of the past. We propose that at least for Thailand, the study of multi-scalar collectivities, including house societies, will also provide fruitful insights for both the metal age and post–metal age states beyond conventional origins of states approaches that have dominated discussions to now.

Re-perceived archaeological evidence facilitates re-prioritization of future research programs. First, excavations of metal age sites, particularly when large areas can be opened (e.g., Ban Non Wat; Higham 2008), provide opportunities to verify or disprove the taphonomic proposal that we postulate. Refined excavation methodologies for non-burial deposits (e.g., by applying insights from studies like Beck 2006) may identify discrete "houses" in multiphase, multicomponent sites, and burial clusters may be specifically related to discrete residential units. Second, the intra-site groupings of burials (clusters and rows) can be more systematically compared for biological relationships and for evidence of material distinctions in both grave goods and ritual expression to explore discrete house identities. Third, variation in grave clustering can be investigated locally within individual sites, and regionally and temporally. Does Talbot's (2007) suggestion for Noen U-Loke that stress resulted in intensification of grave clustering explain other examples of clustering at sites with earlier mortuary deposits, such as Khok Phanom Di or lower Early Period Ban Chiang? Is clustering an expression of strengthened identification with village subunits that waxes and wanes based on site-specific stresses or other processes?

Fourth, more materials research and intensive site surveys are needed to more concretely define the technological, stylistic, economic, chronological, and geographic attributes of all ceramic subregions, as well as their histories, including their emergence by the second millennium B.C.E. and disappearance in the first millennium C.E. Defining the relationships between ceramic subregions and metal technological provinces (White and Hamilton 2009) is also a key topic.

Using residential burial evidence to examine collective identities and culturally defined landscapes is a linchpin for exploring the prehistoric development of Thailand in its own right. Enhanced understanding of the sociopolitical, settlement, and ritual systems of metal age Thailand should also support a deeper grasp of the nature of subsequent states in the region.

Acknowledgments

This essay is the product of years of discussions with team members and colleagues. In particular, the "Ban Chiang Gang," the core members of the Ban Chiang team at the University of Pennsylvania Museum, are gratefully acknowledged for giving feedback on the interpretation of residential burial over innumerable weekly brown bag discussions since White first considered the taphonomic interpretation. Elizabeth Hamilton in particular brought useful references and concepts to the attention of White. White also is in debt to co-author Eyre for sharing her personal experiences with death during her upbringing in Thailand. Eyre's survey project was funded by a Wenner-Gren Dissertation grant (Gr. 6846). We are very grateful to Ron Adams, Michele Toomay-Douglas, Stacie King, David Welch, Dougald O'Reilly, Surapol Natapintu, and the anonymous reviewers for their suggestions on the text. Ardeth Abrams prepared the illustrations. Special thanks are given to Ron Adams for helping to develop the session on residential burial at the 2007 SAA meetings in Austin, Texas, and for doing such a great job in recruiting stellar participants.

Notes

1. In this essay we follow White 2002 in the use of the lowercase in Southeast Asian applications of the Three Age System.

References

Adams, Ron L.
2007 Maintaining Cohesion in House Societies of West Sumba, Indonesia. *In* The Durable House: House Society Models in Archaeology. R. A. Beck Jr., ed. Pp. 344–362. Occasional Paper 35. Carbondale: Center for Archaeological Investigations, Southern Illinois University.

Anschuetz, Kurt F., Richard H. Wilshusen, and Cherie L. Scheick

2001 An Archaeology of Landscapes: Perspectives and Directions. Journal of Archaeological Research 9:157–211.

Ashmore, Wendy, and A. Bernard Knapp
1999 Archaeological Landscapes: Constructed, Conceptualized, Ideational. *In* Archaeologies of Landscape: Contemporary Perspectives. W. Ashmore and A. B. Knapp, eds. Pp. 1–30. Oxford: Blackwell.

Bacus, Elisabeth A.
2006 Social Identities in Bronze Age Northeast Thailand: Intersections of Gender, Status and Ranking at Non Nok Tha. *In* Uncovering Southeast Asia's Past: Selected Papers from the 10th International Conference of the European Association of Southeast Asian Archaeologists. E. A. Bacus, I. C. Glover, and V. C. Pigott, eds. Pp. 105–115. Singapore: National University of Singapore Press.

Barber, Paul
1988 Vampires, Burial and Death: Folklore and Reality. New Haven, CT: Yale University Press.

Bayard, Donn T.
1984 Rank and Wealth at Non Nok Tha: The Mortuary Evidence. *In* Southeast Asian Archaeology at the XV Pacific Science Congress: The Origins of Agriculture, Metallurgy, and the State in Mainland Southeast Asia. D. T. Bayard, ed. Pp. 87–122. University of Otago Studies in Prehistoric Anthropology, 16. Dunedin, New Zealand: University of Otago.

1996–97 Bones of Contention: The Non Nok Tha Burials and the Chronology and Context of Early Southeast Asian Bronze. *In* Ancient Chinese and Southeast Asian Bronze Age Cultures, vol. 2. D. Bulbeck and N. Barnard, eds. Pp. 889–940. Proceedings of a conference held at the Edith and Joy London Foundation property, Kioloa, NSW, Australia, 8–12 February 1988. Taipei: SMC.

Beck, Lane Anderson, ed.
1995 Regional Approaches to Mortuary Analysis. New York: Plenum.

Beck, Margaret E.
2006 Midden Ceramic Assemblage Formation: A Case Study from Kalinga, Philippines. American Antiquity 71:27–51.

Boyd, William E.
2007 The Geoarchaeology of Noen U-Loke and Non Muang Kao. *In* The Origins of the Civilization of Angkor, vol. 2: The Excavation of Noen U-Loke and Non Muang Kao. C. F. W. Higham, A. Kijngam, and S. Talbot, eds. Pp. 29–53. Bangkok: The Thai Fine Arts Department.
2008 Social Change in Late Holocene Mainland SE Asia: A Response to Gradual Climate Change or a Critical Climatic Event? Quaternary International 184(1):11–23.

Chesson, Meredith S., ed.
2001 Social Memory, Identity, and Death: Anthropological Perspectives in Mortuary Rituals. Archeological Papers of the American Anthropological Association, 10. Arlington, VA: American Anthropological Association.

Dewar, Robert E.
2003 Rainfall Variability and Subsistence Systems in Southeast Asia and the Western Pacific. Current Anthropology 44:369–388.

Eyre, Chureekamol Onsuwan
2006 Prehistoric and Proto-historic Communities in the Eastern Upper Chao Phraya River Valley, Thailand: Analysis of Site Chronology, Settlement Patterns, and Land Use. Ph.D. dissertation, Department of Anthropology, University of Pennsylvania. Ann Arbor, MI: University Microfilms International.
2010 Social Variation and Dynamics in Metal Age and Proto-historic Central Thailand: A Regional Perspective. Asian Perspectives 49(1):43–84.

Gillespie, Susan D.
2000a Beyond Kinship: An Introduction. *In* Beyond Kinship: Social and Material Reproduction in House Societies. R. A. Joyce and S. D. Gillespie, eds. Pp. 1–21. Philadelphia: University of Pennsylvania Press.
2000b Lévi-Strauss: Maison and Société à Maisons. *In* Beyond Kinship: Social and Material Reproduction in House Societies. R. A. Joyce and S. D. Gillespie, eds. Pp. 22–52. Philadelphia: University of Pennsylvania Press.

2000c Maya "Nested Houses": The Ritual Construction of Place. *In* Beyond Kinship: Social and Material Reproduction in House Societies. R. A. Joyce and S. D. Gillespie, eds. Pp. 135–160. Philadelphia: University of Pennsylvania Press.

2000d Rethinking Ancient Maya Social Organization: Replacing "Lineage" with "House." American Anthropologist 102:467–484.

2001 Personhood, Agency, and Mortuary Ritual: A Case Study from the Ancient Maya. Journal of Anthropological Archaeology 20:73–112.

Glanzman, William D., and Stuart J. Fleming

1985 Ceramic Technology at Prehistoric Ban Chiang, Thailand: Fabrication Methods. MASCA Journal 3(4):114–121.

Glover, Ian C., Pisit Charoenwongsa, B. Alvey, and N. Kamnounket

1984 The Cemetery of Ban Don Ta Phet, Thailand: Results from the 1980–1 Season. *In* Southeast Asian Archaeology 1981. B. Allchin and M. Sidell, eds. Pp. 319–330. Cambridge: Cambridge University Press.

Goldstein, Lynne G.

1980 Mississippian Mortuary Practices: A Case Study of Two Cemeteries in the Lower Illinois Valley. Scientific Papers 4. Evanston, IL: Northwestern University Archaeological Program.

2002 Visible Death: Mortuary Site and Mortuary Landscape in Diachronic Perspective. *In* The Space and Place of Death. H. Silverman and D. B. Small, eds. Pp. 201–205. Archeological Papers of the American Anthropological Association, 11. Arlington, VA: American Anthropological Association.

González-Ruibal, Alfredo

2006 House Societies vs. Kinship-Based Societies: An Archaeological Case from Iron Age Europe. Journal of Anthropological Archaeology 25:144–173.

Henriksen, Merette A.

1982 The First Excavated Prehistoric House Site in Southeast Asia. *In* The House in East and Southeast Asia. K. Izikowitz and P. Sørensen, eds. Pp. 17–24. London: Curzon.

Higham, Charles F. W.

1989 The Archaeology of Mainland Southeast Asia from 10,000 B.C. to the Fall of Angkor. Cambridge: Cambridge University Press.

1993 The Bone, Antler, and Turtle Carapace Technology. *In* The Excavation of Khok Phanom Di, a Prehistoric Site in Central Thailand, vol. 3: The Material Culture (Part I). C. F. W. Higham and R. Thosarat, eds. Pp. 1–44. Reports of the Research Committee, 50. London: Society of Antiquaries.

1996 The Bronze Age of Southeast Asia. Cambridge: Cambridge University Press.

2002 Early Cultures of Mainland Southeast Asia. Bangkok: River Books.

2006 Crossing National Boundaries: Southern China and Southeast Asia in Prehistory. *In* Uncovering Southeast Asia's Past: Selected Papers from the 10th International Conference of the European Association of Southeast Asian Archaeologists. E. A. Bacus, I. C. Glover, and V. C. Pigott, eds. Pp. 13–21. Singapore: National University of Singapore Press.

2007 Summary and Conclusions. *In* The Origins of the Civilization of Angkor, vol. 2: The Excavation of Noen U-Loke and Non Muang Kao. C. F. W. Higham, A. Kijngam, and S. Talbot, eds. Pp. 595–609. Bangkok: The Thai Fine Arts Department.

2008 Ban Non Wat: The First Five Seasons. *In* From Homo erectus to the Living Traditions. J.-P. Pautreau, A.-S. Coupey, V. Zeitoun, and E. Rambault, Pp. 83–90. Chiang Mai: European Association of Southeast Asian Archaeologists.

2009a The Excavation of Ban Non Wat, Part One: Introduction. The Origins of the Civilization of Angkor, vol. 3. Bangkok: The Thai Fine Arts Department.

2009b Thailand's Bronze Age Superburials: The Aristocrats of Ban Non Wat. Current World Archaeology 35:38–43.

N.d. The Bronze Age of Southeast Asia: New Insight on Social Change from Ban Non Wat. Unpublished MS, Department of Anthropology, University of Otago.

Higham, Charles F. W., and Rachanie Bannanurag

1990 The Excavation of Khok Phanom Di, a Prehistoric Site in Central Thailand, vol. 1: The Excavation, Chronology and Human Burials.

Reports of the Research Committee, 47. London: Society of Antiquaries.

Higham, Charles F. W., and Thomas Higham
2008 A New Chronological Framework for Prehistoric Southeast Asia, Based on a Bayesian Model from Ban Non Wat. Antiquity 82:1–20.

Higham, Charles F. W., and Amphan Kijngam
1984a The Excavations of Ban Na Di, Ban Muang Phruk and Non Kao Noi. *In* Prehistoric Investigations in Northeast Thailand. C. F. W. Higham and A. Kijngam, eds. Pp. 22–56. BAR International Series, 231(i). Oxford: Archaeopress.
1984b The Cultural and Chronological Framework for Northeast Thai Prehistory. *In* Prehistoric Investigations in Northeast Thailand. C. F. W. Higham and A. Kijngam, eds. Pp. 698–730. BAR International Series, 231(iii). Oxford: Archaeopress.
1984c The Mortuary Ritual and Its Implications. *In* Prehistoric Investigations in Northeast Thailand. C. F. W. Higham et al., eds. Pp. 413–545. BAR International Series, 231(ii). Oxford: Archaeopress.

Higham, Charles F. W., and Dougald J. W. O' Reilly
2004 Social Aspects of the Ban Lum Khao Cemetery. *In* The Excavation of Ban Lum Khao. C. F. W. Higham and R. Thosarat, eds. Pp. 301–323. The Origins of the Civilization of Angkor, vol. 1. Bangkok: The Thai Fine Arts Department.

Higham, Charles F. W., and Rachanie Thosarat
1994 Khok Phanom Di: Prehistoric Adaptation to the World's Richest Habitat. Fort Worth: Hartcourt Brace.
1998 Conclusions and Summary of Results. *In* The Excavation of Nong Nor, a Prehistoric Site in Central Thailand. C. F. W. Higham and R. Thosarat, eds. Pp. 523–539. University of Otago Studies in Prehistoric Anthropology, 18. Dunedin, New Zealand: Department of Anthropology, University of Otago.
2004a Conclusions: Introduction. *In* The Excavation of Ban Lum Khao. C. F. W. Higham and R. Thosarat, eds. Pp. 325–328. The Origins of the Civilization of Angkor, vol. 1. Bangkok: The Thai Fine Arts Department.
2004b The Excavation of Khok Phanom Di, a Prehistoric Site in Central Thailand, vol. 7: Summary and Conclusions. Reports of the Research Committee, 72. London: Society of Antiquaries.
2006 Ban Non Wat: The First Three Seasons. *In* Uncovering Southeast Asia's Past: Selected Papers from the 10th International Conference of the European Association of Southeast Asian Archaeologists. E. A. Bacus, I. C. Glover, and V. C. Pigott, eds. Pp. 98–104. Singapore: University of Singapore Press.

Higham, Charles F. W., and Rachanie Thosarat, eds.
2004 The Excavation of Ban Lum Khao. The Origins of the Civilization of Angkor, vol. 1. Bangkok: The Thai Fine Arts Department.

Ho, Chui-mei
1992 An Analysis of Settlement Patterns in the Lopburi Area. *In* Early Metallurgy, Trade and Urban Centres in Thailand and Southeast Asia. I. Glover, P. Suchitta, and J. Villiers, eds. Pp. 39–45. Bangkok: White Lotus.

Hodder, Ian, and Craig Cessford
2004 Daily Practice and Social Memory at Çatalhöyük. American Antiquity 69:17–40.

Holliman, Sandra E.
2001 Death, Gender, and the Chumash Peoples: Mourning Ceremonialism as an Integrative Mechanism. *In* Social Memory, Identity, and Death: Anthropological Perspectives on Mortuary Rituals. M. S. Chesson, ed. Pp. 41–55. Archeological Papers of the American Anthropological Association, 10. Arlington, VA: American Anthropological Association.

Joyce, Rosemary A.
2001 Burying the Dead at Tlatilco: Social Memory and Social Identities. *In* Social Memory, Identity, and Death: Anthropological Perspectives on Mortuary Rituals. M. S. Chesson, ed. Pp. 12–26. Archeological Papers of the American Anthropological Association, 10. Arlington, VA: American Anthropological Association.

Joyce, Rosemary A., and Susan D. Gillespie, eds.
2000 Beyond Kinship: Social and Material Reproduction in House Societies. Philadelphia: University of Pennsylvania Press.

Källén, Anna
2004 And Through Flows the River: Archaeology and the Pasts of Lao Pako. Ph.D. thesis, Department of Archaeology and Ancient History, Uppsala University.

Kirch, Patrick V.
2000 Temples as "Holy Houses": The Transformation of Ritual Architecture in Traditional Polynesian Societies. *In* Beyond Kinship: Social and Material Reproduction in House Societies. R. A. Joyce and S. D. Gillespie, eds. Pp. 103–114. Philadelphia: University of Pennsylvania Press.

Kuijt, Ian
2001 Place, Death, and the Transmission of Social Memory in Early Agricultural Communities of the Near Eastern Pre-Pottery Neolithic. *In* Social Memory, Identity, and Death: Anthropological Perspectives on Mortuary Rituals. M. S. Chesson, ed. Pp. 80–99. Archeological Papers of the American Anthropological Association, 10. Arlington, VA: American Anthropological Association.

Leach, Edmund Roland
1954 Political Systems of Highland Burma: A Study of Kachin Social Structure. Cambridge, MA: Harvard University Press.

Lévi-Strauss, Claude
1982 The Way of the Masks. London: Jonathan Cape.

Lewis, Paul, and Elaine L. Lewis
1998 Peoples of the Golden Triangle. London: Thames and Hudson.

MacDonald, William K.
1980a The Bang Site, Thailand: An Alternative Analysis. Asian Perspectives 21(1):30–51.
1980b Some Implications of Societal Complexity: Organizational Variability at Non Nok Tha, Thailand (2000–0 B.C.). Ph.D. dissertation, Department of Anthropology, University of Michigan. Ann Arbor, MI: University Microfilms International.

McCaw, M.
2007 The Faunal Remains: Results and Conclusions. *In* The Origins of the Civilization of Angkor, vol. 2: The Excavation of Noen U-Loke and Non Muang Kao. C. F. W. Higham, A. Kijngam, and S. Talbot, eds. Pp. 513–536. Bangkok: The Thai Fine Arts Department.

McGovern, Patrick E., William W. Vernon, and Joyce C. White
1985 Ceramic Technology at Prehistoric Ban Chiang, Thailand: Physiochemical Analyses. MASCA Journal 3(4):104–113.

McGrath, R. J., and W. E. Boyd
2001 The Chronology of the Iron Age 'Moats' of Northeast Thailand. Antiquity 75:349–360.

McNeill, Judith R.
1997 Muang Phet: Quaritch Wales' Moated Site Excavations Re-Appraised. Bulletin of the Indo-Pacific Prehistory Association 16:167–175.

Mudar, Karen Mari
1993 Prehistoric and Early Historic Settlement Patterns on the Central Plain: Analysis of Archaeological Survey in Lopburi Province, Thailand. Ph.D. dissertation, Department of Anthropology, University of Michigan.

Onsuwan, Chureekamol
2000 Excavation of Ban Mai Chaimongkol, Nakhon Sawan Province, Central Thailand: A Study of Site Stratigraphy, Chronology and Its Implications for the Prehistory of Central Thailand. M.A. thesis, Department of Anthropology, University of Pennsylvania.

O'Reilly, Dougald J. W.
2003 Further Evidence of Heterarchy in Bronze Age Thailand. Current Anthropology 44:300–306.
2007a The Excavation of Non Muang Kao. *In* The Origins of the Civilization of Angkor, vol. 2: The Excavation of Noen U-Loke and Non Muang Kao. C. F. W. Higham, A. Kijngam, and S. Talbot, eds. Pp. 545–559. Bangkok: The Thai Fine Arts Department.
2007b Non Muang Kao in a Regional Perspective. *In* The Origins of the Civilization of Angkor, vol. 2: The Excavation of Noen U-Loke and Non Muang Kao. C. F. W. Higham, A. Kijngam, and S. Talbot, eds. Pp. 575–587. Bangkok: The Thai Fine Arts Department.

2008 Multivallate Sites and Socio-economic Change: Thailand and Britain in Their Iron Age. Antiquity 82:377–389.

O'Reilly, Dougald J. W., and Pheng Sytha
2001 Recent Excavations in Northwest Cambodia. Antiquity 75:265–266.

Parker Pearson, Mike
1999 The Archaeology of Death and Burial. College Station: Texas A&M University Press.

Pautreau, Jean-Pierre, Patricia Mornais, and Tasana Doy-Asa
2001 Ban Wang Hai: Un cimetière de l'âge du fer en Thaïlande du Nord. Chiang Mai: Silkworm Books.

Pigott, Vincent C., Andrew D. Weiss, and Surapol Natapintu
1997 The Archaeology of Copper Production: Excavations in the Khao Wong Prachan Valley, Central Thailand. *In* South-east Asian Archaeology 1992. R. Ciarla and F. Rispoli, eds. Pp. 119–157. Proceedings of the 4th International Conference of the European Association of South-east Asian Archaeologists, Rome, 28 September–4 October 1992. Serie Orientale Roma., 77. Rome: Istituto Italiano per L'Africa e L'Oriente.

Rakita, Gordon F. M., and Jane E. Buikstra
2005 Introduction. *In* Interacting with the Dead: Perspectives on Mortuary Archaeology for the New Millennium. G. F. M. Rakita, J. E. Buikstra, L. A. Beck, and S. R. Williams, eds. Pp. 1–11. Gainesville: University Press of Florida.

Rakita, Gordon F. M., Jane E. Buikstra, Lane A. Beck, and Sloan R. Williams, eds.
2005 Interacting with the Dead: Perspectives on Mortuary Archaeology for the New Millennium. Gainesville: University Press of Florida.

Rispoli, Fiorella
1997 Late Third-Mid Second Millennium B.C. Pottery Traditions in Central Thailand: Some Preliminary Observations in a Wider Perspective. *In* South-east Asian Archaeology 1992. R. Ciarla and F. Rispoli, eds. Pp. 59–97. Proceedings of the 4th International Conference of the European Association of South-east Asian Archaeologists, Rome, 28 September–4 October 1992. Serie Orientale Roma., 77. Rome: Istituto Italiano per L'Africa e L'Oriente.
2008 The Incised and Impressed Pottery Style of Mainland Southeast Asia: Following the Paths of Neolithization. East and West 57(1–4):235–304.

Rousseau, Jérôme
2006 Rethinking Social Evolution: The Perspective from Middle-Range Societies. Montreal: McGill-Queen's University Press.

Saitta, Dean J.
1999 Prestige, Agency, and Change in Middle-Range Societies. *In* Material Symbols: Culture and Economy in Prehistory. J. E. Robb, ed. Pp. 136–149. Occasional Papers, 26. Carbondale: Center for Archaeological Investigations, Southern Illinois University.

Salganik, Matthew J., Peter Sheridan Dodds, and Duncan J. Watts
2006 Experimental Study of Inequality and Unpredictability in an Artificial Cultural Market. Science 311:854–856.

Scarry, John F.
1999 Elite Identities in Apalachee Province: The Construction of Identity and Cultural Change in a Mississippian Polity. *In* Material Symbols: Culture and Economy in Prehistory. J. E. Robb, ed. Pp. 342–361. Occasional Papers, 26. Carbondale: Center for Archaeological Investigations, Southern Illinois University.

Silverman, Helaine
2002 Introduction: The Space and Place of Death. *In* The Space and Place of Death. H. Silverman and D. B. Small, eds. Pp. 1–11. Archeological Papers of the American Anthropological Association, 11. Arlington, VA: American Anthropological Association.

Silverman, Helaine, and David B. Small, eds.
2002 The Space and Place of Death. Archeological Papers of the American Anthropological Association, 11. Arlington, VA: American Anthropological Association.

Sørensen, Per
1967 Archaeological Excavations in Thailand: The Thai-Danish Prehistoric Expedition 1960–62, vol. 2, part 1. Copenhagen: Munksgaard.

Spielmann, Katherine A.
1998 Ritual Craft Specialists in Middle Range Societies. *In* Craft and Social Identity. C. L. Costin and R. P. Wright, eds. Pp. 153–159. Archeological Papers of the American Anthropological Association, 8. Arlington, VA: American Anthropological Association.

Stark, Miriam
2006 Early Mainland Southeast Asian Landscapes in the First Millennium A.D. Annual Review of Anthropology 35:407–432.

Talbot, Sarah
2007 The Analysis of the Mortuary Record. *In* The Origins of the Civilization of Angkor, vol. 2: The Excavation of Noen U-Loke and Non Muang Kao. C. F. W. Higham, A. Kijngam, and S. Talbot, eds. Pp. 305–351. Bangkok: The Thai Fine Arts Department.

Theunissen, Robert George
2003 Agate and Carnelian Beads and the Dynamics of Social Complexity in Iron Age Mainland Southeast Asia. Ph.D. dissertation, Department of Arts and Sciences, University of New England.

Upham, Steadman
1987 A Theoretical Consideration of Middle Range Societies. *In* Chiefdoms in the Americas. R. D. Drennan and C. A. Uribe, eds. Pp. 345–367. New York: University Press of America.

Upham, Steadman, ed.
1990 The Evolution of Political Systems: Sociopolitics in Small-Scale Sedentary Societies. School of American Research Advanced Seminar Series. New York: University of Cambridge Press.

Vincent, Brian A.
1984 The Petrographic Analysis of Prehistoric Pottery from Ban Na Di and Related Sites. *In* Prehistoric Investigations in Northeast Thailand. C. F. W. Higham and A. Kijngam, eds. Pp. 644–697. BAR International Series, 231(iii). Oxford: Archaeopress.

Voelker, J.
2007 The Ceramics. *In* The Origins of the Civilization of Angkor, vol. 2: The Excavation of Noen U-Loke and Non Muang Kao. C. F. W. Higham, A. Kijngam, and S. Talbot, eds. Pp. 487–493. Bangkok: The Thai Fine Arts Department.

Waterson, Roxana
2000 House, Place, and Memory in Tana Toraja (Indonesia). *In* Beyond Kinship: Social and Material Reproduction in House Societies. R. A. Joyce and S. D. Gillespie, eds. Pp. 177–188. Philadelphia: University of Pennsylvania Press.

Welch, David J., and Judith R. McNeill
1991 Settlement, Agriculture and Population Changes in the Phimai Region, Thailand. Bulletin of the Indo-Pacific Prehistory Association 11:210–228.

White, Joyce C.
1986 A Revision of the Chronology of Ban Chiang and Its Implications for the Prehistory of Northeast Thailand. Ph.D. dissertation, Department of Anthropology, University of Pennsylvania. Ann Arbor, MI: University Microfilms International.
1995a Incorporating Heterarchy into Theory on Socio-Political Development: The Case from Southeast Asia. *In* Heterarchy and the Analysis of Complex Societies. R. M. Ehrenreich, C. L. Crumley, and J. E. Levy, eds. Pp. 101–123. Archeological Papers of the American Anthropological Association, 6. Arlington, VA: American Anthropological Association.
1995b Modeling the Development of Early Rice Agriculture: Ethnoecological Perspectives from Northeast Thailand. Asian Perspectives 34(1):37–68.
1997 A Brief Note on New Dates for the Ban Chiang Cultural Tradition. Bulletin of the Indo-Pacific Prehistory Association 16:103–106.
2002 Series Editor's Preface. *In* Ban Chiang: A Prehistoric Village Site in Northeast Thailand I: The Human Skeletal Remains. By M. Pietrusewsky and M. Toomay Douglas. Pp. xvi–xvii. Philadelphia: University of Pennsylvania Museum of Archaeology and Anthropology
2008 Dating Early Bronze at Ban Chiang, Thailand. *In* From *Homo erectus* to the Living Traditions. J.-P. Pautreau, A.-S. Coupey, V. Zeitoun, and E. Rambault, eds. Pp. 91–104. Chiang Mai: European Association of Southeast Asian Archaeologists.

White, Joyce C., and Elizabeth Hamilton
2009 The Transmission of Bronze Metallurgy to Thailand: New Perspectives. Journal of World Prehistory 22:357–397.

White, Joyce C., Daniel Penny, Lisa Kealhofer, and Bernard Maloney
2004 Vegetation Changes from the Late Pleistocene through the Holocene from Three Areas of Archaeological Significance in Thailand. Quaternary International 113(1):111–132.

White, Joyce C., and Vincent C. Pigott
1996 From Community Craft to Regional Specialization: Intensification of Copper Production in Pre-state Thailand. *In* Craft Specialization and Social Evolution: In Memory of V. Gordon Childe. B. Wailes, ed. Pp. 151–175. University Museum Monograph 93. Philadelphia: University of Pennsylvania Museum of Archaeology and Anthropology.

White, Joyce C., William W. Vernon, Stuart J. Fleming, William D. Glanzman, Ron Hancock, and Andrew Pelcin
1991 Preliminary Cultural Implications from Initial Studies of the Ceramic Technology at Ban Chiang. Bulletin of the Indo-Pacific Prehistory Association 11:188–203.

Wobst, H. Martin
1977 Stylistic Behavior and Information Exchange. *In* Papers for the Director: Research Essays in Honor of James B. Griffin. C. E. Cleland, ed. Pp. 317–342. Anthropological Papers, 67. Ann Arbor: Museum of Anthropology, University of Michigan.
1999 Style in Archaeology or Archaeologists in Style. *In* Material Meanings: Critical Approaches to the Interpretation of Material Culture. E. Chilton, ed. Pp. 118–132. Salt Lake City: University of Utah Press.

Yin Shaoting
2001 People and Forests: Yunnan Swidden Agriculture in Human-Ecological Perspective. Kunming, China: Yunnan Education Publishing House.

6

Residential Burial, Gender Roles, and Political Development in Late Prehistoric and Early Cherokee Cultures of the Southern Appalachians

Lynne P. Sullivan
University of Tennessee
and
Christopher B. Rodning
Tulane University

ABSTRACT

Native people in the southern Appalachians began placing graves in and around residences in the 13th century C.E. Burials previously were placed in specialized burial mounds that likely belonged to individual kin groups. For several centuries, the practice of residential burial was contemporaneous with burial in or near public buildings that sometimes were built on platform mounds. During this time, residential versus 'public' burial became related to spatial symbolism of gender and leadership roles. These changes suggest a developmental trajectory that distinguishes southern Appalachian societies from their contemporaries elsewhere in the southeastern U.S. [Mississippian, Cherokee, gender, North Carolina, Tennessee]

Archaeologists have long recognized that the locations where people choose to place graves often have social meaning and may relate to cultural constructs of identity, including kinship and status (Goldstein 1980; Parker Pearson 2000). The focus of this volume is on the placement of graves within domestic space, the various meanings that such grave placement may have for specific social groups or cultures, and the broader anthropological implications for the practice of such grave placement. We focus here on one geographic area, the southern Appalachian region of southeastern North America, where American Indian peoples practiced residential burial for five centuries. Of particular interest is that residences were not the only burial locations used during this time span in this region. Graves also were placed in nonresidential public places and buildings. Even more interesting are the demographic patterns of the individuals interred in the graves associated with these two locations.

We explore how this dual tradition of residential and public-area burial in the southern Appalachians relates to social processes in the region, including spatial symbolism in gender and leadership roles and the genesis of long-term corporate residences. We have argued elsewhere that gender-related differences observed in these mortuary programs correlate with gender-specific differences in political leadership and with how men and women acquired prestige (Rodning 2001a, 2001b, 2002, 2009a, 2009b; Sullivan 2001, 2006; Sullivan and Rodning 2001). We specifically examine four archaeological sites: Toqua, Dallas, and Chota-Tanasee in eastern Tennessee, and the Coweeta Creek site in southwestern North Carolina (Figure 6.1). Dallas and Toqua represent two late prehistoric (C.E. 1200–1500)

ARCHEOLOGICAL PAPERS OF THE AMERICAN ANTHROPOLOGICAL ASSOCIATION, Vol. 20, Issue 1, pp. 79–97, ISSN 1551-823X, online ISSN 1551-8248. DOI: 10.1111/j.1551-8248.2011.01029.x.

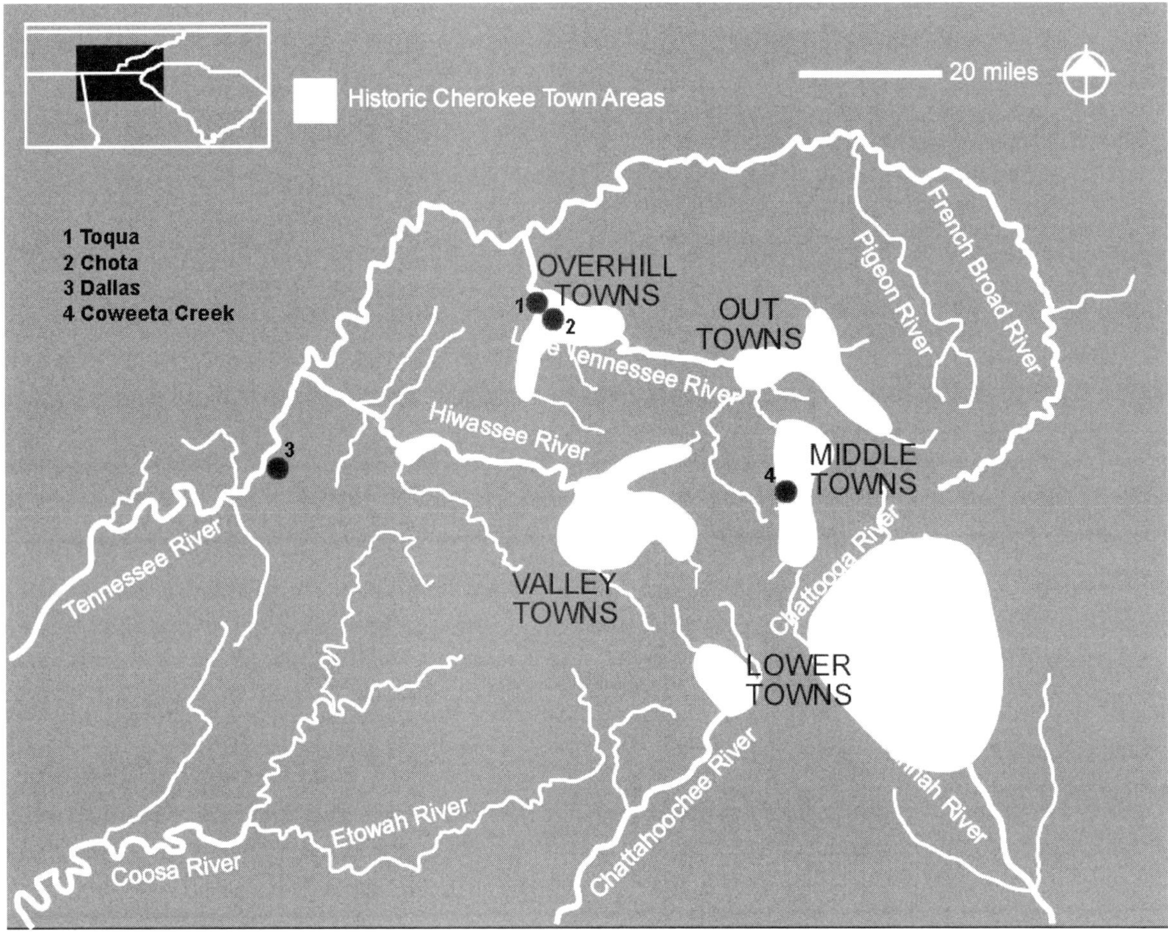

Figure 6.1. Locations of discussed sites in southern Appalachia.

towns that cannot be directly associated with a specific ethnic group from the historic period. Coweeta Creek and Chota are Cherokee towns dating to the 1600s and 1700s, respectively. Chota superceded the adjacent town of Tanasee.

Our study contributes to broader interests in the archaeology of burials within dwellings and in the vicinity of domestic architecture, and it also contributes to broader interests in relationships between gender and architecture in settlements and societies (Spain 1992). For example, as demonstrated by Vanessa Lea (1995, 2001), Kayapo villages in the Brazilian Amazon include male-dominated social and spatial domains associated with centrally located village plazas and men's houses, as well as domestic structures and related social domains dominated by women and situated along the outer edges of villages. At first glance, houses and households—the domain of women—seem peripheral or marginal, both spatially and in terms of practices of social production, inheritance, and community structure. On the contrary, these gendered architectural spaces manifest different social domains, both necessary to the vitality of Kayapo communities—including men's space at the village centers and women's space that encloses villages, differentiating the local village from the surrounding cultural landscape. Similarly, archaeologists have noted close relationships between women and longhouses in Iroquoian villages of northeastern North America (Kapches 1995; Prezzano 1997), and the presence of men's houses situated both at the centers and, in some cases, at the edges of tribal villages of Papua New Guinea (Roscoe 2008).

The Archaeological and Historical Background

During the 13th century C.E., prehistoric American Indians in the southern Appalachians began burying their dead in and around residences. Residential burial continued into the 18th century and was practiced in the region by the historically known Cherokee. Although this 500-year-long tradition of residential burial documents one aspect of cultural continuity among peoples in this region, other aspects (e.g., pottery and other technological traditions) do not show such continuity. There are major gaps in knowledge of the disruption and devastation caused by contacts with Europeans to native social and political groupings, beginning with the Spanish in the mid-sixteenth century. As a result, a lineal connection between the late prehistoric towns and the Cherokee towns examined for this study cannot be made at this time. We also stress that while there may be commonalities among societies that practice residential burial, significant differences in the details of implementation of this tradition may shed light upon differences in cultural practices that relate to distinct cultural identities within the greater southern Appalachians, or to abrupt culture change following European contact. We will return to this idea in the last part of this chapter.

The practice of residential burial in the southern Appalachians was preceded by five centuries during which native groups in the ridges and valleys of eastern Tennessee, from present-day Knoxville southward, created specialized burial mounds (Schroedl et al. 1990). Less is known about the earlier mortuary practices of the native peoples in the Blue Ridge Mountains of western North Carolina (but see Dickens 1976, 1978, 1979; Keel 1976; Rodning and Moore 2010). By the 13th century, they too were placing graves in and around houses in a similar fashion.

In addition to residential burials, other graves were placed in or near large public buildings, some of which were built on large, earthen platform mounds. The majority of graves found in the platform mounds and near the public buildings typically contain the remains of males while those in and near residences more typically are the graves of females. Traditional interpretations of these patterns correlate nonresidential burials associated with mounds and public structures with prestige and power, and they correlate residential burials with domesticity. These models interpret gendered patterns of male burials associated with public and ceremonial spaces, and female burials associated with household dwellings, as evidence for male-dominated social and political hierarchies (Hally 2004, 2008; Hatch 1974, 1976, 1987; Peebles 1974; Peebles and Kus 1977). Our interpretation of these gender distinctions in grave placement is that they reflect alternative pathways to power and status for men and women in different domains of social and political life. This perspective is guided largely by ethnographic and ethnohistoric evidence about gender and leadership within 18th-century Cherokee societies (Corkran 1969; Gearing 1962; Perdue 1998; Persico 1979; Sattler 1995).

The Development of Residential Burial in the Southern Appalachians

As we already noted, the development of residential burial in southern Appalachia followed a long period of burial mound use. By C.E. 600, people in eastern Tennessee were building conical-shaped mounds, but evidence of associated settlements is sketchy for the first three centuries of burial mound use (Schroedl et al. 1990; Sullivan and Koerner 2010). Burial mounds likely were built and maintained by particular lineage groups and may have served as territorial markers (Cole 1975; Schroedl et al. 1990:183).

Platform mounds with structures on them were built near burial mounds possibly as early as C.E. 900 (Schroedl et al. 1990; but see Sullivan et al. 2009) and by C.E. 1200, some burials also were placed in these substructural mounds (Sullivan 2007). Towns, with log stockades surrounding public structures, plazas, and domestic dwellings, developed in conjunction with most platform mounds (Figure 6.2a). Within a century thereafter, the burial mounds fell into disuse and graves were placed in and around residential structures as well as in the platform mounds. The same kind of settlements and architectural styles developed in western North Carolina after C.E. 1300, but the changes in preceding centuries are less clear (Dickens 1976, 1978, 1979; Keel 1976; Ward and Davis 1999).

These changes took place during a period of environmental uncertainties that may have set the stage for migrations into the area from drought-stricken regions farther west in Tennessee (Delcourt and Delcourt 2004; Meeks 2006a, 2006b, 2009). Such migrations would have increased populations and could have led to significant social disruption. Intensification of maize agriculture was also part of this scenario. Claiming space and forming attachments between towns and houses and specific places within the landscape may have been critical to community livelihood during this period and in these conditions.

Of particular significance is the observation that these long-term changes in burial practices, from burial mounds to burials in residential and public space, likely were accompanied by the development of corporate social groups who shared residences and joint property (Beck 2007; Carsten and Hugh-Jones 1995; Joyce and Gillespie 2000). Evidence for this type of organization includes the repetitive construction, repair, and replacement of residences in the same places within towns and villages over many years. Furthermore, archaeological town sites dating as early as the late 17th century can be definitely associated with historically known Cherokee groups in the region. Although use of platform mounds had ceased, the typical early Cherokee town

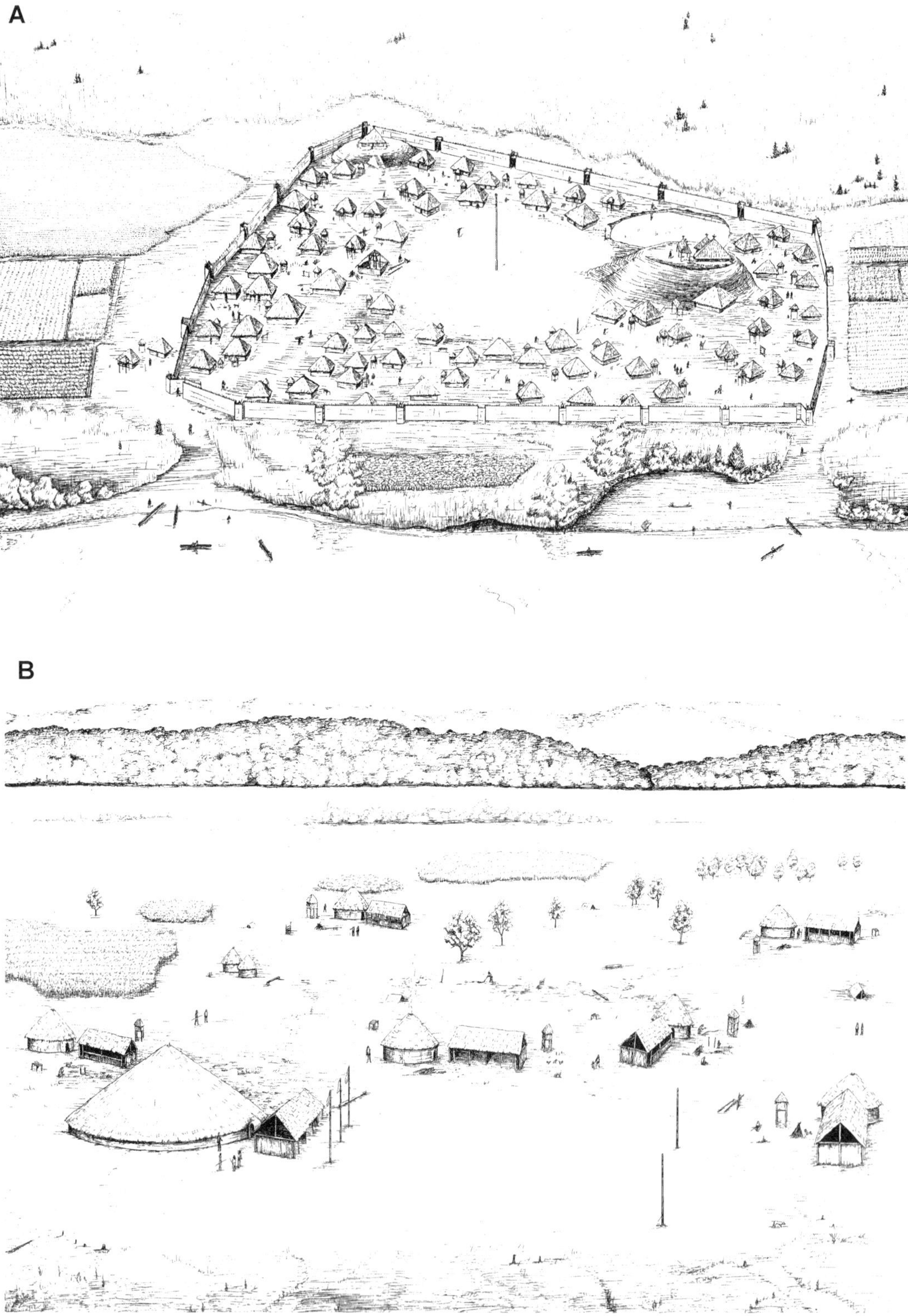

Figure 6.2. Artist's reconstructions of American Indian towns in southern Appalachia. a, Late prehistoric town based on the Toqua site. The smaller buildings near the larger houses were interpreted as corn cribs for this drawing (drawing by Tom Whyte from Polhemus 1987:fig. 13.4). b, Eighteenth-century Cherokee town based on the Chota-Tanasee site (drawing by Tom Whyte from Schroedl 1986:fig. 5.14). (Images courtesy of the Frank H. McClung Museum, The University of Tennessee)

retained the configuration of a central public structure (townhouse) and plaza surrounded by residences (Figure 6.2b). Early Cherokee burial patterns also were similar to those of the late prehistoric groups, with most burials being associated with dwelling houses and some with the townhouse. We can thus trace the development and continued use of residential burial practices in southern Appalachia over some five centuries. In this region, residential burial groupings were created in conjunction with generations of residential groups whose dwellings often occupied the same locations for many decades.

The Contexts of Residential and Nonresidential Burials

The physical contexts of residential and nonresidential burials are quite different. We first describe the physical characteristics of the dwellings and residential burials at late prehistoric through early Cherokee settlements, and then contrast these with the burials and buildings associated with the communal public areas of these settlements. Many late prehistoric and protohistoric domestic and public structures in the southern Appalachian region are analogous to 18th-century Cherokee dwellings and the public structures known as townhouses (Anderson 1994; Faulkner 1978; Polhemus 1990; Rodning 2002, 2007, 2009a; Schroedl 1998, 2000, 2001; Sullivan 1987, 1995). As suggested above, we cannot correlate directly the ethnicity of the prehistoric and protohistoric groups with the Cherokee because of discontinuities in the archaeological and historical records. We do think that at least some or some combination of these groups were ancestral to the Cherokee. Analogies with Cherokee culture therefore are appropriate when warranted by the archaeological evidence and we use these analogies to inform our interpretations of the residential burial patterns at relevant late prehistoric and protohistoric sites.

Typical native residential structures in southern Appalachia included primary dwellings—post-in-ground, woven-walled structures with central clay hearths—and more lightly built structures that likely served as summer shades, kitchens, and storage areas (Dickens 1978; Hally 1994, 2008; Hally and Kelly 1998; Polhemus 1990; Schroedl 1998, 2000, 2001; Sullivan 1995). These two structures often are referenced as "winter" and "summer" houses, following observations of early European explorers (Figure 6.3). Eighteenth-century Cherokee residential structures were similar to the earlier examples, except that the "winter" structures were circular rather than square in plan (Figure 6.4a, b; Schroedl 1986; Sullivan 1995). Anywhere from one to several dozen sets of these residential houses were present within 18th-century Cherokee settlements (Hill 1997; Perdue 1998; Schroedl 2000).

Graves were placed in association with both types of structures. Some graves were placed in the floors of winter houses, while others were in or immediately adjacent to the summer structures (Figure 6.3c, d and Figure 6.4b). In the last case, the graves sometimes were placed in small groupings, forming coherent household cemeteries. Variations exist in the age patterning of individuals interred in and near the two kinds of buildings among sites, and some other aspects of mortuary practices differ across the region. For example, in some areas only infants and young children were interred in the winter house floors while older children and adults were buried in association with summer structures, and in some areas individuals were interred in extended positions while flexed positions were more common elsewhere (Sullivan 1987, 1995). However, the basic pattern of some graves being placed in the floors of the primary residential structures and others being placed in and adjacent to the "summer" houses is consistent from the 14th through 18th centuries throughout the region.

The construction of public, community buildings mimicked that of residences, but on a larger scale (Figures 6.3b, 6.5, and 6.6; Dickens 1978; Hally 1994, 2008; Hally and Kelly 1998; Polhemus 1990; Schroedl 1998, 2000, 2001; Sullivan 1987, 1995). Outdoor plazas usually were maintained in areas beside public buildings (Figure 6.2). In some areas of the Upper Tennessee Valley, prehistoric public buildings were constructed on platform mounds (see Figure 6.2a). In other cases a low mound was created by repeated construction of public buildings in the same location. Graves were placed in the floors of public structures and just outside of them, and sometimes special cemeteries were created adjacent to the plazas. As in some parts of eastern Tennessee, in western North Carolina rebuilding of public buildings in the same locations sometimes created a low mound (Rodning 2002, 2007, 2009a, 2010).

Only those 18th-century Cherokee settlements with large public structures, known as townhouses, were known and named as towns (Schroedl 1998, 2000; Smith 1979). The town to which one belonged was an important aspect of Cherokee identity, and townhouses were the physical embodiment of a Cherokee community. Townhouses formed the hubs of public life (Schroedl 2001) and materialized the identity of a local group of households as a town. The fires kept in townhouse hearths manifested the social and spiritual vitality of towns themselves (Corkran 1969:36; Mooney 1900:396). The townhouse "housed" the community as a

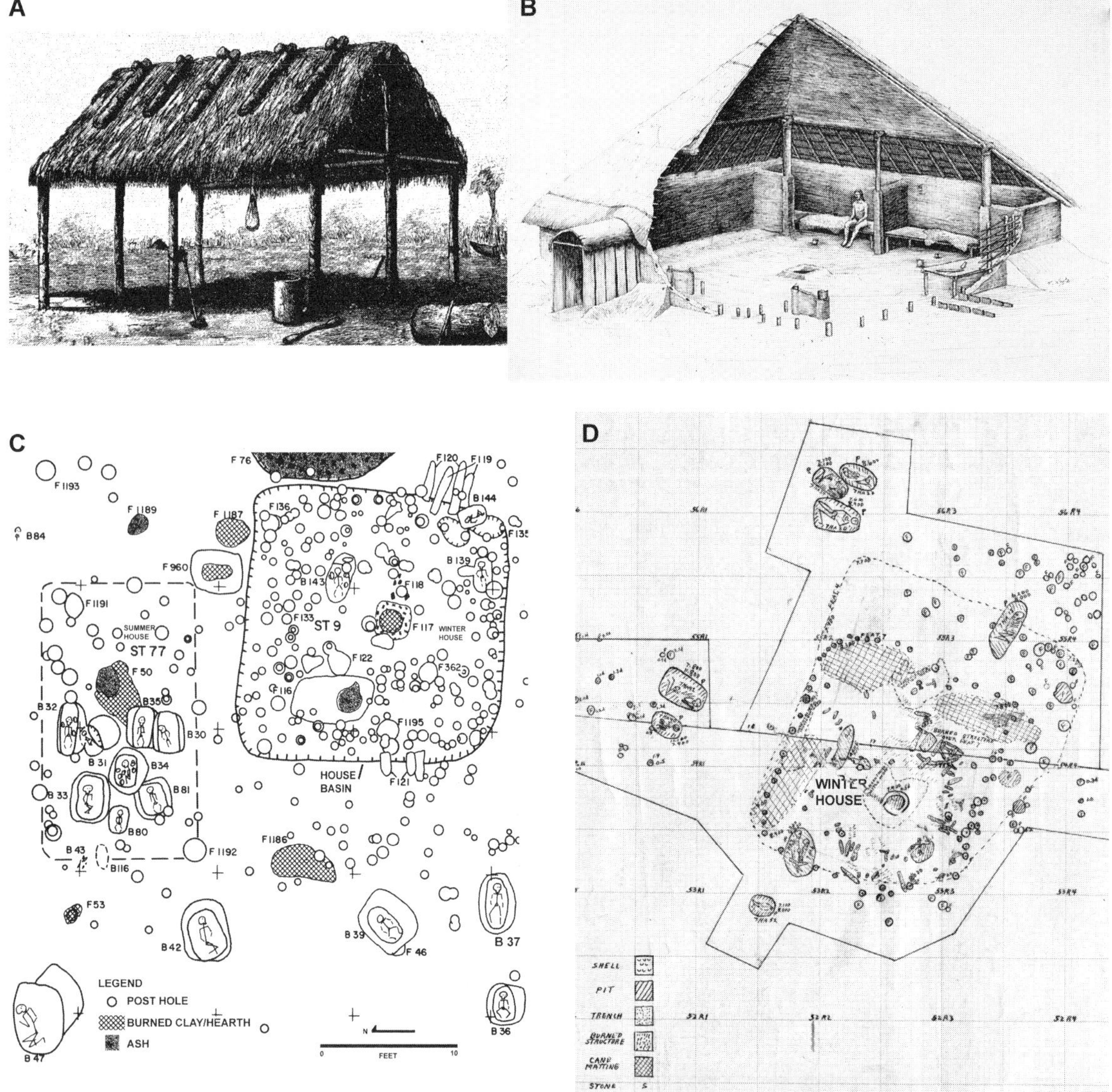

Figure 6.3. Late prehistoric summer and winter houses in southern Appalachia. a, Interpretive illustration of a late prehistoric summer house. This interpretation is derived from a drawing of a Seminole chickee (Swanton 1946:pl. 60), but the southern Appalachian version likely was less formally constructed and was repaired or replaced often, based on the posthole patterns. b, Artist's reconstruction of structure 14 at the Toqua site (drawing by Tom Whyte from Polhemus 1987:fig. 5.32). This particular structure actually was a public building on the mound, but the architecture is identical to that of winter residential houses with the exception that the residential houses were smaller. c, Structure patterns at Toqua showing square winter house and rectangular summer house patterns, and associated burials. Note multiple replacements of exterior wall posts, internal posts denoting partitions or benches, and replacements and relocation of wall-trench entranceways (F119, F120, F121) for the winter house (from Polhemus 1987:fig. 3.14). d, New Deal–era field plat of a winter house pattern at the Dallas site. Summer houses were not recognized by the fieldworkers of this era, but note the burials in the house and the clusters nearby. Indicated grid points on this plat are ten feet apart. (Images b, c, and d are courtesy of the Frank H. McClung Museum, The University of Tennessee)

whole while a domestic dwelling "housed" one of the many households present in a given town. Cherokee townhouses were settings for town council meetings, events related to trade and diplomacy, dances and other rituals, and more casual gatherings of male elders (Corkran 1969; Hill 1997; Williams 1927, 1928, 1930).

Eighteenth-century Cherokee townhouses, like the dwellings, were round as opposed to the earlier, square

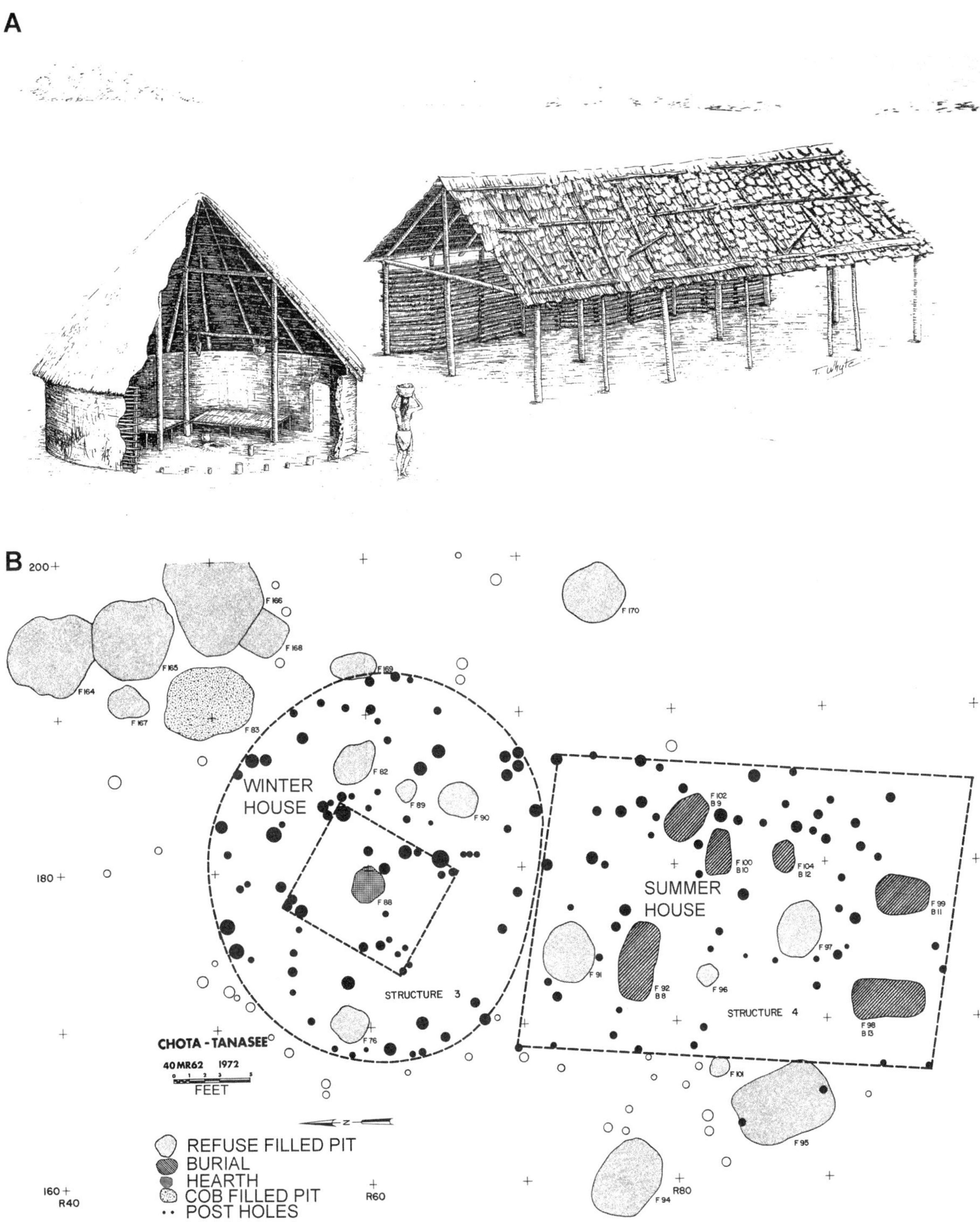

Figure 6.4. *Examples of 18th-century summer and winter houses at the Chota-Tanasee site. a, Reconstructions of Cherokee summer and winter houses (drawing by Tom Whyte from Schroedl 1986:fig. 4.45). b, Structure patterns at Chota-Tanasee showing circular winter house and rectangular summer house patterns, and associated burials. The six burials in the floor of the summer house include one adult female, an adolescent male, one unsexed infant, and three unsexed children (Schroedl 1986:263, fig. 4.39). (All images courtesy of the Frank H. McClung Museum, The University of Tennessee)*

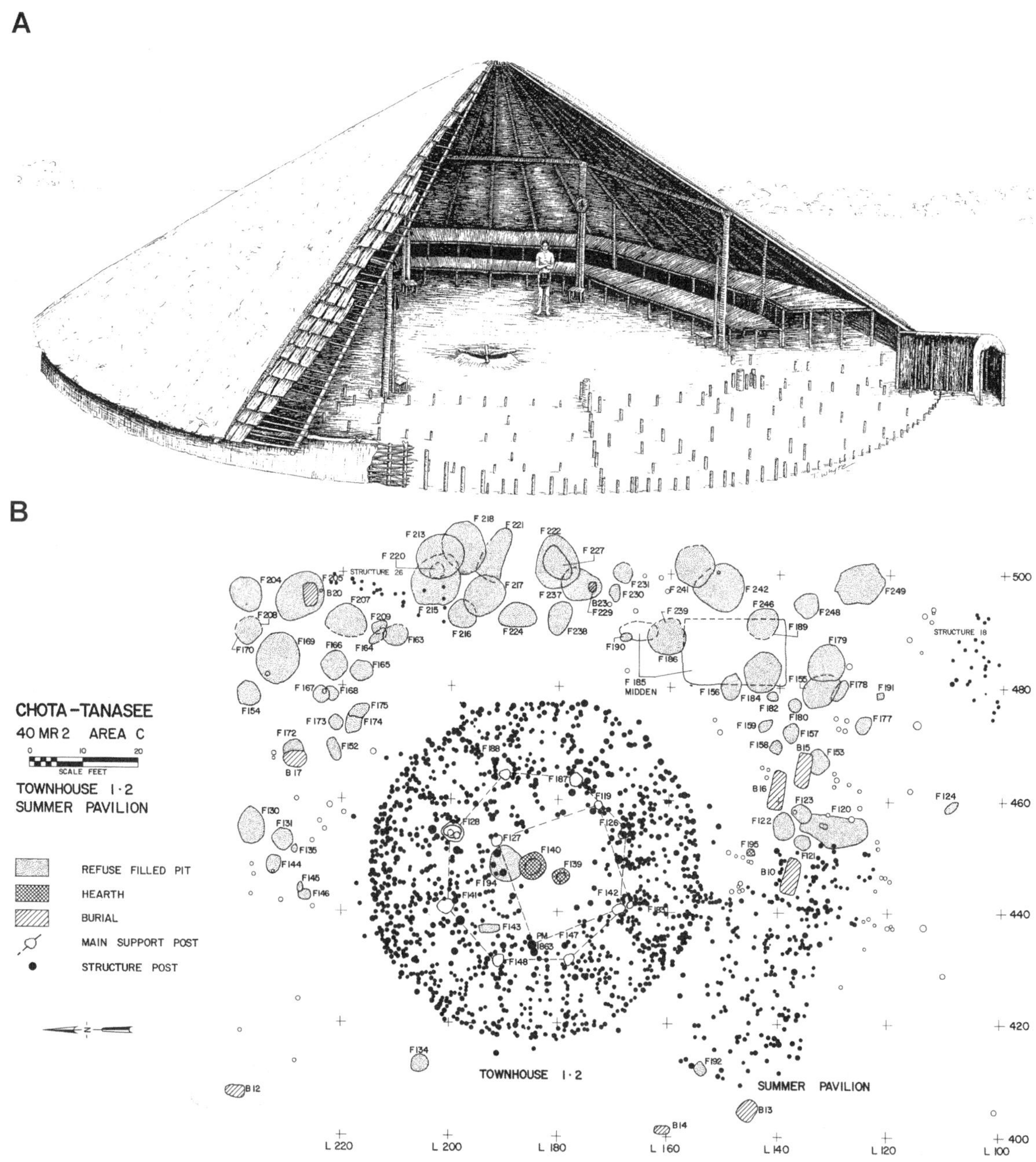

Figure 6.5. The 18th-century Cherokee townhouse at Chota-Tanasee site a, Artist's reconstruction of the townhouse at Chota (drawing by Tom Whyte from Schroedl 1986:fig. 4.43). b, Pattern of a townhouse at Chota, which had been rebuilt. Note the rectangular summer ramada or pavilion to the south of the townhouse entrance. The three burials within this structure all are those of adult males (B10, B15, and B16); B10 was that of Chief Oconostota. Of the two burials immediately to the west, one also is an adult male (B13) and the other was of indeterminate sex and age (B14) (Schroedl 1986:137, 234, fig. 4.2). (Images courtesy of the Frank H. McClung Museum, The University of Tennessee)

buildings (Figure 6.5). Ramadas, pavilions, or sunshades often were situated beside Cherokee townhouses, forming covered areas outside entryways. Some graves were placed just outside townhouse doors, or under or near the ramadas (Figures 6.5b, 6.6, and 6.7).

Gender Traditions and Burial Patterns in Southern Appalachia

Spatial patterns in burial demographics at both Cherokee and prehistoric towns in this region demonstrate

Figure 6.6. Example of a public building or townhouse next to the plaza at the Coweeta Creek site (after Rodning 2009a:642). Note the rectangular ramada, or "summer townhouse," to the southeast of the main building's wall-trench entranceway. This map shows the first of six stages of the Coweeta Creek townhouse, and the density of postholes reflects, in part, the posts and postholes associated with later stages of this structure. The architecture of this building likely was similar to Toqua structure 14 shown in Figure 6.3b.

different gender associations for burials in residential and in public areas. More males typically are buried in association with platform mounds and public buildings than are females, while more female burials typically are associated with residences (Hatch 1974; Peebles 1974; Peebles and Kus 1977; Schroedl 1986; Sullivan 1987). As with the Kayapo settlements discussed above, this patterning initially might seem to suggest dominant and "public" leadership roles for males

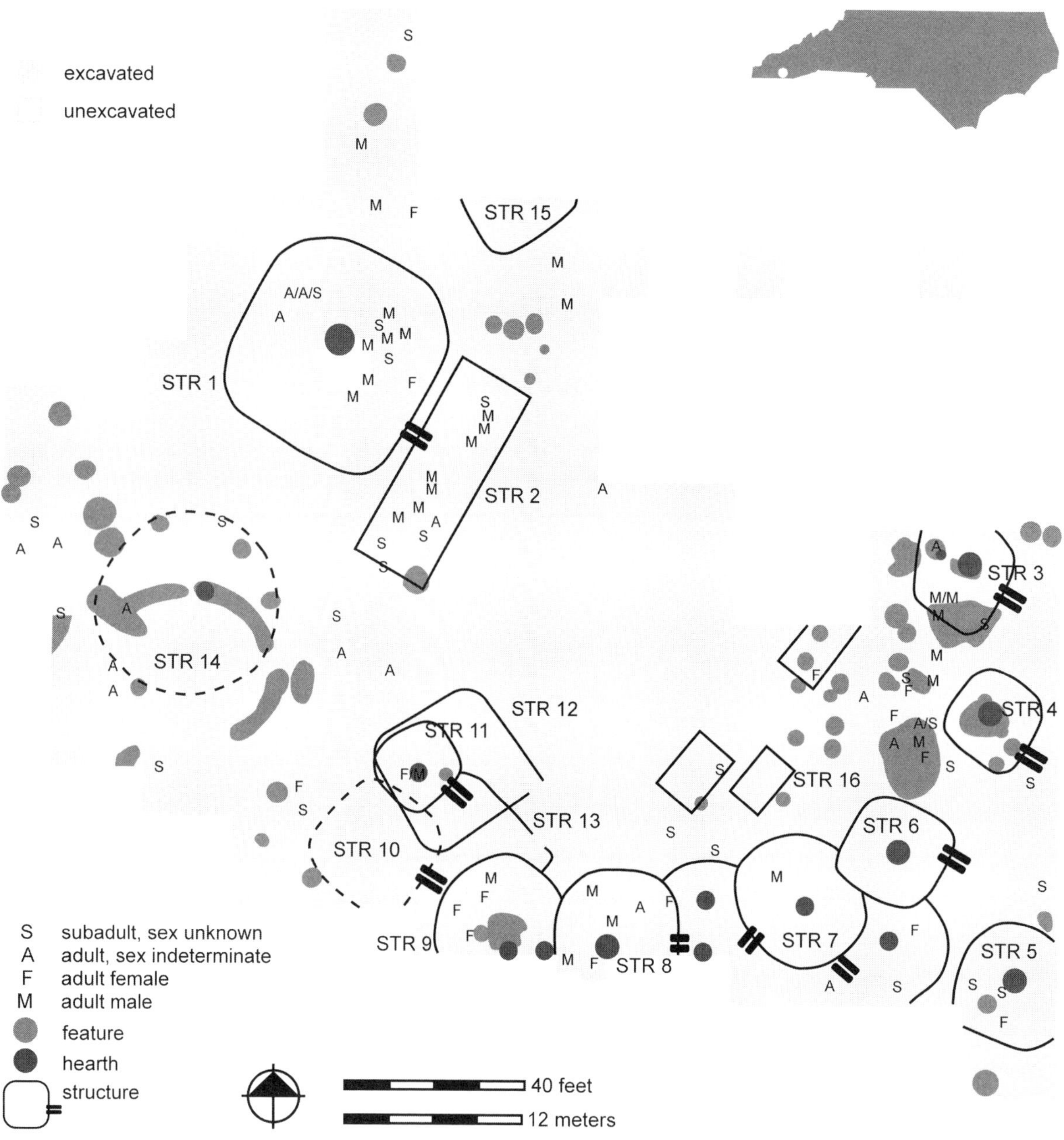

Figure 6.7. Coweeta Creek site plan showing locations of adult male and female burials.

and "domestic" roles for females. We suggest that correlations of public buildings with male dominance and leadership, and of female political "marginality," are too simplistic, and that distinctions between "public" and "domestic" social and spatial domains reflect gender duality rather than gender hierarchy (Rodning 2001a; Sullivan 2001, 2006; Sullivan and Rodning 2001). Interpretations of hierarchy likely misrepresent the power and influence of women in these communities and undermine the significance of residential burial. The 18th-century Cherokee traditions that can be correlated with these burial patterns at Chota-Tanasee provide considerable insight to the observed patterns at Coweeta Creek, the 17th-century Cherokee site, as well as at the prehistoric 14th-century Dallas site and the Toqua site with its late prehistoric occupation spanning the 13th to 16th centuries.

According to ethnohistoric sources, Cherokee dwellings were the realms of women (e.g., Corkran 1969:30–32; Perdue 1998). Men did not own houses; rather, inheritance of houses and clan membership were determined matrilineally, through female lines. Married men lived with their wives' residential groups. In the event of divorce, the husband left the wife's house and returned to the house of his mother or sister. Men with a permanent connection to a household were the brothers and sons of the core female members (Perdue 1998:45). Senior Cherokee women served as clan officers and had considerable authority in these kin groups (Perdue 1998:46; Sattler 1995:222). These women were in charge of families and households, they managed agricultural production, and they derived considerable political power and influence from these realms.

Cherokee women also affected larger community decisions. A number of Cherokee female elders identified as "Beloved Women" or "War Women" are known from early accounts to have been influential leaders (Hatley 1993; Perdue 1998). Although men historically controlled the war organization, Cherokee women could reject men's decisions to go to war (Sattler 1995:222). Hatley (1993:52–63) describes how the clash between the gender traditions of Cherokee and 18th-century European colonial societies led to denigration and ridicule of Cherokee people by the Europeans—even to the point of insulting Cherokee men's masculinity. One English trader commented: "the women rules [*sic*] the roost and wears the breeches and sometimes will beat their husbands within an inch of their lives" (Corkran 1969:30–32). Based on his experiences as an Indian trader in the Southeast in the late 18th century, and referring specifically to relative female freedom in marriage and sexual relations, James Adair referred to a tradition of "petticoat government" in Cherokee towns (Hatley 1993:54; Williams 1930).

In contrast to women's empowerment via management of kindred and residential groups and of agriculture, some Cherokee men were leaders who served as representatives of the entire community and were in charge of intercommunity relationships such as trading and alliances. Each Cherokee town had a history and a set of leaders that differentiated it from others (Gearing 1958, 1962; Gilbert 1943; Goodwin 1977; Persico 1979). Cherokee men also derived prestige via the war organization, an almost exclusively male domain (Gearing 1962). The acquisition of war names and titles was one of the main preoccupations of Southeastern Indian men (Corkran 1969:44–46; Hudson 1976:325; Swanton 1946:696) and some older men successfully negotiated the transition from warriors to community leaders, advisors, and councilors (Gearing 1962). As noted above, the townhouses were where many male-oriented activities occurred, such as events related to trade and diplomacy and more casual gatherings of male elders (Corkran 1969; Hill 1997; Williams 1927, 1928, 1930). As male gathering places, townhouses also were places where men could go to be away from the world of women. Theda Perdue has noted, "Single men often preferred to sleep in the council houses [*sic:* townhouses] rather than in the house of their mothers and sisters" (Perdue 1998:46).

Burial practices at 17th- and 18th-century Cherokee towns follow these gendered statuses and roles. The association between males and public structures is evident in the frequency of adult male burials placed inside and beside the 17th-century townhouse at the Coweeta Creek site in North Carolina (Table 6.1; Figure 6.7; Rodning 1999, 2001a, 2001b) and at the 18th-century Overhill Cherokee settlement at Chota, in Tennessee (Table 6.1; Figure 6.5; Schroedl 1986). All excavated human skeletal remains at these sites were aged and sexed by physical anthropologists at the University of Tennessee and the University of North Carolina during laboratory analyses as reported in Schroedl 1986 and Davis et al. 1996. At Chota, one grave associated with the townhouse is known to be the resting place of Chief Oconostota (Figure 6.5b; King and Olinger 1972).[1] Gerald Schroedl suggests that burial of male elders, known as "Beloved Men," in or associated with the townhouse "would have been appropriate to their standing in Cherokee society" (Schroedl 1986:204).

Most burials in domestic structures at these Cherokee towns are adult women and children (Table 6.1; Figure 6.4b). Except for the male burials associated with the townhouse, other adult males typically were interred in small household cemeteries next to dwellings. Schroedl notes that

> each household was . . . the domain of the wife and her clan-affiliated family members . . . it thus follows that burial in structures might have been restricted to wives and unmarried children . . . adult males whose natal homes would have been elsewhere were likely interred in their village of residence, perhaps in the vicinity of but not within their domiciles. [Schroedl 1986:204]

As discussed in detail above, traditional Cherokee dwellings are places that housed a residential group connected through and identified with women's property, progeny, and power (Perdue 1998). These dwellings were the realms of women, men did not own the houses, inheritance of the houses and clan membership were determined matrilineally, and membership in a clan was a fundamental dimension of Cherokee identity (Gilbert 1943; Perdue 1998). Graves associated with residences also may well reflect an acknowledgment of the ancestors linked to certain residential groups (Schroedl 1986). That is, the graves associated with the households honor the female-linked kin groups associated with these dwellings. In contrast, the graves of men associated with townhouses likely reflect acknowledgment of the interred individuals' participation in community leadership. The placement of burials within and beside such early Cherokee houses and townhouses may have attached

Table 6.1. Sex of Adult Burials by Grave Location and Site

	Grave Location			
	Mound/Public Bldg.		Village/Residential	
Site Name	**♀ (%)**[a]	**♂ (%)**	**♀ (%)**	**♂ (%)**
Chota[b]	0 (0)	4 (14)	39 (100)	24 (86)
Coweeta Creek[c]	2 (13)	17 (61)	13 (87)	11 (39)
Toqua[d]	20 (27)	33 (44)	55 (73)	42 (56)
Dallas[e]	5 (9)	11 (21)	49 (91)	41 (79)

[a]Percentages based on total number of each sex per individual site.
[b]Data from Schroedl 1986.
[c]Data from Davis et al. 1996.
[d]Data from Parham 1987.
[e]Data from Lewis et al. 1995 with updates from McClung Museum inventories.

the memory of preceding generations of houses and towns to these structures themselves. Both the living and the dead were kept in place through the materiality of houses and townhouses. Emplacement of women and men within the built environment was related to the female-empowered residential and kinship context and the male-empowered townhouse and community context.

If we apply these same concepts to late prehistoric towns of the region, a more nuanced understanding of the spatial patterning of graves becomes apparent. We examined these patterns at two late prehistoric towns in eastern Tennessee, the Toqua and Dallas sites (see Figure 6.1) (Sullivan 2001, 2006; Sullivan and Rodning 2001). These sites were excavated in conjunction with Tennessee Valley Authority (TVA) reservoir projects and are now flooded. The Toqua site in the Little Tennessee River valley was a palisaded town with two platform mounds, a central plaza, and a large village area with many domestic houses (Figure 6.2a; Polhemus 1987). It was occupied from the 13th to 16th centuries (Koerner et al. in press; Lengyel et al. 1999). The Dallas site, located on the Tennessee River near present-day Chattanooga, was a similar palisaded town with one small platform mound and a central plaza surrounded by dwellings (Lewis et al. 1995). It was occupied for only about one century, and the entire town was burned down in approximately C.E. 1400 (Sullivan 2007). At both sites, graves were placed in association with the public buildings on the platform mounds, and in and around residences (Figure 6.3c, d). The mounds were entirely excavated at both sites as well as significant portions of the non-mounded village deposits. The Toqua burial sample includes a total of 439 individuals attributable to the late prehistoric occupation, of which 150 adult individuals ($\geq$15 years of age) could be assigned both age and sex. The Dallas site sample includes a total of 279 individuals, of which 106 adults could be aged and sexed. Aging and sexing of the skeletal remains was done through laboratory analysis by University of Tennessee biological anthropologists as reported by Parham (1987) and in Lewis et al. (1995, see xxi for explanation).

The Dallas and Toqua sites also show the typical pattern of more male individuals buried in the mounds and more females buried in residential cemeteries (Table 6.1). More subadults also are in residential graves as opposed to the mounds at Toqua (Parham 1987). This patterning becomes more interesting when we examine specific age cohorts (Sullivan 2006). Figure 6.8 illustrates the patterning of age cohorts by sex and burial location for each site.

The age cohorts shown in Figure 6.8 were assembled using an average age as determined by the physical anthropologists who examined these skeletal remains. For the purposes of the analyses presented below, adult individuals for whom the sex could be determined (estimated age >15 years) were placed into age cohorts consisting of five-year intervals. Those individuals for whom the estimated age ranges, as determined by the physical anthropologists, were more than five years were assigned to the cohorts including the midpoints of the estimated ranges. This procedure undoubtedly misclassified some individuals into age cohorts that are younger or older than their actual (indefinite) ages. The effects of this problem are mitigated because an estimated age range would have to exceed 15 years for an individual to be "misclassified" by more than one cohort, and few estimates exceeded a 15-year range.

In Figure 6.8 each age cohort also is standardized independently to show the percentages of males and females in that cohort who are interred in the mound and "village" (i.e., residential areas). For example, 100 percent of the females in the >40 age cohort are buried in the village at

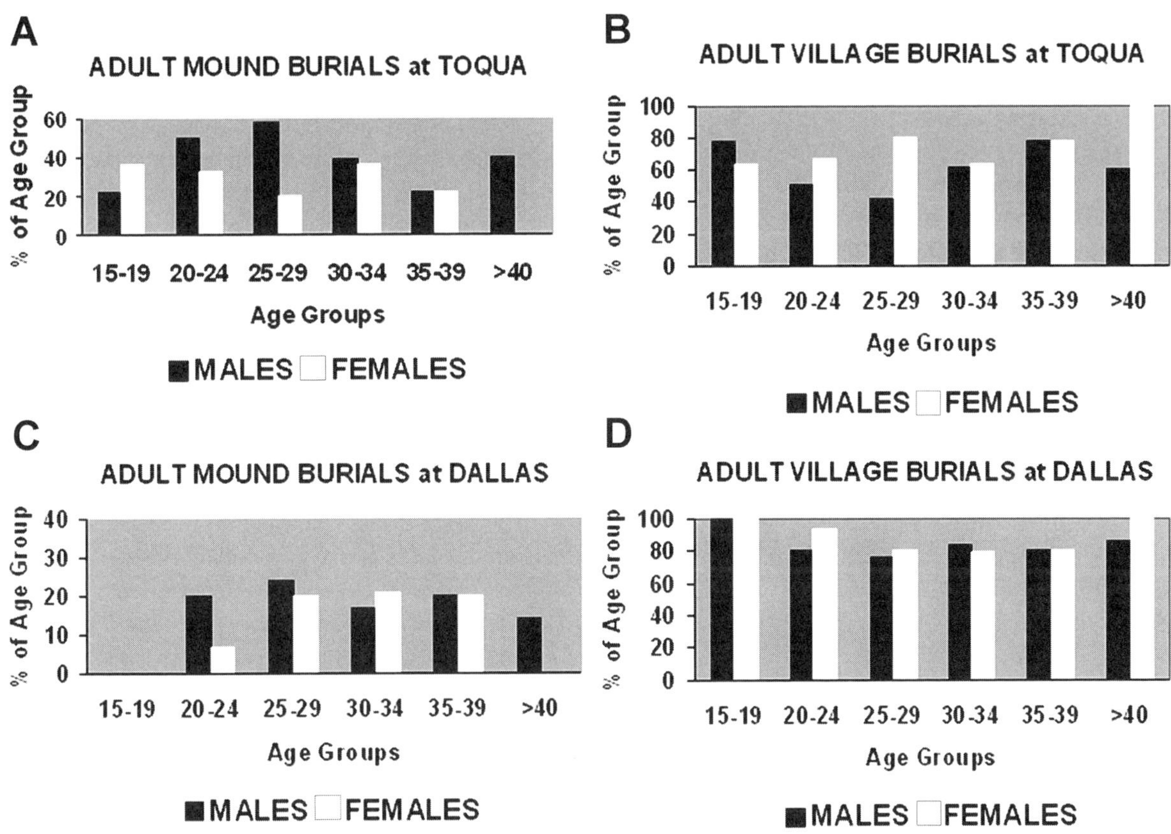

Figure 6.8. Age and sex of adult mound (a, c) and residential (village) (b, d) burials at the late prehistoric Toqua and Dallas sites. Percentages of sexed individuals in each age cohort are shown by burial locations.

both sites. In contrast, small percentages of the males in this age cohort are buried in the mound at each site. This standardization avoids problems posed by archaeological skeletal samples when using simple counts. For example, demographic curves constructed for each site show higher female mortality during the child-bearing years and thus higher than expected numbers of females in younger age categories (Sullivan 2006). By setting the full number of males and females in each cohort at 100 percent, the frequencies of each sex in each location are comparable, regardless of the number of individuals of each sex in the cohort.

Figure 6.8a and c shows that males in the mounds include individuals in all adult age groups, but there are more in the younger age categories (20–29 years). These young males are buried with items that could be associated with warfare, such as ceremonial blades and axes, and clusters of arrow points that likely were quivers of arrows (Hatch 1974, 1987; Polhemus 1987). Some of the oldest men also are buried in the mounds. In contrast, while there are a few younger females in the mounds, as noted above, none of the oldest women are buried in the mounds at either site (Figure 6.8a, c). The oldest females at both sites were, however, interred with more objects than the males of similar age (Sullivan 2001, 2006).

Although there are always problems in relating biological sex to gender to interpret archaeological patterns, in this case we are looking at general patterns and trends that likely follow traditional roles. Judging from the biological patterning, if we were to interpret an individual's prestige and political influence solely by the criterion of mound burial, we would have to conclude that 20-something-year-old males were the most likely group to wield power at these towns and that the eldest women were the least prestigious and influential individuals. This interpretation contradicts cross-cultural research demonstrating that women's prestige and influence often increases with age (Brown and Kerns 1985; Crown and Fish 1996; Eastman 2001), and it suggests that social and political power was entirely in the hands of the "young turks"—another unlikely scenario. Taken together, these trends demonstrate that there was an alternate burial program for women—burial in the village in the location of their houses—as they became older and presumably increasingly responsible for managing households. Mound interment for men is consistent with an increase in prestige during the younger adult years when males would have been active in the war organization. In fact, it is males of this age group that are the main source of the discrepancy between male and female representation in the mounds. Sullivan (2006) has suggested elsewhere that this difference may have been more pronounced at Toqua because there may have been more instances of conflict, and greater numbers of opportunities for males to achieve war honors and prestige during Toqua's 300-year occupation than during the one century of the Dallas site occupation.

After age 30, there is much less difference in the representation of the sexes in the mounds, with the exception of the very oldest members of the population. The general trend is for women to be less likely candidates for mound burial as they age, but this trend does not correlate with decreased likelihood of being buried with grave offerings (Sullivan 2006). These patterns suggest that residential burial for women does not necessarily correlate with decreased prestige or social standing. In fact, burial in a house may be as much of a material "accoutrement" for a female as are some symbolically charged objects interred with males.

While there are some important differences in the mortuary programs between these sites (see Sullivan 2006 for a more in-depth discussion), there also are sufficient similarities between them, and several reasons to infer that the presence of more men in the public cemeteries does not indicate that men had greater access to prestige and power than did women. First, women *are* represented in the mounds, and in some age cohorts are equally represented with men. Second, younger males of warrior age tip the mound population balance towards men. Third, the oldest females at both sites are not buried in the mounds; they are buried in residences, and some with significant numbers of funerary objects. Based on the Cherokee model and cross-cultural research, these "grandmothers" should have been among the most accomplished, politically influential, and beloved members of these prehistoric communities.

We therefore cannot assume that women had little or no political power simply because their graves are not well represented in mounds and public cemeteries. Nor can we assume that households were "peripheral" or "marginal" to the administration, management, and power structure of these societies. Yet, at another scale of social and political organization, the male burials in platform mounds and in townhouses—which symbolically "housed" entire communities—linked these individuals with the spheres of social life and community leadership associated with those structures.

Residential Burial in the Southern Appalachians

At the sites considered here, including late prehistoric and postcontact towns in the southern Appalachians, residential burial appears to have been an integral part of the negotiation and expression of power relationships among men and women, situated within contextualized realms of political influence and the ancestral heritage of localized residential groups. Not only do the integration and negotiations of significant social and gender divisions characterize the social and political dynamics of these societies, but also the burial practices that associated particular graves with specific kinds of architecture physically inscribed these traditions in the archaeological remains.

The longevity of the tradition of residential burial in this region and its correlation with corporate kin groups in long-term houses also indicates strong links between the realm of the ancestors and that of the living. The placement of burials in household and public spaces connected the dead to the living, and even though the burials themselves were essentially invisible, their association with residential and communal buildings and spaces made the dead "visible" within the built environment of the living community. The longevity of the tradition of residential burial in southern Appalachia also demonstrates cultural conservatism in mortuary practices and, in fact, that conservatism is a significant factor in the formation—over generations—of archaeologically recognizable patterns of graves associated with houses.

The presence of winter and summer houses, and graves associated with them, is also seen at late prehistoric and protohistoric settlements in neighboring regions. Of interest is that the gender dimensions of the burials in these other areas (e.g., northern Georgia) do not necessarily follow those we describe for eastern Tennessee and western North Carolina. For example, burial patterns at the 16th-century King site in northern Georgia, as interpreted by Hally (2004, 2008), suggest more of a male-dominated political structure as opposed to the gender balance we propose for Tennessee and North Carolina. At King, females comprise the majority of residential burials, but are associated with far fewer (typically none) funerary objects than either the males at King or the females at the Tennessee and North Carolina sites, and there are no distinctive burial treatments for elder women at King. Hally (2004, 2008) also interprets all of the burials associated with a large public structure on the plaza at King as high-ranking males. While the similarities in the placements of burials among all of the discussed sites may indicate similar corporate and kinship groupings (clans?), the differences in gender dimensions may well correlate with either differing cultural identities (ethnicity?[2]) or the interaction of the King site residents with Spanish conquistadors. On the other hand, burials at the King site demonstrate a pattern we also see at sites in western North Carolina and eastern Tennessee: that of burials placed inside domestic and public architecture, as statements about the enduring relationships between those structures and the community members—both the living and the dead—that are "housed" within them (Hally 2008; Rodning 2001a; Sullivan 2001, 2006; Sullivan and Rodning 2001).

The studies in this volume suggest that societies that practice residential burial may have similar organizational features in the form of long-term corporate residences. Our examples from eastern Tennessee and western North Carolina show that other information about important cultural practices can be gleaned from the details of burial demographics and individual treatments—perhaps especially when interment in association with residences is not the only form of burial. Comparisons of such details may reveal significant cultural differences in otherwise similar, and conservative, mortuary practices. The identification of such differences in burial practices among otherwise generally similar, neighboring archaeological complexes may assist in discerning significant distinctions in cultural practices, such as gender dynamics, that may relate to differences in cultural identities.

Acknowledgments

Thanks to Joyce White and Ron Adams for the invitation to participate in the residential burial symposium at the 2007 Annual Meetings of the Society for American Archaeology in Austin, and to Stacie King for co-editing this volume with Ron. Thanks also to Patricia McAnany and Joe Watkins for their insightful comments and contributions as discussants, and thanks to Tim Pauketat, Brett Riggs, and Jayur Mehta for their feedback on topics covered in this article. Any problems or shortcomings are, of course, our responsibility.

Notes

1. The Cherokee burials from Chota-Tanasee and all other sites excavated by the Tellico Archaeological Project were reinterred in the Little Tennessee River valley in the 1980s.

2. See Harle (2010) for an analysis of biological distance as compared with mortuary practices at protohistoric sites in eastern Tennessee and northern Georgia.

References

Anderson, David G.
1994 The Savannah River Chiefdoms: Political Change in the Late Prehistoric Southeast. Tuscaloosa: University of Alabama Press.

Beck, Robin A., Jr., ed.
2007 The Durable House: House Society Models in Archaeology. Occasional Paper 35. Carbondale: Center for Archaeological Investigations, Southern Illinois University.

Brown, J. K., and V. Kerns, eds.
1985 In Her Prime: A New View of Middle-Aged Women. South Hadley, MA: Bergin/Garvey.

Carsten, Janet, and Stephen Hugh-Jones
1995 Introduction. *In* About the House: Lévi-Strauss and Beyond. Janet Carsten and Stephen Hugh-Jones, eds. Pp. 1–46. Cambridge: Cambridge University Press.

Cole, Patricia E.
1975 A Synthesis and Interpretation of the Hamilton Mortuary Pattern in East Tennessee. M.A. thesis, Department of Anthropology, University of Tennessee.

Corkran, David H., ed.
1969 A Small Postscript on the Ways and Manners of the Indians Called Cherokees, by Alexander Longe. Southern Indian Studies 21:3–49.

Crown, Patricia L., and Suzanne K. Fish
1996 Gender and Status in the Hohokam Pre-Classic to Classic Transition. American Anthropologist 98:803–817.

Davis, R. P. Stephen, Jr., Patricia M. Lambert, Vincas P. Steponaitis, Clark Spencer Larsen, and H. Trawick Ward
1996 NAGPRA Inventory of the North Carolina Archaeological Collection. Chapel Hill: Research Laboratories of Archaeology, University of North Carolina.

Delcourt, Paul A., and Hazel R. Delcourt
2004 Prehistoric Native Americans and Ecological Change: Human Ecosystems in Eastern North America since the Pleistocene. Cambridge: Cambridge University Press.

Dickens, Roy S., Jr.
1976 Cherokee Prehistory: The Pisgah Phase in the Appalachian Summit. Knoxville: University of Tennessee Press.
1978 Mississippian Settlement Patterns in the Appalachian Summit Area. *In* Mississippian Settlement Patterns. Bruce D. Smith, ed. Pp. 115–139. New York: Academic Press.
1979 The Origins and Development of Cherokee Culture. *In* The Cherokee Indian Nation: A Troubled History. Duane H. King, ed. Pp. 3–32. Knoxville: University of Tennessee Press.

Eastman, Jane M.
2001 Life Courses and Gender among Late Prehistoric Siouan Communities. *In* Archaeological Studies of Gender in the Southeastern United States. Jane M. Eastman and Christopher B. Rodning, eds. Pp. 57–76. Gainesville: University Press of Florida.

Faulkner, Charles H.
1978 The Origin and Evolution of the Cherokee Winter House. Journal of Cherokee Studies 3:87–94.

Gearing, Frederick O.
1958 The Structural Poses of Eighteenth Century Cherokee Villages. American Anthropologist 60:1147–1158.
1962 Priests and Warriors: Structures for Cherokee Politics in the Eighteenth Century. Memoir 93. Washington, DC: American Anthropological Association.

Gilbert, William H., Jr.
1943 The Eastern Cherokees. Bureau of American Ethnology Bulletin 133, pp. 169–413. Washington, DC: Smithsonian Institution.

Goldstein, Lynne G.
1980 Mississippian Mortuary Practices: A Case Study of Two Cemeteries in the Lower Illinois Valley. Scientific Papers 4. Evanston, IL: Northwestern University Archaeological Program.

Goodwin, Gary C.
1977 Cherokees in Transition: A Study of Changing Culture and Environment Prior to 1775. Research Paper 181. Chicago: University of Chicago, Department of Geography.

Hally, David J.
1994 Lamar Archaeology. *In* Ocmulgee Archaeology, 1936–1986. David J. Hally, ed. Pp. 144–174. Athens: University of Georgia Press.
2004 Mortuary Patterns at a Sixteenth-Century Town in Northwestern Georgia. Southeastern Archaeology 23:166–177.
2008 King: The Social Archaeology of a Late Mississippian Town in Northwestern Georgia. Tuscaloosa: University of Alabama Press.

Hally, David J., and Hypatia Kelly
1998 The Nature of Mississippian Towns in Georgia: The King Site Example. *In* Mississippian Towns and Sacred Spaces: Searching for an Architectural Grammar. R. Barry Lewis and Charles Stout, eds. Pp. 49–63. Tuscaloosa: University of Alabama Press.

Harle, Michaelyn S.
2010 Biological Affinities and the Construction of Cultural Identity for the Proposed Coosa Chiefdom. Ph.D. dissertation, Department of Anthropology, University of Tennessee.

Hatch, James
1974 Social Dimensions of Dallas Mortuary Practices. M.A. thesis, Department of Anthropology, Pennsylvania State University.
1976 Status in Death: Principles of Ranking in Dallas Culture Mortuary Practices. Ph.D. dissertation, Department of Anthropology, Pennsylvania State University.
1987 Mortuary Indicators of Organizational Variability among Late Prehistoric Chiefdoms in the Southeastern U.S. Interior. *In* Chiefdoms in the Americas. Robert D. Drennan and Cathryn A. Uribe, eds. Pp. 9–19. Lanham, MD: University Press of America.

Hatley, Tom
1993 The Dividing Paths: Cherokees and South Carolinians through the Era of Revolution. Oxford: Oxford University Press.

Hill, Sarah H.
1997 Weaving New Worlds: Southeastern Cherokee Women and Their Basketry. Chapel Hill: University of North Carolina Press.

Hudson, Charles M.
1976 The Southeastern Indians. Knoxville: University of Tennessee Press.

Joyce, Rosemary A., and Susan D. Gillespie, eds.
2000 Beyond Kinship: Social and Material Reproduction in House Societies. Philadelphia: University of Pennsylvania Press.

Kapches, Mima
1995 Chaos Theory and Social Movements: A Theoretical View of the Formation of the Northern Iroquoian Longhouse Cultural Pattern. *In* Origins of the People of the Longhouse. André Bekerman and Gary A. Warrick, eds. Pp. 86–96. Proceedings of the 21st Annual Symposium of the Ontario Archaeological Society, Toronto, 1994.

Keel, Bennie C.
1976 Cherokee Archaeology: A Study of the Appalachian Summit. Knoxville: University of Tennessee Press.

King, Duane H., and Danny E. Olinger
1972 Oconastota. American Antiquity 37:222–228.

Koerner, Shannon D., Lynne P. Sullivan, and Bobby R. Braly
In press A Reassessment of the Chronology of Mound A at Toqua. Southeastern Archaeology.

Lea, Vanessa
1995 The Houses of the Mebengokre (Kayapo) of Central Brazil—A New Door to Their Social Organization. *In* About the House: Lévi-Strauss and Beyond. Janet Carsten and Stephen Hugh-Jones, eds. Pp. 206–225. Cambridge: Cambridge University Press.
2001 The Composition of Mebengokre (Kayapo) Households of Central Brazil. *In* Beyond the Visible and the Material. Peter Rivière, Laura M. Rival, and Neil L. Whitehead, eds. Pp. 157–176. Oxford: Oxford University Press.

Lengyel, Stacey N., Jeffery L. Eighmy, and Lynne P. Sullivan
1999 On the Potential of Archaeomagnetic Dating in the Midcontinent Region of North America: Toqua Site Results. Southeastern Archaeology 18:156–171.

Lewis, Thomas M. N., Madeline Kneberg Lewis, and Lynne P. Sullivan (compiler and editor)
1995 The Prehistory of the Chickamauga Basin in Tennessee. 2 vols. Knoxville: University of Tennessee Press.

Meeks, Scott C.
2006a Drought, Subsistence Stress, and Political Instability: Late Prehistoric Abandonment in the Tennessee River Valley. Paper presented at the Annual Meeting of the Southeastern Archaeological Conference, Little Rock, Arkansas.
2006b The Vacant Quarter Hypothesis: Changing Late Prehistoric Political Landscapes in the Tennessee River Valley from a Paleoecological Perspective. Paper presented at the Biennial Meeting of the American Quaternary Association, Bozeman, Montana.
2009 Understanding Cultural Pattern and Process in the Tennessee River Valley: The Role of Cultural Resources Management Investigations in Archaeological Research. *In* TVA Archaeology: Seventy-five Years of Prehistoric Site Research. Erin E. Pritchard, ed. Pp. 169–198. Knoxville: University of Tennessee Press.

Mooney, James
1900 Myths of the Cherokee. Bureau of American Ethnology Annual Report 19, pp. 3–576. Washington, DC: Smithsonian Institution.

Parham, Kenneth
1987 Toqua Skeletal Biology: A Biocultural Approach. *In* The Toqua Site: A Late Mississippian Dallas Phase Town, vol. 1. By Richard R. Polhemus. Pp. 431–552. Report of Investigations 41, Department of Anthropology, University of Tennessee, and Publications in Anthropology 44, Tennessee Valley Authority. Knoxville.

Parker Pearson, Mike
2000 The Archaeology of Death and Burial. College Station: Texas A&M University Press.

Peebles, Christopher S.
1974 Moundville: The Organization of a Prehistoric Community and Culture. Ph.D. dissertation, Department of Anthropology, University of California, Santa Barbara.

Peebles, Christopher S., and Susan M. Kus
1977 Some Archaeological Correlates of Ranked Societies. American Antiquity 42:421–448.

Perdue, Theda
1998 Cherokee Women: Gender and Culture Change, 1700–1835. Lincoln: University of Nebraska Press.

Persico, V. Richard, Jr.
1979 Early Nineteenth-Century Cherokee Political Organization. *In* The Cherokee Indian Nation: A Troubled History. Duane H. King, ed. Pp. 92–109. Knoxville: University of Tennessee Press.

Polhemus, Richard R.
1987 The Toqua Site: A Late Mississippian Dallas Phase Town. 2 vols. Report of Investigations 41, Department of Anthropology, University of Tennessee, and Publications in Anthropology 44, Tennessee Valley Authority. Knoxville.
1990 Dallas Phase Architecture and Sociopolitical Structure. *In* Lamar Archaeology: Mississippian Chiefdoms in the Deep South. Mark Williams and Gary Shapiro, eds. Pp. 125–138. Tuscaloosa: University of Alabama Press.

Prezzano, Susan C.
1997 Warfare, Women, and Households: The Development of Iroquois Culture. *In* Women in Prehistory: North America and Mesoamerica. Cheryl Claassen and Rosemary A. Joyce, eds. Pp. 88–99. Philadelphia: University of Pennsylvania Press.

Rodning, Christopher B.
1999 Archaeological Perspectives on Gender and Women in Traditional Cherokee Society. Journal of Cherokee Studies 20:3–27.
2001a Mortuary Ritual and Gender Ideology in Protohistoric Southwestern North Carolina. *In* Archaeological Studies of Gender in the Southeastern United States. Jane M. Eastman and Christopher B. Rodning, eds. Pp. 77–100. Gainesville: University Press of Florida.
2001b Architecture and Landscape in Late Prehistoric and Protohistoric Western North Carolina. *In* Archaeology of the Appalachian Highlands. Lynne P. Sullivan and Susan C. Prezzano, eds. Pp. 238–249. Knoxville: University of Tennessee Press.
2002 The Townhouse at Coweeta Creek. Southeastern Archaeology 21:10–20.
2007 Building and Rebuilding Cherokee Houses and Townhouses in Southwestern North Carolina. *In* The Durable House: House Society Models in Archaeology. Robin A. Beck Jr., ed. Pp. 464–484. Occasional Paper 35. Carbondale: Center for Archaeological Investigations, Southern Illinois University.
2009a Mounds, Myths, and Cherokee Townhouses in Southwestern North Carolina. American Antiquity 74:627–663.
2009b Domestic Houses at Coweeta Creek. Southeastern Archaeology 28:1–26.
2010 Architectural Symbolism and Cherokee Townhouses. Southeastern Archaeology 29:59–79.

Rodning, Christopher B., and David G. Moore
2010 Mortuary Practices in Late Prehistoric and Protohistoric Southwestern North Carolina. Southeastern Archaeology 29:80–100.

Roscoe, Paul
2008 Settlement Fortification in Village and "Tribal" Society: Evidence from Contact-Era New Guinea. Journal of Anthropological Archaeology 27:507–519.

Sattler, Richard A.
1995 Women's Status among the Muskogee and the Cherokee. *In* Women and Power in Native North America. Laura L. Klein and Lillian A. Ackerman, eds. Pp. 214–229. Norman: University of Oklahoma Press.

Schroedl, Gerald F.
1998 Mississippian Towns in the Eastern Tennessee Valley. *In* Mississippian Towns and Sacred Spaces: Searching for an Architectural Grammar. R. Barry Lewis and Charles Stout, eds. Pp. 64–92. Tuscaloosa: University of Alabama Press.
2000 Cherokee Ethnohistory and Archaeology from 1540 to 1838. *In* Indians of the Greater Southeast: Historical Archaeology and Ethnohistory. Bonnie G. McEwan, ed. Pp. 204–241. Gainesville: University Press of Florida.
2001 Cherokee Archaeology since the 1970s. *In* Archaeology of the Appalachian Highlands. Lynne P. Sullivan and Susan C. Prezzano, eds. Pp. 278–297. Knoxville: University of Tennessee Press.

Schroedl, Gerald F., ed.
1986 Overhill Cherokee Archaeology at Chota-Tanasee. Report of Investigations 38. Knoxville:

Department of Anthropology, University of Tennessee.

Schroedl, Gerald F., C. Clifford Boyd Jr., and R. P. Stephen Davis Jr.
1990 Explaining Mississippian Origins in East Tennessee. *In* The Mississippian Emergence. Bruce D. Smith, ed. Pp. 175–196. Washington, DC: Smithsonian Institution Press.

Smith, Betty Anderson
1979 Distribution of Eighteenth-Century Cherokee Settlements. *In* The Cherokee Indian Nation: A Troubled History. Duane H. King, ed. Pp. 46–60. Knoxville: University of Tennessee Press.

Spain, Daphne
1992 Gendered Spaces. Chapel Hill: University of North Carolina Press.

Sullivan, Lynne P.
1987 The Mouse Creek Phase Household. Southeastern Archaeology 6:16–29.
1995 Mississippian Household and Community Organization in Eastern Tennessee. *In* Mississippian Communities and Households. J. Daniel Rogers and Bruce D. Smith, eds. Pp. 99–123. Tuscaloosa: University of Alabama Press.
2001 "Those Men in the Mounds": Gender, Politics, and Mortuary Practices in Late Prehistoric Eastern Tennessee. *In* Archaeological Studies of Gender in the Southeastern United States. Jane M. Eastman and Christopher B. Rodning, eds. Pp. 101–126. Gainesville: University Press of Florida.
2006 Gendered Contexts of Mississippian Leadership in Southern Appalachia. *In* Leadership and Polity in Mississippian Society. Brian M. Butler and Paul D. Welch, eds. Pp. 264–285. Occasional Paper 33. Carbondale: Center for Archaeological Investigations, Southern Illinois University.
2007 Shell Gorgets, Time, and the Southeastern Ceremonial Complex in Southeastern Tennessee. *In* Southeastern Ceremonial Complex: Chronology, Content, Context. Adam King, ed. Pp. 88–106. Tuscaloosa: University of Alabama Press.

Sullivan, Lynne P., Bobby R. Braly, and Shannon D. Koerner
2009 Revisiting Mississippian Chronology in East Tennessee: The Radiocarbon Reality. Paper presented at the 74th Annual Meeting of the Society for American Archaeology, Atlanta, GA.

Sullivan, Lynne P., and Shannon D. Koerner
2010 New Perspectives on Late Woodland Architecture and Settlement in Eastern Tennessee: Evidence from the DeArmond Site (40RE12). Tennessee Archaeology 5:31–50.

Sullivan, Lynne P., and Christopher B. Rodning
2001 Gender, Tradition, and the Negotiation of Power Relationships in Southern Appalachian Chiefdoms. *In* The Archaeology of Traditions: Agency and History Before and After Columbus. Timothy R. Pauketat, ed. Pp. 107–120. Gainesville: University Press of Florida.

Swanton, John R.
1946 The Indians of the Southeastern United States. Smithsonian Institution, Bureau of American Ethnology, Bulletin 137. Washington, DC: Government Printing Office.

Ward, H. Trawick, and R. P. Stephen Davis Jr.
1999 Time Before History: The Archaeology of North Carolina. Chapel Hill: University of North Carolina Press.

Williams, Samuel Cole, ed.
1927 Lieutenant Henry Timberlake's Memoirs. Johnson City, TN: Watauga Press.
1928 Early Travels in the Tennessee Country, 1540–1800. Johnson City, TN: Watauga Press.
1930 James Adair's History of the North American Indians. Johnson City, TN: Watauga Press.

7

Inside and Outside: Residential Burial at Formative Period Chalcatzingo, Mexico

Susan D. Gillespie
University of Florida

ABSTRACT

At Chalcatzingo, Mexico, an early regional center, the common location for burials was under house floors, but some high-status burials occurred in more open spaces. These latter were also residential burials, interred within the landed domain of social units. Although both "inside" and "outside" burials drew on claims of ancestral continuity, it is important to explore the differences they entailed. Investigating how repeated mortuary practices at Chalcatzingo evoked referential networks—endowing those practices with intelligibility and enabling identity formation over time—can broaden understandings of residential burial practices and bridge various classificatory separations imposed by archaeologists, including those between public and private mortuary spaces. [mortuary practices, citation, social houses, complex society, Mesoamerica]

A focus on residential burial conforms to a recent trend in mortuary analyses to examine the "landscape of the dead" (Parker Pearson 1999:124), part of the growing interest since the 1990s in the anthropology of place (Low and Lawrence-Zúñiga 2003:1). Treating residential burial, typically subfloor interments within a domicile, as a separate category of mortuary practice presumes that certain conditions and implications derive from burial location in direct spatial juxtaposition with the habitation activities of living individuals. The potential for making interpretations of social organization and political economy, as well as religion and ritual, is therefore substantial. This potential is augmented by cross-cultural studies of residential burial practices archaeologically and ethnographically. Nevertheless, isolating residential burial as a classificatory category introduces or reifies certain parameters in archaeological assumptions and inferences. Both the potential and the limitations of this categorizing warrant further elucidation.

The analysis of residential burials as a class of mortuary practices is both an update to an earlier perspective in mortuary archaeology—characterized as the "Saxe-Binford approach" of the 1970s (Brown 1995; Chapman and Randsborg 1981)—and a shift to more contemporary interests—the "ancestral-descendant approach" (Rakita and Buikstra 2005:8; see also McAnany 1995, 1998; McAnany et al. 1999:129) concerned with issues of identity and social memory (e.g., Chesson 2001). Binford (1971) had proposed that systematic differences in disposal of the dead cross-culturally can be correlated with subsistence behaviors and by extension with sociopolitical complexity (Brown 1995:10). Similarly, Saxe's (1970) well-known "Hypothesis 8" linked the presence of formal disposal areas of the dead to territoriality. However, many of these earlier studies dealt with cemeteries distant from the living areas of foraging populations, and the spatial patterning within cemeteries was somewhat neglected (Chapman and Randsborg 1981:14; Goldstein 1981:57).

Nevertheless, similar ideas should apply to the territoriality claimed by agricultural societies in putting their dead within or near their residences. As Parker Pearson observed, "the fixing of the dead in the land is a social and political act which ensures access and rights over natural resources" (Parker Pearson 1999:141). The inferential shift to the ancestral-descendant approach is reflected in a greater

ARCHEOLOGICAL PAPERS OF THE AMERICAN ANTHROPOLOGICAL ASSOCIATION, Vol. 20, Issue 1, pp. 98–120, ISSN 1551-823X, online ISSN 1551-8248. DOI: 10.1111/j.1551-8248.2011.01030.x.

concern for "mortuary space" and the location of the dead "relative to landscape and construction and location relative to other decedents" (Ashmore and Geller 2005:84; see also Silverman and Small 2002). The important difference with residential burial, of course, is the close proximity of the dead to the most intimate spaces of the living, in many cases with minimal physical barriers separating the two. The cohabitation of the living and dead in the same space implies the continued role playing of the dead, usually as ancestors (rather than as ghosts), in the social practices that forge the identities, statuses, and property rights of the living. Residential burials suggest property claims to the land where the residences are situated and to the structures themselves, with rights grounded in appeals to precedence strengthened by the physical presence of predecessors. Sequential burials in the same location manifest the strategic linking of identities of the living inhabitants to the deceased over time (Ashmore and Geller 2005:84; Gillespie 2002; McAnany 1995).

Another important characteristic of residential burial is that interment within the walls of a private residence is less visible than burial in the open spaces of cemeteries or public structures. The dead are thus assumed to become entwined in salient social memories of burial acts within the social field of a household. The knowledge of the placement of the dead shared by, even limited to, household members would contribute to the maintenance of their specific group identity in contrast with parallel identities of other households (Hendon 2000:47–49; Mizoguchi 1993:231). Thus Joyce observed that "burial practices within residential compounds provide the ground against which nonresidential burial practices were distinguished" (Joyce 1999:41). Her analysis of burial practices from Formative period Mesoamerican sites contrasted the marking and emergence of personal and group identities between corporate group-oriented residential burial and the wider social contexts informed by burials within public architecture, notably platform mounds (Joyce 1999:41). The development of the latter out of the former coincided with the rise of complex societies in the Middle Formative period (see Barrett 1990 for a similar British case study).

In sum, substantial inferences derived from residential burial practices have proven useful in archaeological interpretations, but these implications are also being challenged. I use the case study of Formative period Chalcatzingo, Mexico, to comment on some of these embedded assumptions and to explore other ways of treating residential burial, moving beyond categories of mortuary space to examine the shaping of social and material relationships iterated through mortuary practices. By investigating repeated practices that evoke referential networks endowing those practices with intelligibility and allowing for the reproduction of memory, my aim is to broaden understandings of residential burial and to bridge the classificatory distinctions between public and private mortuary spaces. In so doing, I also challenge the classification of "mortuary space" as distinct from other types of spaces (see also Joyce, chapter 3, this volume).

Chalcatzingo

Chalcatzingo is located in the Amatzinac River valley in eastern Morelos state, 100 kilometers southeast of Mexico City (Grove 1987c) (Figure 7.1). The major occupation of the site was during the Middle Formative period, from 900–500 B.C.E. (Before the Christian Era, uncalibrated), when complex societies developed throughout Mesoamerica. During this period, Chalcatzingo was the political center of the Amatzinac valley and one of the most important communities in highland central Mexico, with ties to the Gulf coast Olmec peoples, southwest Mexico, and southeast Mexico into the Maya area (Grove 1987a). Chalcatzingo is also one of the most extensively excavated Middle Formative sites in central Mexico, providing substantial information on domestic life (Grove and Gillespie 2002:11).

The site lies at the base of a highly visible natural landmark, the conjoined volcanic hills (*cerros*) named Cerro Delgado and Cerro Chalcatzingo (Figure 7.2). Major research was conducted in the early 1970s by the Chalcatzingo Archaeological Project led by David Grove, Jorge Angulo, and Raul Arana (Grove 1984; Grove, ed. 1987). Three cultural phases of occupation discussed here are the Early Formative Amate phase (1500–1100 B.C.E.), the Early Middle Formative Barranca phase (1100–700 B.C.E.), and the Late Middle Formative Cantera phase (700–500 B.C.E.; all dates are uncalibrated) (Cyphers Guillén and Grove 1987). During the Cantera phase, the site reached an extent of 40 hectares and included one large stone-faced platform mound along with several smaller stone-faced platforms (Prindiville and Grove 1987:79).

However, the most important modification to the built environment was the terracing of the natural hillside slopes at the start of the Barranca phase (ca. 1100 B.C.E.), creating an initial ten hectares of level fields. Importantly, with the exception of Terrace 1, apparently only one residential structure was placed on each terrace, creating a dispersed settlement pattern that continued through the Cantera phase (Prindiville and Grove 1987:79). The house locations on each terrace had long life spans. Constructed of adobe brick and wattle-and-daub walls with thatched roofs, the structures were intentionally burned at intervals, an act with highly ritualized overtones, and then rebuilt in the same place over

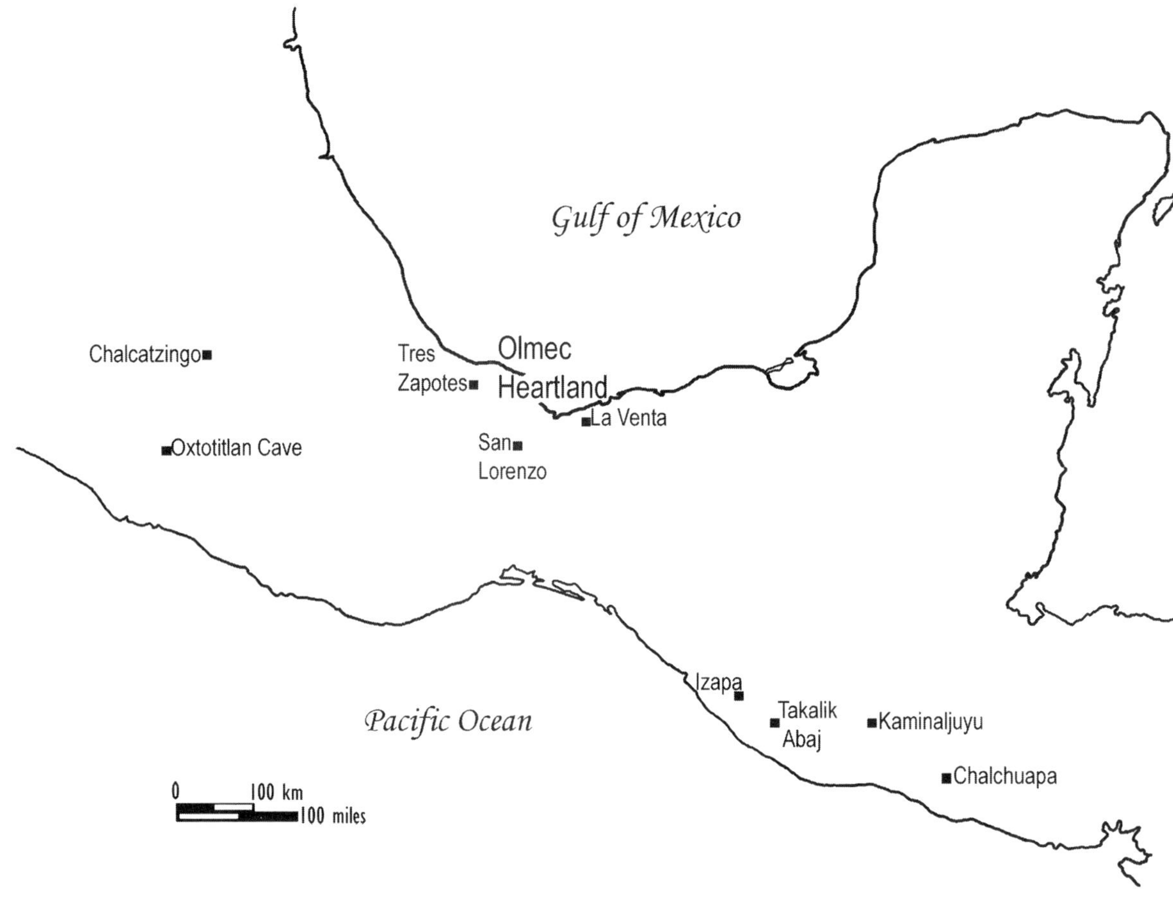

Figure 7.1. Chalcatzingo and selected Formative sites in Mesoamerica.

generations (Grove and Gillespie 2002:17; Prindiville and Grove 1987:74).

Grove (1987b:421; Prindiville and Grove 1987:80) interpreted these practices as evidence for hereditary proprietary rights to the land and the structures on them, rights in which deceased persons whose bodies were incorporated into the structures would have played a role. The buildings had a life cycle with ritually marked moments of birth and death (Grove and Gillespie 2002:17), which must have been implicated in the life cycles of their human inhabitants (see, e.g., Chapman 1994; Gillespie 2000b, 2002; McAnany et al. 1999; Mock 1998). The analytical scale of household mortuary space should therefore extend beyond the walls of the individual residences to consider the patterning of the long-lived house locations, each on its own terrace sloping down (south to north) from the base of the hills.

Eleven Cantera phase domestic structures were excavated partially to nearly completely in the 1970s. They are all large by Mesoamerican standards, with interior walls dividing them into different rooms (Prindiville and Grove 1987:67, 69). Unfortunately, the ground surface is the same today as during the Formative period, so the floors have been plowed away, surface artifact patterns destroyed, and foundation walls partially scattered (Prindiville and Grove 1987:66). Despite these conditions, 143 Formative period burials were recovered, providing a large database for elucidating repeated mortuary practices. Of these, approximately 111 date to the Cantera phase (Merry de Morales 1987a:95, 1987b). The burials include all age categories and ostensibly both sexes. Regrettably, some of the burials were damaged by plowing, and in virtually all cases the skeletal material was too poorly preserved to definitively ascertain sexes of the deceased, and only general age categories could be determined (Merry de Morales 1987a:95).

The principal objective of the 1970s analysis was to assess how burials might reveal social ranks and to distinguish elite individuals based on criteria such as crypt graves, the inclusion of exotics (jade, iron-ore mirrors, and hematite), and the presence of other mortuary furniture such as pottery, figurines, and grinding stones (Merry 1975; Merry de Morales 1987a, 1987b). This objective was in keeping with the Saxe-Binford approach dominant at that time, but it

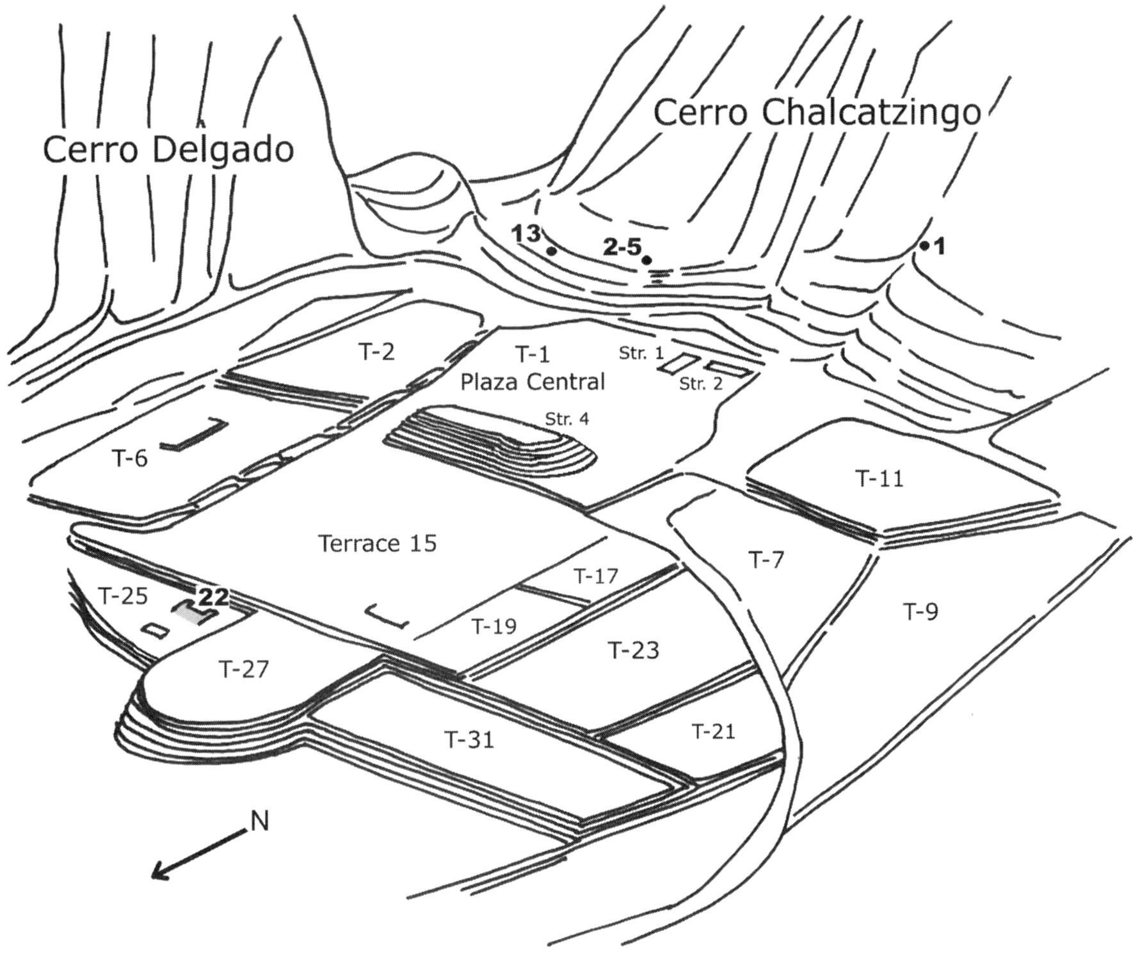

Figure 7.2. Perspective drawing of Chalcatzingo's terraces with some of its Formative period architecture. Monument (sculpture) numbers are in boldface. (Courtesy of David C. Grove)

was also indispensable to broader explanatory goals for the project as a whole concerning the emergence and manifestation of social complexity at this chiefly center. I begin with an overview of how the burial data were interpreted by the Chalcatzingo Project and later commentators to highlight the difficulties and advantages of treating subfloor burials as a category of mortuary practice.

The Normative Pattern of Subfloor Burial: Testing Its Implications

In 1972 when the initial test pits at Chalcatzingo revealed numerous shallow burials in a localized area of the topmost terrace (Terrace 1), the archaeologists believed they had found a cemetery (Merry 1975:26). However, subsequent horizontal excavations and the discovery of stone wall foundations led to the realization that most of the burials were within a single structure. Excavations on other terraces revealed that residences there also had intramural burials. Residential subfloor burial was thus taken to be the general practice at Chalcatzingo, as it was elsewhere in Formative Mesoamerica (e.g., Joyce 1999). In this assessment, the archaeologists adopted the normative approach to mortuary data typical for that time—" the rules a society used" (Goldstein 1981:57; see Chapman and Randsborg 1981:3–4)—useful to characterize demographic profiles, ranking, and other forms of social classification at the level of the community.

More specifically, the project archaeologists concluded that "the majority of Chalcatzingo's Cantera phase burials occur beneath house subfloors and are presumed to be the remains of people who inhabited those houses at least sometime during their life," while burials not under house floors were considered "anomalous" (Prindiville and Grove 1987:73). Major areas of "anomalous" burials were the large platform mound on Terrace 1, a walled sunken patio on Terrace 25, and two caves on the hillside. However, having asserted that subfloor burial was the "normal pattern" (Merry de Morales 1987a:98), the Chalcatzingo archaeologists—notably Merry de Morales, Prindiville, and Grove—questioned the implications that followed from it. They tested the assumption that subfloor burial was the norm for all residents of an individual domicile and revealed this was not the case (for similar conclusions elsewhere, see Chapman 2005:36). The number of burials found relative to estimated population for individual residential structures was too few to account for the entirety of the households that would have occupied those structures over several generations (Prindiville and Grove 1987:73–74, table 6.1).

The archaeologists concluded that an unknown number of Chalcatzingo's inhabitants were not buried under the floors of their residences. This determination would explain the "anomalous" burials of individuals outside the walls of residential structures, including 22 Formative period burials under the floor of a sunken patio unassociated with a domicile. Of these graves the archaeologists asked, "Did these people come from various households?" (Prindiville and Grove 1987:73). There is also the anomaly of one house having a high number of burials, Structure 1 on Terrace 1, known as the *Plaza Central.* Plaza Central Structure 1 (PC Str. 1) was a large building even by Chalcatzingo standards, but its 38 subfloor burials represent nearly four times the number found in the next largest burial inventory, the ten interments in adjacent PC Str. 2. One suggestion (later rejected) was that this residential location was unusually long lived, and thus many generations are represented (Prindiville and Grove 1987:table 6.1; Grove and Gillespie 2002:14).

Furthermore, PC Str. 1 was the only excavated residential structure that contained subfloor burials in stone crypts, and some of them had jade objects (Merry de Morales 1987a:98). The Plaza Central, over one hectare in extent, lies immediately below the talus slopes of Cerro Chalcatzingo, beneath Olmec style Cantera phase boulder and bas-relief carvings on that hillside (Grove and Cyphers Guillén 1987:23). PC Str. 1 was built on the south side of the terrace (adjacent to the *cerro*), while at the north end was the largest structure at Chalcatzingo—the 70-meter-long stone-faced platform mound (PC Str. 4), whose earliest construction stage dates to the Early Formative Amate phase (Grove and Cyphers Guillén 1987:31; Prindiville and Grove 1987:63). Because of its premier location and many high-status burials, PC Str. 1 was deemed an elite residence, home to Chalcatzingo's Cantera phase leaders or "chiefs" (Merry de Morales 1987a:98, 101; Prindiville and Grove 1987:79; see also Grove and Gillespie 1992:193).

PC Str. 1 was rebuilt in the same location several times. At least four building stages were revealed (a–d), the earliest in the Early Cantera subphase. The deepest burial was 120 centimeters below surface (hereafter *cm bs*), but the rest are shallower than 80 cm bs. Significantly, all the burials lay well above the earliest excavated floor (130 cm bs). In fact, the 38 subfloor interments are believed to be associated only with the final building stage (PC Str. 1d) (Grove and Cyphers Guillén 1987:27). They were all dated to the Late Cantera subphase (Merry de Morales 1987a:101) from approximately 600–500 B.C.E. (Cyphers Guillén and Grove 1987) and therefore are not the remains of many generations of inhabitants. Furthermore, the PC Str. 1 burials uniquely express the range of all burial types on the site (Merry de Morales 1987a:98). Thus Grove (1987b:422) suggested that some persons buried under the PC Str. 1 floor were not household residents, and that this was a special burial location. Again, his surmise contradicts the assumption that people were buried under the floors of their own domiciles, incorporated into the structure in acts of domestic or household ritual.

Moreover, the absence of burials in the three earlier iterations of PC Str. 1 (stages a–c) calls into question whether this building was, in fact, a residence. The normative pattern of subfloor burial was actually used to help determine which structures at Chalcatzingo functioned as domiciles. The presence of intramural burials in PC Str. 1 was taken to indicate that it was indeed a house (Grove and Cyphers Guillén 1987:27). The same reason was given for classifying the adjacent PC Str. 2 as a residence. PC Str. 2, which shared a patio area with PC Str. 1, is different from the other buildings in its layout and included artifacts, and it was an area of craft working. However, it had been destroyed and rebuilt several times, and it included ten subfloor burials, which were used to argue that PC Str. 2 was probably a residence (Grove and Cyphers Guillén 1987:29). Nearby PC Str. 6, on the other hand, was called a "house-like structure," but it lacked subfloor burials (Grove and Cyphers Guillén 1987:31). In other words, to say that "subfloor graves were present in every Cantera phase domestic structure excavated at Chalcatzingo," as Grove and I did in a recent article (Grove and Gillespie 2002:13), engages a bit of verbal sleight of hand because the presence of burials was used to determine whether or not a structure had a residential function.

The Chalcatzingo data thereby help to expose the fragility of inferences regarding subfloor interments and some drawbacks in separating subfloor burials from other mortuary spaces. The assumption of a normative burial location for all household members was not sustained. The notion that subfloor burials necessarily imply private or household as opposed to public rituals—those with numerous and more diverse witnesses—is not warranted in the case of the PC Str. 1 burials of individuals from likely multiple households. And if the PC Str. 1 burials were not members of a single household, then the twinned presumptions that that structure was the Cantera phase chiefly residence because of its many high-status burials and that there was a single chiefly residence at the site are jeopardized (Gillespie 2009).

Despite these unwarranted assumptions, there is nevertheless great potential for construing social relationships from the Chalcatzingo mortuary data by focusing on practices that resulted in the various discrete mortuary spaces for multiple interments of generally intact bodies in delimited places on the individual terraces. Interments were almost always primary and did not typically disturb other burials, despite confined intramural mortuary space (see King, chapter 4, this volume). There are definite indications that burial locations were remembered (if not actually marked) over long periods and that there were proscriptions on wantonly disturbing the dead. Two distinctive skull burials were encountered (Burials 37, 111) but there is little other indication of the separation or curation of body parts. All of these patterns indicate meaningful choices made in lieu of known alternatives elsewhere, for example, the distancing of the dead from the living, a single community cemetery, a communal tomb chamber with mixed osseous material, cremation, the circulation of relics, and separate structures for individual burials (e.g., barrows). Some of the implications of these choices are suggested here by examining the contexts for mortuary practices through time.

Mortuary Practices as Material Citation

The synchronic normative approach to mortuary analysis typical of much of 20th-century archaeology continued well into the 1990s (Chapman 2005:27–28), during which time it was increasingly challenged. Manifestations of status indicators in funerary contexts were shown to be dynamic, even cyclical, rendering normative studies problematic (Cannon 1989). Mizoguchi observed that "by concentrating on static patterns, we tend to forget the flow of time through which various human practices were conducted [and the] archaeological study of mortuary practices is no exception" (Mizoguchi 1993:223). More recent approaches in archaeological interpretation, as summarized by Joyce and Lopiparo, reveal "a transformation from an ethnographic emphasis on 'shared' practices to a historical examination of *repeated* practices" (Joyce and Lopiparo 2005:370). The influence of agency and practice theories has resulted in greater attention to "chains, networks, and other images of repetition, such as citationality," that is, to "figures of sequences of action in time" (Joyce and Lopiparo 2005:368, 372).

Jones (2001) recommended citation as a useful tool for analyzing depositional events, including burials. He adapted Butler's (1993) concept of citation—the notion that "in order for a word or thing to make sense it must reiterate components of previous sentences or objects"—to artifacts and their contexts as a form of material citation "in which traces on each artefact establish relations of similitude within a wider matrix of similarities and differences" (Jones 2001:339, 342, 351) and thereby facilitate the reproduction of memory. An advantage of Butler's citation is that it "moves the focus from individual agency alone to individual action within culturally delimited frameworks that make certain kinds of action intelligible" (Joyce 2000:187). Actions become intelligible and meaningful because performances within material spaces and the deposited objects that result from them contribute to "different networks of referentiality" (Jones 2001:339). From this perspective, mortuary customs are no longer seen as reflecting social roles or statuses. Those roles and statuses emerge instead out of routine yet strategic actions and engagements with the material world, including funerary rituals that served as the media for constituting social relations (Barrett 1990:181–182; Chapman 2000:177; Joyce 2001:22).

Jones (2001:340) further borrowed Gell's (1998:232ff.) notion of "distributed objects" as a "citational field" in which objects are considered components of chains of reference to other iterations. They invoke an orientation to the past via memory—recapitulating past actions to create a sense of similarity or identity with precursors. These retrospective and past-oriented actions are retentions, temporal references to that which has already transpired. Modifying, even innovating, actions to create a sense of future-oriented (prospective) difference with past actions nevertheless still make reference to those retentions or precursors, the precursors then becoming protentions, bases for subsequent actions (terms from Gell [1998:235] based on Husserl's [1964] phenomenology of time-consciousness). Indeed, actions are always future oriented (Gell 1998:256) in that they establish the potentiality of and constraints on subsequent actions. To paraphrase Gell (1998:257), each burial becomes a "project" for future burials, whether or not that project is fulfilled.

Similar concepts have already been applied to mortuary analyses (e.g., Barrett 1990, 1994; Chapman 2000; Joyce 2001; Mizoguchi 1993) that treat burials as complex citations, each of whose individual criteria (grave type, orientation, position, furniture, etc.) can be seen as components of individual and multidimensional networks of referentiality. The networks become historical artifacts referenced by individuals and groups as they emerge from practices over time, providing the context for endowing those practices with signification and value. Subjects or actors are "acted upon" (Munn 1986:14) by these practices and their inherent materiality, such that their social subjectivities are formed or transformed, rather than merely reflected, by their actions.

Examining burials as referential chains, as citations of prior actions, is best done where there is good control over the dating of the interments, for example, through radiocarbon dating of bone (Chapman 2005) or tight stratigraphic sequencing. Neither of these options is available for the Chalcatzingo burials, nor as a general rule is burial depth a reliable indicator of relative dating. Nevertheless, those burials occurred over several centuries, and there are subgroups of burials for which sequencing data are available. Indeed, investigating mortuary practices at Chalcatzingo in terms of citation has the advantage of accounting for the many small-scale patterns noted by the Chalcatzingo archaeologists that were unintelligible at a synoptic community-wide scale (Merry de Morales 1987a:99). This approach can also bridge the conceptual divide between subfloor and non-subfloor mortuary spaces, so that the latter are no longer seen as "anomalous." It further obviates the classificatory distinctions usually made between human interments and related depositional practices such as subfloor caches of objects and animal burials (see Jones 2001:346; Joyce, chapter 3, this volume).

Networks of referentiality (citational fields) and the dynamic social fields they engage—the "spacetime of self-other relationships formed in and through acts and practices" (Munn 1986:9)—can be construed at multiple temporal and spatial scales. Rather than distinguish burial practices at Chalcatzingo as either subfloor or anomalous at the level of the site as a whole, chains of mortuary practices can be examined at the minimal spatial scale within a single interment and within a single structure, the medial scale of the artificially built terrace, and the maximal scale of the community as a whole vis-à-vis other communities. From this perspective, the interments on the Plaza Central, which include subfloor burials in PC Strs. 1 and 2 as well as special crypt burials in the great platform mound (PC Str. 4), can be shown to reference citational fields that distinguish them from other burial locations, including those in the sunken patio on Terrace 25. On the other hand, the Terrace 25 and Plaza Central burials, constituting the "elite" or "high-status" burials at the site, have more in common with one another than they do with the "non-elite" residential burials on the other terraces. These citational fields are briefly traced here, focusing on the Plaza Central and Terrace 25, the two areas of the site with the highest densities of burials.

The Vertical Perspective: Paired Burials

To distinguish the different kinds of intersubjective relationships that emerge from citations, I modify for heuristic purposes Strathern's (1994:51) "vertical perspective" (referring to the linear relationship between an agent and individuals now deceased) and "horizontal perspective" (focusing on the substantive linkages between an agent and other living persons), recognizing that both come into play in mortuary practices. The vertical perspective is useful in interpreting the continued burial of individuals in the same residential space. Sequentiality, accomplished through such repetition, is essential to notions of duration or longevity, of making connections to past generations that are valorized as sources of legitimacy, identity, and rights to property (Gillespie 2000a:12). The first burials establish a precedent that is cited by subsequent burials in the same locale. The burials are more than just a commemoration of the dead; they are a material index of the agency of ancestors (Gell 1998: 256).

The placement of founding burials in structures on the individual terraces marked a within-community difference that was sustained by succeeding burials. The longevity of corporate group property rights, as Grove (1987b:421; Prindiville and Grove 1987:80) earlier noted, was also manifested in such material citations as the rebuilding of structures that sheltered the sequentially placed interments in the same location. These data support the modeling of Chalcatzingo's social organization as a Lévi-Straussian "house society" (Gillespie 2009). They indicate strategic actions to objectify the perpetuity of house identity and property, with the "houses"—which are long-lived property-owning social units—operating as corporate agents (Gillespie 2000a, 2000c, 2007; see in this volume Adams and Kusumawati, chapter 2; King, chapter 4; and White and Eyre, chapter 5). Social houses maintain their existence, status, and property by the continuity of such practices, including citations that reference the memories and objects associated with predecessors. These practices inscribe a link or identity to precursors in those cases where actions involve materiality.

Later interments in the same locale did not merely copy past actions, because the physical setting and familial relationships had been changed by earlier deaths. Instead, they became part of strategies to reorder the dead with regard to the living (Barrett 1990:182). PC Str. 1, with its 38 Late Cantera subphase burials, exemplifies the resort to such strategies as burial space became restricted over time, rendering this structure, in Barrett's phrase, "an increasingly elaborate topography of the dead" (Barrett 1990:182). Merry de Morales (1987a) observed several interesting within-structure patterns in the graves that could not be explained strictly by rank differences or changes in shared customs over time. One such pattern was a notable set of differences in burial furniture and grave orientation on either side of an imaginary east–west line that divided the structure into northern and southern halves (Merry de Morales 1987a:103–104). These two halves may have been thought of as separate burial locations within the same structure, revealing different citational histories.

PC Str. 1 Paired Burials

Another important within-structure pattern was formed by paired burials. Paired burials consist of two interments made at different points in time positioned on top of one another or side by side, separated by at least several centimeters of earth (as opposed to double burials in which two individuals were buried together at the same time, which also occurred at Chalcatzingo). They provide a measure of sequencing even though the exact time difference between the two cannot be ascertained, and as a minority practice, imply some kind of relationship among the individuals so treated (see Chapman 2000; Gilchrist and Sloane 2005:158). Six burial pairs were identified among the 38 interments of PC Str. 1 by Merry de Morales (1987a:104–106, table 8.2). Three are in the northern half (#21/31, #19/32, #15/30) and three in the southern half (#3/33, #5/34, #10/27) of the structure (Figure 7.3). While some pairs could be coincidental (e.g., #19/32)—a consequence of limited space or imperfect memories of earlier interments, given that subfloor burials were typically not disturbed—most appear to have been deliberately placed (Merry de Morales 1987a:104). Their orientations varied: in three cases the bodies were parallel in alignment (heads in the same direction), while in the other three they were perpendicular to one another (Table 7.1). Crypt burials were paired with other crypt types; direct (non-crypt) interments with others of the same type. The uppermost burials of the pairs occurred in the plow zone, 20–25 cm bs, while the earlier burials ranged in depth from 50 to 75 cm bs.

The most compelling burial pairs are #3/33 and #5/34. The earlier burials of each pair, #33 and #34, were interments of individuals in extended position, bodies oriented east–west, laid feet-to-feet in graves lined and capped with flat stones (called crypts in the 1987 site report and rock tombs in Merry 1975). These two were among a small cluster of five such crypts in the southern half of the structure at approximately 60 cm bs (#28, #33 [at 75 cm bs], #34, #36, and #37—the last a small stone box with only a skull). Of these five, #33 and #34 were the only interments oriented east–west and were the northernmost of the crypt burials in the southern half of the structure (one crypt burial, #26, was found in the northern half). Also, #33 and #34 were paired in identical fashion by later interments, #3 and #5 respectively, also in crypts but oriented north–south, with heads to the north in both cases. The later bodies were laid perpendicularly over the lower portions of the human remains placed earlier. They therefore form double pairs.

Merry de Morales (1987a:105) and Grove (2006) suggested that #33 and #3 constituted a male–female pair, #33 being the male. Burial 33 had a jade Olmec style figurine and a jade awl fragment ("blood-letter"), the latter an object found with probable males in Cantera phase contexts (and elsewhere in Formative Mesoamerica; Joyce 2000:46). Burial 3 had a grinding stone that may have been a marker of female gender. More significantly, a carved stone head (broken off a statue) included in Burial 3 apparently was that of a female based on the head covering worn, and Grove (2006; Grove and Gillespie 1992:195) has indicated some likelihood that the statue represented the deceased individual. Merry de Morales (1987a:105) further noted that these two crypt burials, #3 and #33, contained the "most truly Olmec artifacts found" during the excavations—the figurine and the statue head—which was another manifestation of their pairing.

While some of the pairs may indeed represent male–female dyads, possibly spouses, the inability to accurately sex the vast majority of the Chalcatzingo burials leaves this issue unresolved (Merry de Morales 1987a:106). Furthermore, Burial 5 was a juvenile in a crypt burial, and there could be many reasons that two interments of different mortuary events were placed one atop the other or side by side (Merry de Morales 1987a:104). Significantly, Merry de Morales (1987a:106) observed that examples of the common funerary types of ceramic vessels (double-loop handle censer, *cantarito* [small bottle], shallow bowls, composite bowls, and, in PC Str. 1 only, shallow bowls in mouth-to-mouth orientation) did not co-occur across a burial pair (see Table 7.1). That is, if one grave had a particular vessel type or configuration, its pair did not. She therefore suggested that the first interment was remembered, and the second was devised to form its complement in some fashion.

Although Merry de Morales (1987a:106) considered those behaviors to mark some sort of "social dichotomy," such as gender, expressed by the two deceased individuals, the complementary mortuary furniture and body positions may more simply have resulted from the intentional reference to the earlier burial when creating the second as a material citation (Table 7.1 reveals the absence of a consistent pattern of pairing any two vessel types). The spatial juxtaposition of the artifacts in the two graves indicates a recapitulation of the earlier act (a retention). Interestingly,

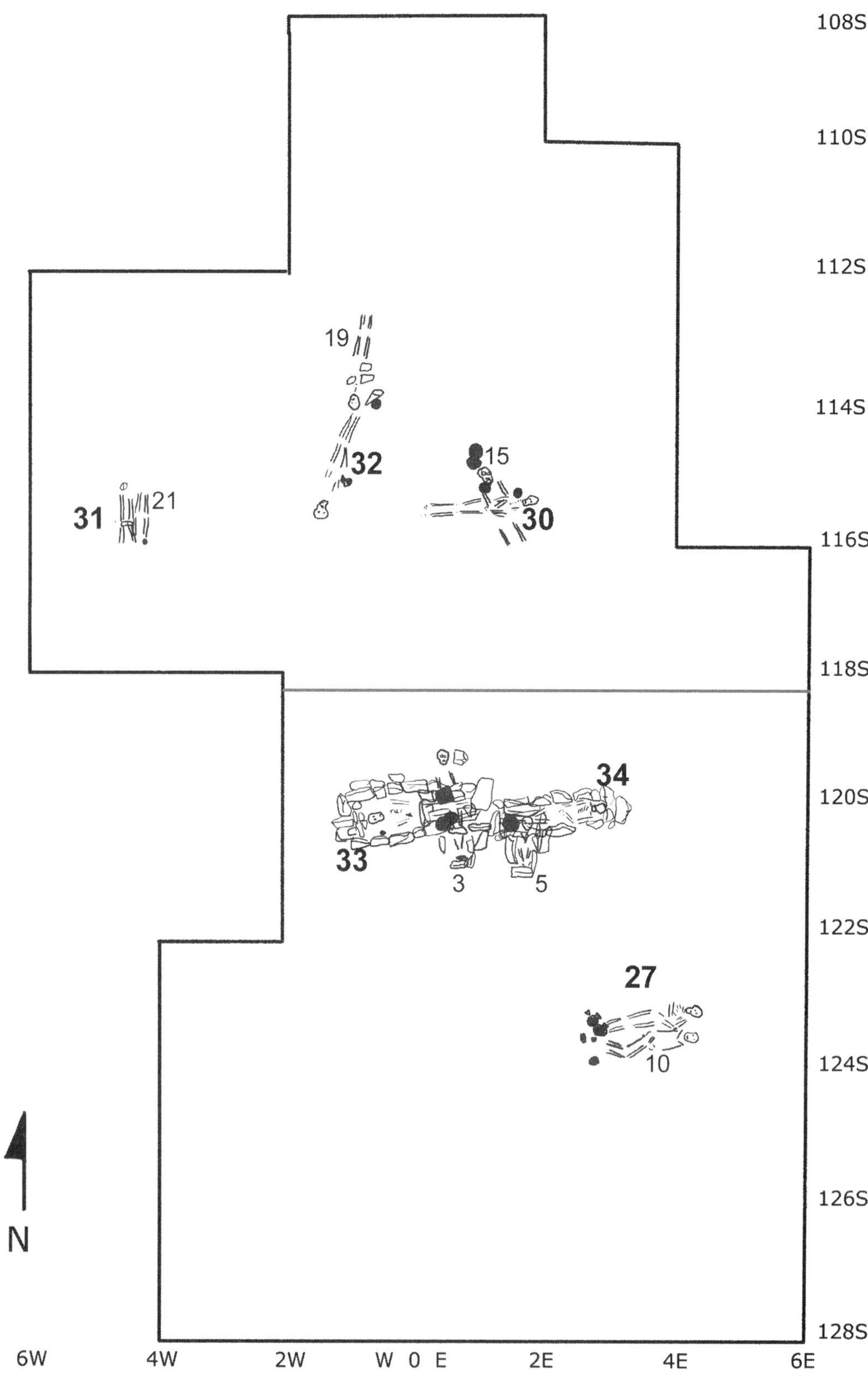

Figure 7.3. The paired burials within PC Str. 1 (based on Merry 1975:figs. 1–6). Decrease in font size indicates the later burial in each pair. The horizontal line across the middle of the excavation unit roughly divides the space into northern and southern halves.

Table 7.1. Paired Burials within PC Str. 1d

Burial	Depth (cm bs)	Quadrant	Relationship to Other (Head/Feet)	Type*	Age**	Double-Loop Handle Censer	Shallow Bowl	Shallow Bowls Mouth-to-Mouth	Cantarito	Cantarito in a Shallow Bowl	Composite Bowl
27	60	122–124S/2–4E	Parallel E/W	D	A	X					
10	25	122–124S/2–4E	Parallel E/W	D	A					X	
30	70	114–116S/0–2E	Perpendicular E/W	D	A	X		X			
15	27	114–116S/0–2E	Perpendicular NW/SE	D	YA		X				
34	60	119–121S/1–4E	Perpendicular E/W	Crypt	YA	X					
5	20	120–122S/0–2E	Perpendicular N/S	Crypt	J						X
33	75	118–120S/1W-1E	Perpendicular W/E	Crypt	A					X	
3	20	118–120S/0–2E	Perpendicular N/S	Crypt	A				X		X
32	56	114–116S/0–2W	Parallel S/N	D	A				X		
19	22	112–114S/0–2W	Parallel S/N	D	A			X			
31	50	114–116S/4–6W	Parallel S/N	D	A						
21	20	114–116S/4–6W	Parallel S/N?	D	A						X

Note: Based on Merry de Morales 1987a:104–106, table 8.2, 1987b. Earlier burial is listed first in each pair.
*Type categories: crypt or simple, direct interment (D).
**Age categories: adult (A), young adult (YA), juvenile (J).

only certain interments were chosen for this role as precursors (protentions) for future pairings. However, the complementarity of the included ceramic objects may indicate more than the marking of difference between the earlier and later interments. It could have signified an act of completion or wholeness, the two individuals so treated forming a totality whose parts were separated in time but brought together at the death of the survivor.

Terrace 25 Paired Burials

Burial pairs were not limited to PC Str. 1. Two Cantera phase burial pairs (#95/105 and #97/102) were identified by Merry de Morales (1987a:108) within the other area with many Formative burials—Terrace 25 (Figure 7.4). At the south end of this terrace was a sunken patio, walled with several courses of flat stone slabs on at least its eastern, southern, and western sides. Its size cannot be determined because the northern wall(s) have been destroyed and the patio's edges changed over time, but its minimal size was 40 square meters (Fash 1987:85, fig. 7.4). Near the center of the southern wall a rectangular construction jutted into the patio, composed of some 20 large, rectangular, shaped stones arranged on three sides around an earthen core. This structure was a 4.4-meter-long north-facing table-top bench/altar, labeled Monument 22, similar in form to monolithic altars at Gulf coast Olmec centers (Figure 7.5). Relief carving on the front face stones was identified as the large eyes and eyebrows of the deified earth (Fash 1987:82).

Burial 105 had been placed within the earthen fill of the bench/altar's center, and Burial 95 was placed above and slightly south of Burial 105 (Table 7.2). Although the bodies were laid within the preexisting larger stone construction, both interments had their own crypts made of flattish stones placed around and above them. The earlier burial was east–west, head to east, while its pair was west–east, head to west, to form a complement. However, there is no obvious pattern of complementarity among the ceramic offerings between them or for the other Cantera phase burial pair on Terrace 25, #97/102 (Burial 102, the earlier of the two, had no grave furniture).

Significantly, the Terrace 25 patio had a burial "triplet," because under the #95/105 pair was an earlier burial, #109, dating to the preceding Barranca phase (Figure 7.4). This earliest burial was a subfloor residential burial, one of at least two (the other is #112) placed under a Barranca phase residence (Fash 1987:86). Just outside of that structure a large pit was dug deep into the subsoil hardpan (*tepetate*), into and upon which other Barranca phase burials were placed. However, instead of being continuously rebuilt, as was the pattern

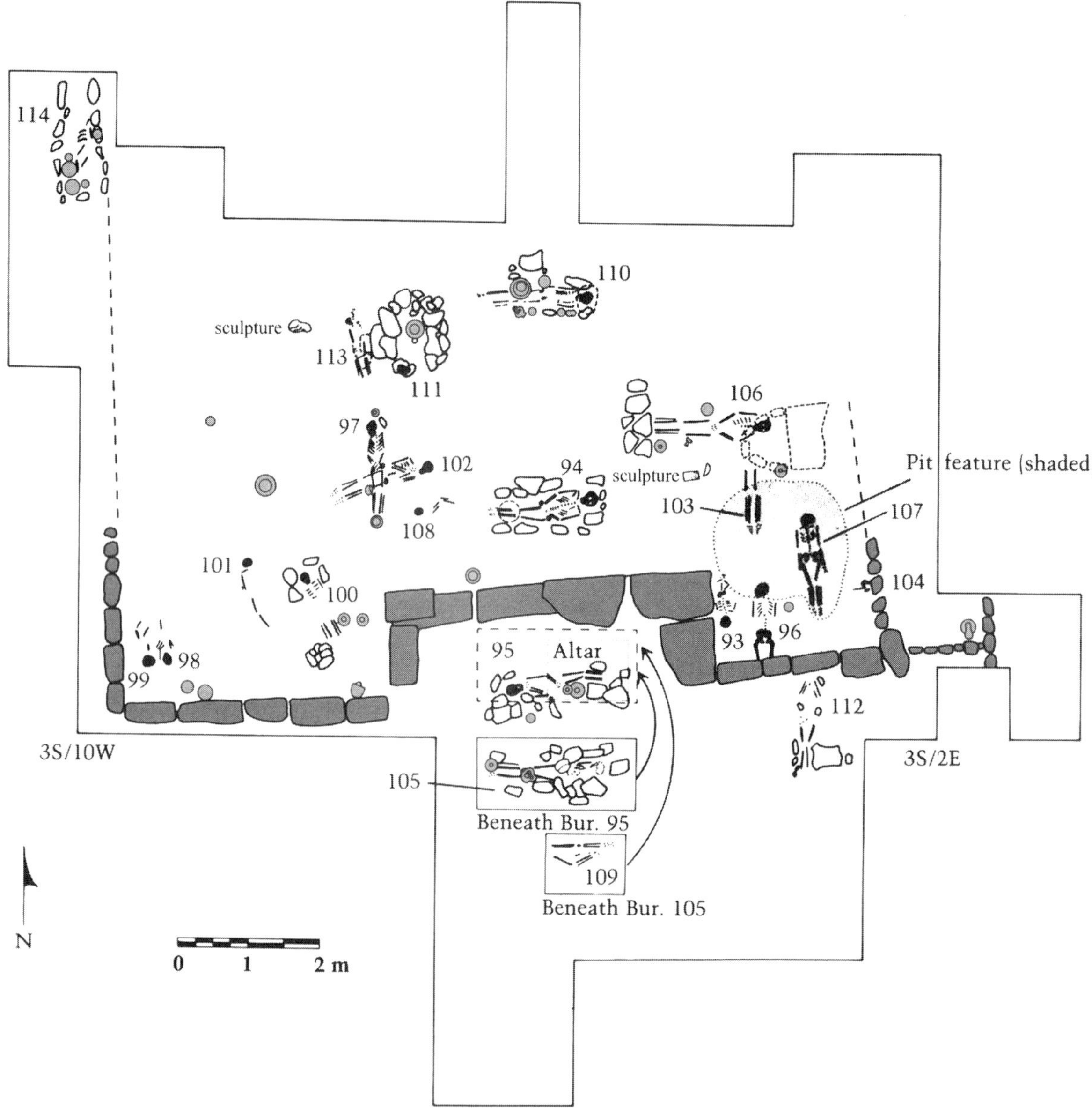

Figure 7.4. Plan map of Terrace 25 excavations showing the bench/altar (Monument 22), patio, Burials 93 to 114, and some of the whole vessels deposited in the patio (modified from Fash 1987:fig. 7.1).

elsewhere at Chalcatzingo, this residence became the locale for the southern extent of the sunken patio. The bench/altar and subsequently Cantera phase Burials 105 and 95 were placed precisely atop Burial 109, which was oriented west–east, the same orientation as the two burials above it and the bench/altar construction. The upper half of the Burial 109 adult, probably male, body (Merry de Morales 1987b:473) was impacted by the positioning of the crypt for Burial 105. The individual's teeth with traces of "red paint," mandible, and some long bones were found in fragments just beneath the crypt (Arana 1973). Fash, who excavated Terrace 25 in 1974, doubted that this placement was a coincidence, suggesting that the altar's direct association with the Barranca phase residence and Burial 109 indicates "a long-standing 'sacred' importance for this location" (Fash 1987:94). The Cantera phase burials postdated the original erection of the bench/altar atop the earlier house foundations, and the significance of this place may have changed once again to that of a "shrine" (Fash 1987: 94).

Figure 7.5. Drawing of the bench/altar face (Monument 22) and stone walls of the Terrace 25 patio. (Courtesy of David C. Grove)

Although the architectural function of this locale was greatly transformed in the Cantera phase, the citation of the Barranca phase burial was made in the same way as at PC Str. 1. We might consider that the bench/altar was erected on that spot as a part of the future-oriented "project" established by the social house that included Burial 109 as its property, the only one of the ten Barranca phase and five Late Barranca/Early Cantera phase burials found at Chalcatzingo that included a valuable jade object (tubular bead) (Merry de Morales 1987b). These sequential actions bridged what archaeologists see as a Barranca to Cantera phase boundary in the citation of the precursor subfloor burial by the two Cantera phase crypt graves, all of them represented as "elite" individuals. Those actions also blurred the classificatory distinction between private subfloor and public non-subfloor burials.

Although the sequence of three bench/altar burials was noted by the Chalcatzingo archaeologists, two other paired burials in the Terrace 25 patio (Table 7.2) are less obvious and were not so recognized (Figure 7.6). These interments also spanned the Barranca to Cantera phase change, and the burials were discussed separately by time period by Merry de Morales (1987a). By focusing on chains of practices rather than separating the data according to changes in archaeological cultural phases over time, these sequences of actions become more apparent. The other pairs are #111/113 (Cantera/Barranca) and #106/103 (Cantera/Late Barranca-Early Cantera) in the patio area north of the altar's west and east corners, respectively. In both cases the earlier burials (#113, #103) were disturbed, the upper halves of the bodies missing (like #109 under the bench/altar), and they lacked grave furniture. The #106/103 pair is perpendicular in orientation, whereas the #111/113 pairing is more unusual in that the Cantera phase Burial 111 consists of a skull perched atop a stone, part of a larger ring of stones (recall the Cantera skull in its own crypt in PC Str. 1, Burial 37).

The citation of the three earlier interments as precursors in Terrace 25 therefore extended over some centuries, unlike what is known for the PC Str. 1d burials, all of which dated to the Late Cantera subphase. These material citations created or reiterated linkages among the more ancient dead, the recently deceased, and the living that could have been construed as genealogy or precedence with or without demonstrated biological ties, as a way of asserting the long-lived property rights and identities of social houses (Gillespie 2009). Fash (1987:94) suggested that the individuals buried in the patio area may have lived in, or been associated with, a Cantera phase residence and platform mound on the north end of Terrace 25. This architectural placement mimics that of the Plaza Central, which likewise had a structure with many burials on the south end and a platform mound on the north end.

Burials Within a Horizontal Referential Network

Terrace 25

The walled sunken patio on Terrace 25 was an open space where, one presumes, funerary rituals were part of a display of status and property rights among a larger audience of witnesses than that available for residential subfloor interments. From these public actions more extensive social fields would have been created or strengthened out of the shared experience and social memories of the participants (Barrett 1990:186). The function of the patio with its bench/altar is uncertain; it is unique at the site. Furthermore, this locale was subjected to a series of architectural transformations in the Cantera phase after the Barranca phase house was razed. The altar was erected more than once, its carved front side was later blocked from view by large stones, and the size of the patio was modified several times (Fash 1987; David C. Grove, personal communication, 2008). Importantly, the patio was used for ritual deposition activities of various sorts. Some bodies and objects were laid down on the original ground surface and covered with earthen fill when the patio

Table 7.2. Terrace 25 Formative Burials

Burial	Depth (cm bs)	Quadrant	Orientation (Head/Feet)	Phase*	Type**	Age***	Ceramics	Other	Remarks
93	100	0–2S/0–1W	S/N	C	D	I			sacrifice; next to NE corner of altar
94	150	0–1N/2–4W	E/W	C	Crypt	YA		obsidian flake	in front of altar
95	120	2–3S/2–4W	W/E	C	Crypt	YA	2 ollas	tubular jade bead	within altar (topmost)
96	150–165	0–2S/0–1W	N/S	LB/EC	D	YA		obsidian blade	under patio wall
97	120	1–1S, 0–2N/5–7W	N/S	C	D	A	3 bowls		paired with 102
98	100	1–2S/8–9W	S/N	C	D	YJ	1 bowl?		double with 99; uncertain which has the bowl
99	100	1–2S/8–9W	S/N	C	D	YJ			double with 98
100	95	0–2S/6–7W	N/S	C	Stone	J	3 bowls		double with 101
101	100	0–2S/7–8W	N/S	C	D	J			double with 100; has pile of stones near feet
102	100	0–1N/5–7W	E/W	C	D	A			paired with 97; associated with 108
103	200	0–1N/0–1W	N/S	LB/EC	Stone	A			upper half gone; rattlesnake carving nearby
104	100	0–1S/0–1E	?	C	Dist	A			fragments; legs under wall
105	130–160	1–2S/2–4W	E/W	C	Crypt	A	5 bowls, 1 olla, 1 eccentric bowl		inside altar (middle of the 3)
106	152	1–2N/0–2W	E/W	C	D	A	7 bowls, 1 censer		large stone slab later placed over head area
107	220	0–1S/0–1E	N/S	LB	D	J	1 jar	stingray spine	buried within a deep Barranca phase pit
108	110	0–1N/4–6W	?	C	Dist	J	4 bowls	tubular jade bead	near 102, probably associated
109	170	1–2S/2–3W	W/E	B	Dist	A		tubular jade bead	on tepetate, under altar; upper half disturbed
110	120	2–4N/2–5W	E/W	C	Stone	A	7 bowls, 1 censer	metate	
111	80	2–3N/5–6W	?	C	Stone	A	3 bowls	jade bead	skull only on ring of stones
112	170	2–4S/0–1E	N/S	B	Dist	A			no skull
113	120	2–3N/6–7W	N/S	B	D	A			upper half gone; animal carving nearby
114	70	4–6N/9.5–11W	N/S	C	Crypt	A	4 bowls, 1 olla		just outside patio wall, which precedes it

Note: Based on Arana 1973; Fash 1974; Merry de Morales 1987b. N = 22.
*Phase: Cantera (C), Barranca (B), Late Barranca/Early Cantera (LB/EC).
**Type categories: crypt; simple, direct interment (D); stone associated (stone); disturbed (dist).
***Age categories: adult (A), young adult (YA), juvenile (J), young juvenile (YJ), infant (I).

Figure 7.6. The paired burials on Terrace 25. Decrease in font size indicates later burials in each group.

was first laid out and leveled; others were buried in pits dug down into the layers of that fill. Various objects, including whole pottery vessels, stone sculptures, dog bones, piles of rocks, rock walls, and stone pavements were recovered here in addition to human bodies (Arana 1973; Fash 1974).

The published map of the patio excavations (Fash 1987:fig. 7.1) gives a first impression of randomness in the positioning of artifacts, vessels, stones, and bodies shown there (and not all buried objects were depicted in the published drawing). Nevertheless, there are recognizable patterns at the sub-patio spatial scale. For examples, Burials 105 (in the altar), 94, and 110 form three east–west–oriented (head to east) crypt interments, creating a north–south axis with the center front face of the bench/altar, spaced almost equidistant from one another. Two perpendicular burial pairs appear about one meter north of the east and west corners of the bench/altar (#103/106 and #102/97, respectively). It may not be a coincidence that the two Formative period portable sculpture fragments discovered in the patio—a headless jaguar (Grove 1987d:fig. 20.6) and a cylinder fragment resembling rattlesnake rattles (Grove 1987d:fig. 20.7)—occurred in near association with the Barranca/Cantera burial pairs outside the bench/altar (#113/111 with the jaguar sculpture; #103/106 with the rattlesnake rattle). However, these sculptures were not recognized as burial furniture or as associated in some way with the interments, despite the fact that Burial 113 and the jaguar carving were both lying directly on the natural *tepetate* layer at 115–120 cm bs, were drawn in the same one-by-two-meter unit, and were described as having been covered with earthen fill as no intrusive pits were observed in the profile to account for their positioning at different moments in time (Fash 1974).

The archaeologists considered the degree of spatial association prerequisite for inclusion in the category of "grave furniture" to be either among or very close to the skeletal remains, with evidence that the objects were deposited at the same time as the body. However, if one considers the burial to be part of a chain of actions, then contemporaneous spatially juxtaposed actions, spatially separated actions at the same time, and subsequent actions of a different kind in the same place may be implicated as part of the same citational network. The archaeological separation of human burials as distinct features forming a bounded classificatory type may therefore limit our understanding of the practices of which they were a part (for example, caches can be indistinguishable from burials; Becker 1992; Coe 1965; see Joyce, chapter 3, this volume). The immediate vicinity of the Burial 103/106 pair also includes a cluster of dog bones and a ring of stones, one of them a very large shaped slab, in the upper strata (Arana 1973). This same spot was repeatedly marked by depositions of different materials, and not all of them are necessarily archaeologically visible (see Joyce 2006 for a similar phenomenon at a Formative Honduras site). Apparently only certain locales in the patio area were subjected to such repeated, though variable, depositional actions. Thus, it was likely intended that the southeast patio wall should cover parts of three earlier burials (#96, #104, #112), just as it was no accident that the bench/altar and Burials 95 and 105 were placed over the earlier Burial 109.

In sum, acts of citation can be recognized as far more frequent and significant than what can be ascertained from mapping the burials alone if one allows for the citations to make references to other related (not identical) practices, and also to include similar practices that may have been repeated elsewhere in the area, the site, and spatial locations farther afield. This latter allowance adds a "horizontal perspective" to the network, a complement to the vertical one, dealing with how individuals and groups form connections across space as well as over time to other individuals and groups and the places associated with them. Networks of referentiality were thereby created and recapitulated, linking the burials (and the social personae they indexed) to one another and to the other objects in these spaces.

PC Str. 1

The Terrace 25 burials were considered "anomalous" because they fell outside the normal pattern of interring the dead under the floors of houses. No doubt the walled sunken patio was the locale for many ritual actions that differentiated it from other structures at the site. However, the residences, too, were sites of ritual activity, including the deposition of objects beneath the floor (Grove and Gillespie 2002), so it is unwise to draw too strong a distinction between ritual and domestic architectural settings. PC Str. 1 was an unusual residence that may have become as much a shrine as was the Terrace 25 patio (Grove and Gillespie 2002:17–18). As noted above, Terrace 25's burials are comparable to those on the Plaza Central in the use of stone slabs for lining and capping the graves (crypts) and in the pairing of burials. Crypts were not found elsewhere at the site (although there were other "stone-associated" burials; Merry de Morales 1987b:479), so the crypt burials in the one area cited the crypt burials in the other.

The PC Str. 1 excavations also revealed clusters of whole vessels, areas of stone paving, and piles of "debris" deposited upon and under the floors of the various construction stages (Merry 1975), not unlike those occurrences in the patio of Terrace 25. These intramural deposits included a portable stone sculpture, although the similarity of that act to the placement of the two stone sculptures in the Terrace 25 patio was not recognized by the Chalcatzingo Project archaeologists. Near the center of the northern half of the structure (111–113S/1E-1W) a large pit was dug down to 150 cm bs, some 20 centimeters below the earliest (Early Cantera subphase) floor (Merry 1975:fig. 4, 7). The top of this Late Cantera subphase intrusion was traced at about 70 cm bs (Grove and Cyphers Guillén 1987:27; Merry 1975:52). This feature was labeled a "trash pit," although as such it is virtually unique among the interiors of the excavated residences. It did contain cultural materials that appeared to be debris; however, at its base was an upright stone sculpture (the "winged phallus"; Grove 1987d:fig. 20.12) along with *metate* (grinding stone) fragments—such fragments commonly occurred in graves. The top edge of the pit was partially marked by stone walls, and it may have had adobe lining (Merry 1975:43). Rather than consider this pit a place for managing household trash, given that it co-occurred in space and time with Late Cantera subphase practices of interring human remains (Burial 19 at 22 cm bs partially overlies it), this feature should be seen as an intentional deposit, an act of citation that therefore referenced those burials.

In sum, the anomalous burials in open spaces outside of the residences, as at Terrace 25, were components of dynamic citational fields that included the more common private burials inside residences, most notably within PC Str. 1. Nevertheless, the differences between them must be considered within the network of references—citations are parts of a matrix of similarities and differences—within distinct social fields. The issue of visibility, noted above, remains important because "the degree of this overt visibility [of burials] relates to power" dependent on the witnessing of those acts (Hendon 2000:49). Varying scales of intimacy and visibility form a better means for assessing contrasting social settings than a simple domestic–public dichotomy of space (Joyce and Hendon 2000:155). Increasing the number of witnesses and the degree of emotionally charged memories created in funeral events requires more effective and elaborate forms of display, including "the mound as an elevated platform" (Barrett 1990:186). In this respect the open space of the Terrace 25 patio was trumped by the innovation of burials within the great linear stone-faced platform mound, PC Str. 4.

PC Str. 4

Even in its eroded state this long platform still has a commanding presence, and it looks substantially taller from the downhill view, on the lower terraces where the vast majority of the residents lived. Looking south towards the platform mound from these other terraces, one sees Cerro Chalcatzingo immediately behind with the carved reliefs on its rock surface. At least three, possibly four, Cantera phase subsurface burials were found at different locations on the top of the platform mound: relatively intact crypt Burials 39 and 40, a unique elaborate tomb structure that was looted in about 1970, and a possible additional stone-lined grave (Grove and Cyphers Guillén 1987:31). Although the traces of any surface structures have probably disappeared, one may nevertheless consider these burials to be residential in the sense that the mourners who prepared them were members of the elite social house that claimed the Plaza Central, treating the entire terrace as a spatial determinant of a house's landed property. The Chalcatzingo archaeologists assumed that the individuals interred under the surface of the platform mound lived in, or were directly associated with, the PC Str. 1 residence (Merry de Morales 1987a:100–101).

While it has been argued (above) that PC Str. 1's many burials probably do not all represent members of the immediate household, they must have been persons claimed as having membership in or alliance with the Plaza Central social house. Place of burial is always a strategic decision, and it can be used to strengthen or challenge claims to the deceased by the survivors of the multiple houses with which the deceased may have had affiliation (house of birth, house of parent, house of spouse, etc.). Disputes over bodies in such situations are not uncommon (Bloch 1995; Waterson 1995). For the members of the PC Str. 1 house to have interred so many bodies within the walls of their principal domicile was a material sign of their status and of the strength of their alliances with other houses.

The objects found in graves, especially exotics, such as jade beads or other greenstone ornaments, were likely indexes or tokens of the wealth, prestige, and identity of the house(s) that buried them. Even the PC Str. 1 graves with little other indication of "wealth" had such tokens, suggesting that greenstone objects are not indisputable markers of high social status asserted by individuals in life and death (Merry de Morales 1987a:99). Merry de Morales (1987a:99) observed that jade beads were usually singular inclusions, unbroken and placed in or near the mouth. She thereby saw them as different from other jade objects, which were usually individual fragments variously positioned in a grave. Nevertheless, the beads were equally fragments of a larger costume element—a necklace or belt. Both the beads and the other greenstone bodily adornments are incomplete, their remaining parts likely retained by the survivors (an example of "disjunction"; see Joyce, chapter 3, this volume).

Joyce (1999:41) has suggested that for Formative Mesoamerica in general, personal identities that emerge and are played out within the social field of the corporate group (house) are manifested in residential burial practices. There is a great deal of intra-interment variability at Chalcatzingo, as Merry de Morales (1987a:99) observed in her analysis, which may reflect those individual identities. However, the inclusion of the fragmented items also indicates a sense of collectivity, of being parts of a whole. The deceased joined the collective house ancestors, whose physical aspects were incorporated in the structure itself, buried under the floors. When a residential structure went through life-cycle rites of razing and burning, small greenstone earspool fragments were deposited in the floor fill before rebuilding (Grove and Gillespie 2002:17), a possible material citation linking the life cycle of residences and the human beings who inhabited them both in life and after death.

The two intact PC Str. 4 crypt burials show similarities and differences with the PC Str. 1 graves, indicating the intelligibility of certain of their aspects to the members of the house responsible for the burials even as they manifest innovations (Table 7.3).[1] Both mortuary spaces have in common crypt graves, the inclusion of jade objects, and the fact that hematite was present in the two PC Str. 4 burials and in two of the 38 subfloor interments of PC Str. 1 (#28, #33), which were also in crypts and had jade grave furniture (Merry de Morales 1987a:98) (Table 7.4). However, in those latter cases, the hematite was present only as a smear on a single vessel in Burial 28 and a clump of hematite in the crypt of Burial 33. In contrast, the complete bodies and all the grave furniture in the PC Str. 4 crypts were stained with

Table 7.3. PC Str. 4 (Platform Mound) Cantera Phase Burials

Burial	Depth (cm bs)	Quadrant	Orientation (Head/Feet)	Type	Age	Furniture	Miscellaneous
39	60	22–24S/1W-2E	W/E	Crypt	Adult	2 jadeite earspools (worn) 49 jade beads as a necklace 8 jade beads (belt) greenstone adze? on chest Laca shallow bowl Amatzinac White cantarito inside bowl	entire body stained with hematite
40	39	23–25S/3–5W	W/E	Crypt	Adult	2 jade earspools near upper left arm 1 jade bead, probably in mouth 1 tubular jadeite bead between upper legs 16 jade beads in pelvis (belt?) 11 jade beads as necklace; with knotted sinew thread concave hematite mirror atop mandible fragment of second mirror 94 tiny pieces of turquoise (mosaic) near skull piece of worked shell in one earspool Amatzinac White shallow bowl Peralta Orange cantarito inside bowl	likely crypt; covering stones destroyed in plow zone; entire body and all grave furniture stained with hematite
(no #)		east end of PC Str. 4	bone fragments found in backdirt			jadeite from a mosaic disk	2-m-long, 1.5-m-wide mound of stone with a stone wall facing east, having a stone-filled doorway; the tomb was looted in about 1970

Note: Based on Grove and Cyphers Guillén 1987; Merry de Morales 1987b.

Table 7.4. PC Str. 1 Burials 28, 33 Related to Str. 4 Burials

Burial	Depth (cm bs)	Quadrant	Orientation (Head/Feet)	Type	Age	Furniture	Miscellaneous
28	60	121–123S/1–2E	N/S	Crypt	Adult	partial jade earspool, in 2 separated pieces small jade bead between lower legs 2 obsidian blades, 1 to west of each hand Amatzinac White bowl with 4 rim lugs Amatzinac White composite bowl Amatzinac White double-loop handle censer, east side of crypt Amatzinac White double-loop handle censer, west side of crypt unslipped cantarito (not in bowl) Peralta Orange animal effigy vessel (jaguar?)	hematite smeared on interior of Amatzinac White bowl with 4 rim lugs, "killed," placed beneath skull
33	75	118–120S/1W-1E	W/E	Crypt	Adult	Olmec style serpentine figurine by right hand jade awl fragment beneath skull Amatzinac White shallow bowl unslipped cantarito inside the bowl 3 groups (4, 9, 12) of smooth pebbles in crypt 2 groups (10, 11) pebbles below crypt stones	small clump of hematite north of pelvis included as grave furniture

Note: Based on Merry de Morales 1987b.

hematite, even into the holes of the jade beads (Merry de Morales 1987b:463).

There were other important differences with the platform burials. In addition to the fact that they "obviously fall outside the normal pattern of house subfloor interments . . . the most striking aspect was the tremendous amount of jade in the two unlooted burials here (nos. 39, 40), more than was found in all other burials combined, and the fact that only these two individuals had been wearing the jade as jewelry at the time of burial" (Merry de Morales 1987a:98). This evidence is more than a material indication of the highest status individuals at Cantera phase Chalcatzingo, the conclusion reached by Merry de Morales (1987a:98). Unlike the PC Str. 1 burials, these two individuals were historically distinct persons. Their identities were implicated in their inalienable association with specific, likely named, intact items of house property that remained on their bodies in death rather than being broken up and retained by survivors. The social personae of these individuals were known and memorialized within a much wider social field than simply that of their own house (and allied houses). The increased display capabilities of interment atop the highly visible platform mound suggest the development of funerary spectacles with the capability of drawing more witness-participants into the ceremonies, while at the same time providing a spatial distance between the witnesses (below) and the officiants (above) (see Barrett 1990:186 for a similar Bronze Age British case). At the same time, the citation of practices elsewhere on the Plaza Central (crypt interment, jade inclusion) reveals a continuity, a reference to precursors, that would have muted the presumed innovation of a new political strategy in the eyes of the participants (following Mizoguchi 1993:232).

For Formative Mesoamerica, Joyce suggested that, in contrast with residential burials, "mound burials embody personal identity completely abstracted from the residential group context and its social claims . . . individuals buried in prominent nonresidential locations wear costumes that are standardized within communities and even in some cases between communities" (Joyce 1999:41). Her analysis of the Chalcatzingo PC Str. 4 burials alongside elite interments at the Middle Formative Olmec center of La Venta and at Los Naranjos, Honduras, revealed the repeated use of the same costume items, especially jade earspools and bead belts. These practices spanned cultural and linguistic differences and great spatial distances. They indicate a network of persons of an elite category whose identities therefore transcended their local spheres of influence (Joyce 1999:38–39).

Chalcatzingo's Middle Formative connections with the Gulf coast Olmecs are evident in specific similarities between bedrock carvings on the Cerro Chalcatzingo hillside and some sculptures from La Venta, the preeminent Middle Formative Olmec center (Grove 1989:134), although Chalcatzingo also developed its own repertory of motifs that has not been found on the Gulf coast (Grove 2000). In addition, the elite "burials" placed in the ritual precinct of La Venta manifest the practices of wearing complete sets of jade jewelry (earspools, bead belts) and the inclusion of red pigment in association with the grave (Drucker 1952; Drucker et al. 1959), like the PC Str. 4 platform mound burials. Nevertheless, there are also strong similarities between La Venta and some subfloor burials of Chalcatzingo PC Str. 1, as noted by Merry de Morales (1987a:103), which suggests once again that the "inside" and "outside" burials are part of the same referential network.

As previously stated, PC Str. 1 Burial 3 had at the pelvis a stone anthropomorphic head broken off a statue (Merry de Morales 1987a:103). The decapitation of statues conforms to a pattern of sculpture mutilation more commonly known among the Gulf coast Olmecs (Grove 1981). Burial 3's earlier counterpart, Burial 33, included an anthropomorphic figurine in the La Venta Olmec style, a jade awl, five groups of rounded pebbles around the crypt's interior edges, and a clump of hematite. Grove (2006) has recently compared this latter crypt and grave furniture to the cist Tomb C at La Venta (Drucker 1952:67–68, fig. 22).[2] Like Burial 33, Tomb C is a Late Middle Formative east–west–oriented, stone slab-lined tomb.

An important difference is that Tomb C (like all but one of the tombs at La Venta Complex A) was a pseudo-burial (Drucker 1952:71; Drucker et al. 1959:162). The persona of the "deceased" was indexed by costume ornaments positioned as if worn on a body, but there were no human remains (Gillespie 2008:131). Two jade earspools were positioned as if on either side of a head, and a jade bead belt and jade awl (blood-letter) were placed over what would have been the pelvis area. Tomb C also included a serpentine anthropomorphic figurine positioned "mid-body," like Chalcatzingo Burial 33, and clusters of serpentine and jade celts along the edges of the crypt suggestive of the similarly placed clusters of pebbles in Burial 33. The contents of the Tomb C cist were covered in a thick layer of red pigment. La Venta Tomb C therefore references PC Str. 1 Burial 33 rather directly, even as the "wearing" of greenstone ornaments among the La Venta pseudo-burials shows greater similarities to the Chalcatzingo PC Str. 4 burials. Because this sandstone-lined cist is unique to La Venta (the sandstone having to be imported), whereas crypt burials using abundant natural stone are not uncommon at Chalcatzingo or elsewhere in the highlands (Grove 1987a:435), one may suggest that the Olmecs of La Venta cited their Chalcatzingo counterparts, rather than the usual interpretation that Chalcatzingo's elites were influenced by ideas and practices originating on the Gulf coast. As for Terrace 25, its stone-walled sunken patio and bench/altar share greater similarities with sites in Guerrero state to the west than with Olmec centers to the southeast (Fash 1987:82; Grove 1989:142–143, 2000:287).

Conclusion

At Chalcatzingo, the notion of residential burial should not be confined to the space of a residential structure. Although subfloor burial was the common pattern, the spatial domains of the long-lived social houses were the individual human-made terraces, and other mortuary spaces were created on some of those terraces, notably on the Plaza Central and Terrace 25. Rather than pursue the normative, synoptic, and classificatory approach to the Formative Chalcatzingo burial corpus, I adopted a citational approach to investigate small-scale patterns evident in mortuary practices as repeated actions over time. Joyce and Lopiparo argued that attention to "figures of sequences of action in time . . . shift[s] our emphasis productively . . . to attending to what people were doing as they recapitulated valued practices of the past and innovated within the constraints exercised by past practices and articulated traditions" (Joyce and Lopiparo 2005:372).

By examining some of the Chalcatzingo mortuary data as repeated practices, insights are made into vertical connections—especially with the paired burials—and horizontal connections linking burial practices that transcend the various types of mortuary spaces across the site. Despite the substantial differences implicated in practices of hidden residential subfloor burial and funerary displays in more open areas, the "anomalous" public burials in the platform mound and the patio area were shown to be components of citational referential networks that included the private burials inside the structures. Moreover, the mortuary rituals themselves were entwined with other depositional practices in these same spaces, including the burial of pottery vessels, portable stone sculptures, and animals (or their body parts), which become more intelligible to us in this context. This practice-based approach therefore transcends classificatory limitations in the analytical distinctions separating "inside" and "outside" burials, residential and nonresidential spaces, and "mortuary" and "non-mortuary" deposits.

Acknowledgments

I am grateful to David C. Grove for sharing his personal recollections, slides, and field notes from the Chalcatzingo Archaeological Project; for his patience in answering my many questions about the project; and for his comments on early drafts of this chapter. I remain responsible for any errors or omissions. I also wish to thank Joyce C. White and Ron L. Adams for inviting me to participate in their 2007 SAA symposium on residential burial, and Ron and Stacie King for taking on the task of bringing the papers to publication.

Notes

1. The operating assumption is that the PC Str. 4 burials postdate at least some of the PC Str. 1 crypt burials. While this assumption is reasonable, the relative chronology of burials in the two structures cannot be determined. PC Str. 4 was not built as a burial mound, and its earliest construction predates the Cantera phase by centuries.

2. Another similarity between burials at La Venta and Chalcatzingo involves a certain grave inclusion: the placing of a *cantarito* (small bottle) within a shallow bowl as the sole ceramic offerings in Burial 10 and in crypt Burial 33 in PC Str. 1 and in the two intact crypt burials on PC Str. 4, Burials 39 and 40. Significantly, the same vessel pair constituted the lone pottery artifacts in La Venta Offering 5 (Drucker et al. 1959:162–167), another pseudo-burial in Complex A that predates the Tomb C feature (Merry de Morales 1987a:99; see Grove and Gillespie 1992:197). Although the *cantarito* in a shallow dish was considered to be a little-understood marker of high status at Chalcatzingo (Merry de Morales 1987a:99), it may reference more directly the Plaza Central social house, given that no *cantaritos* at all were found in the Cantera phase graves on Terrace 25 (Grove and Gillespie 1992:197–198).

References

Arana, Raul
1973 Terrace 25 Field Notes. Chalcatzingo Archaeological Project. Notes in the possession of David C. Grove, University of Florida.

Ashmore, Wendy, and Pamela L. Geller
2005 Social Dimensions of Mortuary Space. *In* Interacting with the Dead: Perspectives on Mortuary Archaeology for the New Millennium. Gordon F. M. Rakita, Jane E. Buikstra, Lane A. Beck, and Sloan R. Williams, eds. Pp. 81–92. Gainesville: University Press of Florida.

Barrett, John C.
1990 The Monumentality of Death: The Character of Early Bronze Age Mortuary Mounds in Southern Britain. World Archaeology 22:179–189.
1994 Fragments from Antiquity: An Archaeology of Social Life in Britain, 2900–1200 BC. Oxford: Blackwell.

Becker, Marshall J.
1992 Burials as Caches; Caches as Burials: A New Interpretation of the Meaning of Ritual Deposits among the Classic Period Lowland Maya. *In* New Theories on the Ancient Maya. Elin C. Danien and Robert J. Sharer, eds. Pp. 185–196. University Museum Symposium Series, 3. Philadelphia: The University Museum, University of Pennsylvania.

Binford, Lewis R.
1971 Mortuary Practices: Their Study and Their Potential. *In* Approaches to the Social Dimensions of Mortuary Practices. James A. Brown, ed. Pp. 6–29. Memoirs of the Society for American Archaeology, 25. Washington, DC.

Bloch, Maurice
1995 People into Places: Zafimaniry Concepts of Clarity. *In* The Anthropology of Landscape: Perspectives on Place and Space. Eric Hirsch and Michael O'Hanlon, eds. Pp. 63–77. Oxford: Clarendon Press.

Brown, James A.
1995 On Mortuary Analysis—With Special Reference to the Saxe-Binford Research Program. *In* Regional Approaches to Mortuary Analysis. Lane Anderson Beck, ed. Pp. 3–26. New York: Plenum.

Butler, Judith
1993 Bodies That Matter: On the Discursive Limits of "Sex." New York: Routledge.

Cannon, Aubrey
1989 The Historical Dimension in Mortuary Expressions of Status and Sentiment. Current Anthropology 30:437–458.

Chapman, John C.
1994 The Living, the Dead, and the Ancestors: Time, Life Cycles and the Mortuary Domain in Later European Prehistory. *In* Ritual and Remembrance: Responses to Death in Human Societies. Jon Davies, ed. Pp. 40–85. Sheffield, U.K.: Sheffield Academic Press.
2000 Tension at Funerals: Social Practices and the Subversion of Community Structure in Later

Hungarian Prehistory. *In* Agency in Archaeology. Marcia-Anne Dobres and John Robb, eds. Pp. 169–195. London: Routledge.

Chapman, Robert
2005 Mortuary Analysis: A Matter of Time? *In* Interacting with the Dead: Perspectives on Mortuary Archaeology for the New Millennium. Gordon F. M. Rakita, Jane E. Buikstra, Lane A. Beck, and Sloan R. Williams, eds. Pp. 25–40. Gainesville: University Press of Florida.

Chapman, Robert, and Klavs Randsborg
1981 Approaches to the Archaeology of Death. *In* The Archaeology of Death. Robert Chapman, Ian Kinnes, and Klavs Randsborg, eds. Pp. 1–24. Cambridge: Cambridge University Press.

Chesson, Meredith S., ed.
2001 Social Memory, Identity, and Death: Anthropological Perspectives on Mortuary Rituals. Archeological Papers of the American Anthropological Association, 10. Arlington, VA: American Anthropological Association.

Coe, William R.
1965 Caches and Offertory Practices of the Maya Lowlands. *In* Handbook of Middle American Indians, vol. 2: The Archaeology of Southern Mesoamerica, part 1. Robert Wauchope and Gordon R. Willey, eds. Pp. 462–469. Austin: University of Texas Press.

Cyphers Guillén, Ann, and David C. Grove
1987 Chronology and Cultural Phases at Chalcatzingo. *In* Ancient Chalcatzingo. David C. Grove, ed. Pp. 56–62. Austin: University of Texas Press.

Drucker, Philip
1952 La Venta, Tabasco: A Study of Olmec Ceramics and Art. Smithsonian Institution Bureau of American Ethnology Bulletin 153. Washington, DC: Government Printing Office.

Drucker, Philip, Robert F. Heizer, and Robert J. Squier
1959 Excavations at La Venta, Tabasco, 1955. Smithsonian Institution Bureau of American Ethnology Bulletin 170. Washington, DC: Government Printing Office.

Fash, William, Jr.
1974 Terrace 25 Field Notes. Chalcatzingo Archaeological Project. Notes in the possession of David C. Grove, University of Florida.
1987 The Altar and Associated Features. *In* Ancient Chalcatzingo. David C. Grove, ed. Pp. 82–94. Austin: University of Texas Press.

Gell, Alfred
1998 Art and Agency: An Anthropological Theory. Oxford: Clarendon Press.

Gilchrist, Roberta, and Barney Sloane
2005 Requiem: The Medieval Monastic Cemetery in Britain. London: Museum of London Archaeology Service.

Gillespie, Susan D.
2000a Beyond Kinship: An Introduction. *In* Beyond Kinship: Social and Material Reproduction in House Societies. Rosemary A. Joyce and Susan D. Gillespie, eds. Pp. 1–21. Philadelphia: University of Pennsylvania Press.
2000b Maya "Nested Houses": The Ritual Construction of Place. *In* Beyond Kinship: Social and Material Reproduction in House Societies. Rosemary A. Joyce and Susan D. Gillespie, eds. Pp. 135–160. Philadelphia: University of Pennsylvania Press.
2000c Rethinking Ancient Maya Social Organization: Replacing "Lineage" with "House." American Anthropologist 102:467–484.
2002 Body and Soul among the Maya: Keeping the Spirits in Place. *In* The Space and Place of Death. Helaine Silverman and David B. Small, eds. Pp. 67–78. Archeological Papers of the American Anthropological Association, 11. Arlington, VA: American Anthropological Association.
2007 When Is a House? *In* The Durable House: House Society Models in Archaeology. Robin A. Beck Jr., ed. Pp. 25–50. Occasional Paper 35. Carbondale: Center for Archaeological Investigations, Southern Illinois University.
2008 History in Practice: Ritual Deposition at La Venta Complex A. *In* Memory Work: Archaeologies of Material Practices. Barbara J. Mills and William H. Walker, eds. Pp. 109–136. Santa Fe, NM: School for Advanced Research Press.
2009 Chalcatzingo, Morelos, durante el Formativo: Una "Sociedad de Casas." *In* Las Sociedades Complejas del Occidente de México en el Mundo Mesoamericano: Homenaje al Dr. Phil C. Weigand. Eduardo Williams, Lorenza López

Mestas, and Rodrigo Esparza, eds. Pp. 393–410. Zamora, Mexico: El Colegio de Michoacán.

Goldstein, Lynne G.
1981 One-Dimensional Archaeology and Multi-Dimensional People: Spatial Organisation and Mortuary Analysis. *In* The Archaeology of Death. Robert Chapman, Ian Kinnes, and Klavs Randsborg, eds. Pp. 53–69. Cambridge: Cambridge University Press.

Grove, David C.
1981 Olmec Monuments: Mutilation as a Clue to Meaning. *In* The Olmec and Their Neighbors: Essays in Honor of Matthew W. Stirling. Elizabeth P. Benson, ed. Pp. 49–68. Washington, DC: Dumbarton Oaks.
1984 Chalcatzingo: Excavations on the Olmec Frontier. London: Thames and Hudson.
1987a Chalcatzingo in a Broader Perspective. *In* Ancient Chalcatzingo. David C. Grove, ed. Pp. 434–442. Austin: University of Texas Press.
1987b Comments on the Site and Its Organization. *In* Ancient Chalcatzingo. David C. Grove, ed. Pp. 420–433. Austin: University of Texas Press.
1987c Introduction. *In* Ancient Chalcatzingo. David C. Grove, ed. Pp. 1–5. Austin: University of Texas Press.
1987d Ground Stone Artifacts. *In* Ancient Chalcatzingo. David C. Grove, ed. Pp. 329–342. Austin: University of Texas Press.
1989 Chalcatzingo and Its Olmec Connection. *In* Regional Perspectives on the Olmec. Robert J. Sharer and David C. Grove, eds. Pp. 122–147. Cambridge: Cambridge University Press.
2000 Faces of the Earth at Chalcatzingo, Mexico: Serpents, Caves, and Mountains in Middle Formative Period Iconography. *In* Olmec Art and Archaeology in Mesoamerica. John E. Clark and Mary E. Pye, eds. Pp. 277–295. Washington, DC: National Gallery of Art.
2006 Chalcatzingo y los Olmecas. Paper presented in the Encuentro Internacional de Olmequistas, Xalapa, Veracruz, Mexico.

Grove, David C., ed.
1987 Ancient Chalcatzingo. Austin: University of Texas Press.

Grove, David C., and Ann Cyphers Guillén
1987 The Excavations. *In* Ancient Chalcatzingo. David C. Grove, ed. Pp. 21–55. Austin: University of Texas Press.

Grove, David C., and Susan D. Gillespie
1992 Archaeological Indicators of Formative Period Elites: A Perspective from Central Mexico. *In* Mesoamerican Elites: An Archaeological Assessment. Diane Z. Chase and Arlen F. Chase, eds. Pp. 191–205. Norman: University of Oklahoma Press.
2002 Middle Formative Domestic Ritual at Chalcatzingo, Morelos. *In* Domestic Ritual in Ancient Mesoamerica. Patricia Plunket, ed. Pp. 11–19. Cotsen Institute of Archaeology, Monograph 46. Los Angeles: University of California.

Hendon, Julia A.
2000 Having and Holding: Storage, Memory, Knowledge, and Social Relations. American Anthropologist 102:42–53.

Husserl, Edmund
1964 The Phenomenology of Internal Time-Consciousness. Martin Heidegger, ed. James S. Churchill, trans. Bloomington: Indiana University Press.

Jones, Andrew
2001 Drawn from Memory: The Archaeology of Aesthetics and the Aesthetics of Archaeology in Earlier Bronze Age Britain and the Present. World Archaeology 33:334–356.

Joyce, Rosemary A.
1999 Social Dimensions of Pre-Classic Burials. *In* Social Patterns in Pre-Classic Mesoamerica. David C. Grove and Rosemary A. Joyce, eds. Pp. 15–47. Washington, DC: Dumbarton Oaks.
2000 Gender and Power in Prehispanic Mesoamerica. Austin: University of Texas Press.
2001 Burying the Dead at Tlatilco: Social Memory and Social Identities. *In* Social Memory, Identity, and Death: Anthropological Perspectives on Mortuary Rituals. Meredith S. Chesson, ed. Pp. 12–26. Archeological Papers of the American Anthropological Association, 10. Arlington, VA: American Anthropological Association.
2006 Struggling with the Memory of Things. Paper presented at the 10th Theoretical Archaeology Group Conference, University of Exeter, Exeter, UK.

Joyce, Rosemary A., and Julia A. Hendon
2000 Heterarchy, History, and Material Reality: "Communities" in Late Classic Honduras. *In* The Archaeology of Communities: A New World Perspective. Marcello A. Canuto and Jason Yaeger, eds. Pp. 143–160. London: Routledge.

Joyce, Rosemary A., and Jeanne Lopiparo
2005 PostScript: Doing Agency in Archaeology. Journal of Archaeological Method and Theory 12:365–374.

Low, Setha M., and Denise Lawrence-Zúñiga
2003 Locating Culture. *In* The Anthropology of Space and Place: Locating Culture. Setha M. Low and Denise Lawrence-Zúñiga, eds. Pp. 1–47. Malden, MA: Blackwell.

McAnany, Patricia A.
1995 Living with the Ancestors: Kinship and Kingship in Ancient Maya Society. Austin: University of Texas Press.
1998 Ancestors and the Classic Maya Built Environment. *In* Function and Meaning in Classic Maya Architecture. Stephen D. Houston, ed. Pp. 271–298. Washington, DC: Dumbarton Oaks.

McAnany, Patricia A., Rebecca Storey, and Angela Lockard
1999 Mortuary Ritual and Family Politics at Formative and Early Classic K'axob, Belize. Ancient Mesoamerica 10:129–146.

Merry, Marcia Paulette
1975 Investigation of a Middle Formative Area of Burials, Chalcatzingo, Morelos, Mexico. M.A. thesis, Department of Anthropology, University of the Americas, Cholula, Puebla, Mexico.

Merry de Morales, Marcia
1987a Chalcatzingo Burials as Indicators of Social Ranking. *In* Ancient Chalcatzingo. David C. Grove, ed. Pp. 95–113. Austin: University of Texas Press.
1987b The Chalcatzingo Burials. *In* Ancient Chalcatzingo. David C. Grove, ed. Pp. 457–480. Austin: University of Texas Press.

Mizoguchi, Koji
1993 Time in the Reproduction of Mortuary Practices. World Archaeology 25:223–235.

Mock, Shirley Boteler
1998 Prelude. *In* The Sowing and the Dawning: Termination, Dedication, and Transformation in the Archaeological and Ethnographic Record of Mesoamerica. Shirley Boteler Mock, ed. Pp. 3–18. Albuquerque: University of New Mexico Press.

Munn, Nancy D.
1986 The Fame of Gawa: A Symbolic Study of Value Transformation in a Massim (Papua New Guinea) Society. Cambridge: Cambridge University Press.

Parker Pearson, Mike
1999 The Archaeology of Death and Burial. College Station: Texas A&M University Press.

Prindiville, Mary, and David C. Grove
1987 The Settlement and Its Architecture. *In* Ancient Chalcatzingo. David C. Grove, ed. Pp. 63–81. Austin: University of Texas Press.

Rakita, Gordon F. M., and Jane E. Buikstra
2005 Introduction. *In* Interacting with the Dead: Perspectives on Mortuary Archaeology for the New Millennium. Gordon F. M. Rakita, Jane E. Buikstra, Lane A. Beck, and Sloan R. Williams, eds. Pp. 1–11. Gainesville: University Press of Florida.

Saxe, Arthur A.
1970 Social Dimensions of Mortuary Practices. Ph.D. dissertation, Department of Anthropology, University of Michigan, Ann Arbor.

Silverman, Helaine, and David B. Small, eds.
2002 The Space and Place of Death. Archeological Papers of the American Anthropological Association, 11. Arlington, VA: American Anthropological Association.

Strathern, Andrew J.
1994 Keeping the Body in Mind. Social Anthropology (Journal of the European Association of Social Anthropologists) 2:43–53.

Waterson, Roxana
1995 Houses, Graves, and the Limits of Kinship Groupings among the Sa'dan Toraja. Bijdragen tot de Taal-, Land- en Volkenkunde 151:194–217.

8

A Family Affair: The Use of Intramural Funerary Chambers in Mesopotamia during the Late Third and Early Second Millennia B.C.E.

Nicola Laneri
Istituto Italiano per l'Africa e l'Oriente—Rome, Italy

ABSTRACT

Among ancient and modern societies, the transformation in funerary customs can represent a clear indicator of changes in the social fabric of a given society. It is within this perspective that archaeologists should thus correlate the information available from the "world of the living" with those recognizable in funerary contexts. For the purpose of reaching this target, the focus of this paper is on the residential graves found in Mesopotamian contexts of the late third and early second millennia BCE, and on the relationship between changes in funerary customs, socioeconomic transformations and the emergence of new social groups among Mesopotamian communities during this specific period. [ancient Mesopotamia, funerary chambers, ancestors, household, merchants]

The increasing interest in the study of residential burials is demonstrated not only by this edited volume but also by other recent publications that interpret the disposal of the dead within houses or city limits of ancient societies (Bartoloni 2008; Gillespie 2001; Hodder and Cessford 2004; Kuijt 2001; Laneri 2007a; Lull 2000; McAnany 1995). However, the focus of these funerary studies as well as those concentrated on the analysis of more "traditional" extramural funerary depositions has been on specific burial customs rather than the dynamic processes encountered when dealing with socioeconomic reasons for changes in burial practices. Furthermore, synchronic analyses of burial customs have outnumbered those oriented towards defining a diachronic and transformational approach in the relationship between changes in burial customs and transformation in the community's social organization (Laneri 2007b). This is particularly evident when archaeologists face changes in the disposal of buried corpses from extramural to intramural or residential funerary depositions. More specifically, the transformation of burial customs, from communal extramural cemetery to residential burials built within private dwellings, should be interpreted as an important indicator of changes that have taken place in the socioeconomic dynamics of a given society. In fact, the necessity of incorporating within a family's house selected dead, thereby transforming them into familial ancestors, appears as pivotal to the reinforcement of the household lineage in moments of dramatic socioeconomic transformation. This is for example the case of the ancient Near East during the late third and early second millennia B.C.E., at which time there is an increasing visibility of emerging social groups (i.e., private merchants and entrepreneurs [Adams 1974; Lamberg-Karlovsky 1996]) evident from both written sources (e.g., the written cuneiform tablets of private Assyrian merchants in the Anatolian commercial harbor of Kültepe/Kanish of the early second millennium B.C.E.) and the archaeological data (e.g., the transformation of the urban fabric of numerous Mesopotamian city-states characterized by the presence of large private dwellings inhabited by merchants). Furthermore, it is during this phase that we witness the increasing presence of residential funerary chambers built within private dwellings at numerous Mesopotamian sites.

ARCHEOLOGICAL PAPERS OF THE AMERICAN ANTHROPOLOGICAL ASSOCIATION, Vol. 20, Issue 1, pp. 121–135, ISSN 1551-823X, online ISSN 1551-8248. DOI: 10.1111/j.1551-8248.2011.01031.x.

Within this context, the presence of residential funerary chambers within private dwellings is central for the construction of the social memory of the household (see Adams and Kusumawati, chapter 2, this volume). In this case, we should follow Hodder and Cessford's (2004:31) perspective that envisions memory as "an active process of memorializing that is socially embedded." In fact, the mnemonic process of remembering the ancestors by the community of the living is not just mental, but rather a practical and active one strongly entwined with the daily activities of the household (see King, chapter 4, this volume). Thus, after a first phase of physical and mental incorporation of the dead ancestors within the "house" (see White and Eyre, chapter 5, this volume), their continuous remembrance and commemoration "contribute to a series of actions through which the dwelling itself was made more solid over time" (see Joyce, chapter 3, this volume).

Thus, the aim of this chapter is to investigate this general theoretical perspective through an empirical analysis of specific case studies from Mesopotamian contexts belonging to the late third and early second millennia B.C.E. More specifically, I will emphasize the role that residential funerary chambers had in reinforcing kin-based social relationships among descent groups and how the construction of funerary crypts within private dwellings had the purpose of affirming socioeconomic differentiations between emerging families, such as those of private merchants and entrepreneurs, and institutional authorities. Using a diachronic perspective, I will first emphasize the relationship between the construction of residential funerary chambers in private dwellings and changes in economic subsistence strategies as evidenced by the case of a northern Mesopotamian city-state (i.e., Titriş Höyük) during the second half of the third millennium B.C.E. In the second section of this chapter, my focus will shift to the construction of residential funerary crypts and the memorialization of ancestors in early second millennium B.C.E. Mesopotamian societies, for the purpose of affirming the socioeconomic and political role conquered by new social classes of merchants and entrepreneurs in an environment until then controlled only by institutional power (i.e., the temple and the palace).

A Transforming Society

The period ranging from the third to the early second millennia B.C.E. is of fundamental importance to the development of complex societies within ancient Mesopotamia (Stein 2004; Yoffee 2005) (Figure 8.1). It is during this phase that Mesopotamian societies express an increasing level of socioeconomic complexity characterized by the first known forms of kingship as well as systems of long-distance commercial exchange that facilitated the movement of commodities and finished products between Mesopotamian city-states and communities located in Anatolia, Iran, Afghanistan, and the Gulf regions.

In fact, it is the establishment of long-distance trade during the third and early second millennia B.C.E. that stimulates the economic development of Mesopotamian societies that did not have direct access to raw materials and whose economic subsistence was based on a combination of agricultural and pastoral activities (Adams 1974; Algaze 2008; Edens 1992; Lamberg-Karlovsky 1996; Larsen 1987; Van de Mieroop 1997). The combined use of archaeological and textual data allows an interpretation of long-distance trade in which, using Lamberg-Karlovsky's words, "by the second half of the third millennium both state personnel and private agents were involved" (Lamberg-Karlovsky 1996:86). According to Van Driel, it is during this specific archaeological phase that "gains [in long-distance trade] were for trading agents (i.e., merchant = *dam-gàr* in Sumerian and *tamkāru* in Akkadian), not for the institution [i.e., the palace or the temple]" (Van Driel 1999:31).

In this perspective, trade appears as a driving force in establishing the economic power of specific Mesopotamian cities, especially during the late third and early second millennia B.C.E. (Van de Mieroop 1992). The entwined relations between private and public created a complex economic system in which the value of certain commodities was based on the relationship between supply and demand regulated by specific prices (Goddeeris 2002:382–385). This system of prices was based on forms of equivalences mostly regulated by the use of silver as the primary form of pre-coinage currency (Powell 1999; Veenhof 1999). Another element that can be added to the picture of this system is the different forms of loans that could be issued by both private and public institutions (Van de Mieroop 1992:204). Loans were usually made in the form of silver (and in minor cases barley), and followed two main types (Goddeeris 2002:385–390): (a) consumptive loans (for the survival of families following a poor harvest season) and (b) commercial or entrepreneurial loans.

As a result, during the early second millennium B.C.E. merchants had the power to collect taxes and lend money. Furthermore, within this system merchants received a grant from the palace to acquire and convert specific commodities acquired from gardeners, fishermen, and shepherds (e.g., dates, vegetables, fish, and wool) into silver (Van de Mieroop 1992:113).

The data available from the early second millennium B.C.E. bring to light a more complex picture in which newly wealthy individuals and their associated families have

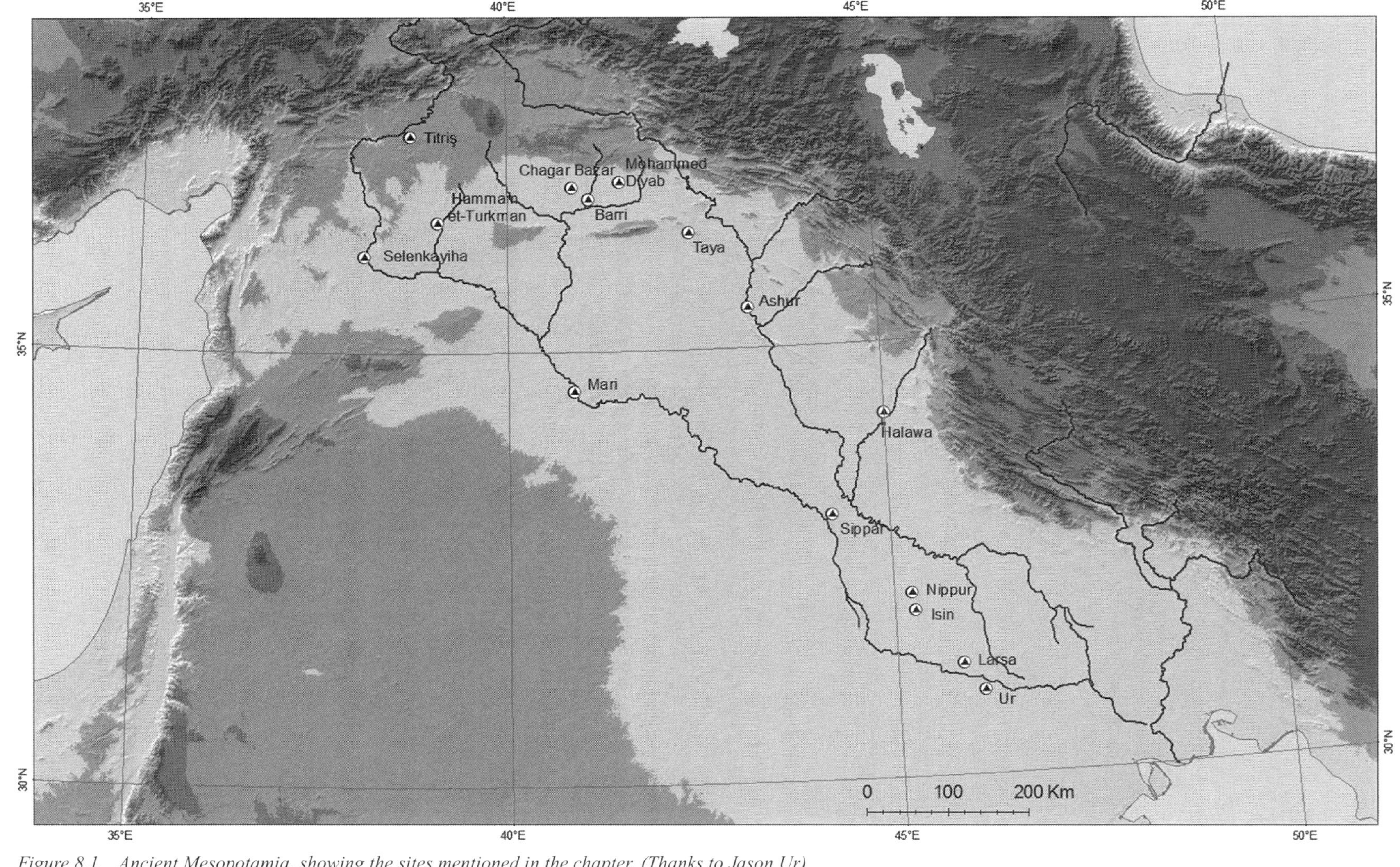

Figure 8.1. Ancient Mesopotamia, showing the sites mentioned in the chapter. (Thanks to Jason Ur)

greater visibility and independence from the palatial and temple authorities, although the latter were still pivotal in the control and organization of the subsistence economy (Van de Mieroop 1992:77–119). The independence of these households is particularly emphasized by their economic surpluses obtained from agricultural productions and, then, invested in "long distance trade and eventually metal and cloth industry" (Goddeeris 2002:402). In this perspective, "entrepreneurial activities" (Stone 1999) appear to be fundamental in generating the economic prosperity of private households that challenged the economic power of central authorities in Mesopotamia both before and after political centralization (e.g., the Akkad and Ur III dynasty during the second half of the third millennium B.C.E., and the Old Babylonian dynasty during the first quarter of the second millennium B.C.E.). Thus, as pointed out by Lamberg-Karlovsky, in ancient Mesopotamia "during times of a powerful state, the state attempted to monopolize all property and establish all production by state command; when the state was weak property and production fell into the hands of private families and individuals" (Lamberg-Karlovsky 1996:97).

In terms of the archaeological record, the settlement pattern of the major Mesopotamian regional city-states of the period considered in this chapter is mostly characterized by the presence of temples, palaces, and administrative centers, generally located at one edge of the ancient site, with the remainder of the city used to house an increasing presence of private dwellings divided into broader neighborhoods (Stone 1999:210–219). These neighborhoods were clustered around the public areas (e.g., at Titriş Höyük, Ur, Nippur; Matney and Algaze 1995; Stone 1987), although in the case of the site of Larsa, the houses of wealthy families were located in a secluded space at the northeastern edge of the city, with houses separated from each other by open spaces (Calvet 2003:figs. 3–4). Another important feature of town planning during the third and second millennia B.C.E. is the use of fortification systems in order to protect the city and, in some circumstances, an inner citadel in which the public buildings were located (Cooper 2006).

The urban fabric of this period was also characterized by the creation of commercial ports within or near the city-states. Although it is difficult to identify the exact location of markets from archaeological excavations, the commercial port (*karum* in Akkadian) of the Assyrian merchants was discovered at the early second millennium B.C.E. central Anatolian site of Kültepe/Kanish (Özguç 2003). It is at this locale that archaeologists have found thousands of written cuneiform tablets within the private dwellings documenting the long-distance commercial exchange that occurred between the Assyrian private merchants and the local Anatolian counterpart (Larsen 1987; Michel 2001). Even though this site is not in Mesopotamia proper, it was used by traders coming from the northern Mesopotamian site of Assur, and it is possible to hypothesize that other commercial harbors were located in a similar position outside of the main citadel (Van de Mieroop 1992:188–194).

When viewed together, these data demonstrate the increasing role played by wealthy families in both the political and the mercantile issues of Mesopotamian cities during this particular phase (Goddeeris 2002:178–179). This is recognizable in both the archaeological data (e.g., the increasing visibility of private dwellings in the urban fabric) and the written sources (e.g., the cuneiform tablets written by the private Assyrian merchants found at the site of Kültepe/Kanish) (Stone 1996).

A main feature of this period's private dwellings is the frequent occurrence of residential funerary depositions, which appear to be fundamental for understanding the socioeconomic importance gained by specific segments of Mesopotamian communities in this chronological phase (Laneri 2007a). These residential funerary depositions can vary in type and mostly consist of large constructed funerary chambers, simple pits, *pithoi* or clay coffins, and, for the subadults, urns or cooking pots placed as subfloor interments. In addition, the graves are usually clustered in specific sectors of the house, primarily in the back. In the case of the funerary chambers, we encounter the custom of multiple depositions, which means the tomb was reopened to bury the most recent deceased either in an articulated or disarticulated manner.

The Case of Titriş Höyük

As demonstrated by archaeological research, the use of residential graves has been widely embedded with the construction of social identities by numerous Near Eastern communities since prehistoric times (Hodder and Cessford 2004). However, in Mesopotamia, it is during the third millennium B.C.E. that the burial custom of disposing selected deceased in graves built within the private dwellings is more coherently recognizable in the archaeological record. In southern Mesopotamia, residential graves are found at sites like Kish, Khafajah, and Abu Salabikh since the beginning of the third millennium B.C.E., and are mostly located within large private dwellings that are built, as in the case of Khafajah, near the religious center (Algaze 1983–84; Delougaz et al. 1967; Postgate 1980).

The residential graves found inside private dwellings in northern Mesopotamian sites are recognizable during the second half of the third millennium B.C.E., as is visible at sites like Tell Taya, Titriş Höyük, Selenkahiye, and Mari (Jean-Marie 1999; Laneri 2004, 2007a; Reade 1982; Van Loon 2001). These residential funerary chambers are a key element in structuring the social memory of specific groups in the urbanization process that marks northern Mesopotamian city-states during the Early Bronze Age. In this social transformation, the urban fabric of northern Mesopotamian city-states is divided into a fortified citadel that incorporates the public buildings (i.e., the palace, the temples, and the administrative sectors), a surrounding area that is marked by the presence of well-planned neighborhoods with private dwellings, and an outer fortification system (Cooper 2006; Matney and Algaze 1995; Reade 1982; Ristvet 2007).

One of the best examples of these northern Mesopotamian city-states is the site of Titriş Höyük located in the Urfa province in southeastern Turkey (Figure 8.1). Here archaeologists have been able to bring to light a coherent stratigraphy of layers belonging to the Early Bronze Age period (i.e., the entire third millennium B.C.E.), thereby presenting a unique opportunity for a truly diachronic perspective on the transformation of the settlement's socioeconomic organization (Algaze et al. 2001; Laneri 2004, 2007a; Matney and Algaze 1995).

During the Mid-Early Bronze Age (hereinafter MEBA, ca. 2600–2400 B.C.E.) the settlement reached its maximum extension of about 43 hectares. Corresponding to this phase is the construction of a possible public building with massive foundation walls recovered in the Outer Town (Matney and Algaze 1995). The site was also characterized by a series of dispersed suburbs (about nine) that were probably used for housing specialized workshops, as demonstrated by the discovery of a flint workshop situated approximately 400 meters east of the site's limits (Algaze et al. 2001).

The presence of extramural cemeteries is another important feature in determining the settlement pattern of this phase (Honça and Algaze 1998). The largest of these is located about 400 meters west of the settlement and consists of a series of funerary chambers, smaller cist graves, and *pithoi*. The topographic distribution of these graves is based on clusters of small cist graves and *pithoi* located about 20 meters from and surrounding a large funerary chamber (Laneri 2004).

The dramatic transformation that occurred in the following Late-Early Bronze Age period (hereinafter LEBA, i.e., 2400–2100 B.C.E.) is characterized by the contraction of the site—now totaling about 35 hectares—and by a complete re-foundation of the city's urban fabric (Matney and Algaze 1995). The whole settlement was then rebuilt following a city plan characterized by the construction of a thick fortification structure over a stone foundation, by a possible relocation of the public buildings to the main mound, and by the construction of private dwellings based on standardized measurements that are also recognizable at other northern Mesopotamian sites (e.g., Tell Taya; Reade 1982:77, fig. 58). These were made up of a main courtyard linked to the residential, kitchen, storage, and working areas (Figure 8.2). Specialized working activities were now performed either within the private houses or in specific areas dedicated to specialized production activities (e.g., pottery and flint-knapping; Algaze et al. 2001:37–40). The complete re-planning of Titriş Höyük's urban fabric with greater emphasis on the construction of large private dwellings appears to the archaeologists as a clear example of the close involvement of the private households in planning the whole city in collaboration with the royal authorities. In addition, we witness a radical transformation in the economic subsistence with an increase in the production of wine, probably exchanged as a precious commodity with other Mesopotamian city-states. This is demonstrated by the higher number of carbonized grapes, pips, and seeds from among the paleobotanical samples found in the LEBA contexts as well as by the presence of plaster basins unearthed in numerous single private dwellings of this phase (Algaze et al. 2001:41–44; Laneri 2007a) (Figure 8.3). The presence of tartaric acid confirmed through the analysis of one sample taken from the surface of one of the six plaster basins found at Titriş Höyük reinforces the idea that these architectural features were most probably used for the processing of grapes related to the production of wine (Matney and Algaze 1995).

The important use of wine as an elite commodity in Near Eastern culture during this period is clearly evident from both archaeological and written data available from contexts dating to the mid-late third and the early second millennia B.C.E. Texts from the early second millennium B.C.E. clearly indicate that wine was produced in southeastern Anatolia and exported by private merchants from local city-states (e.g., the site of Carchemish located along the Euphrates River about 70 kilometers southwest of Titriş Höyük) to other Mesopotamian capitals (Dalley 2002:90–91; Forlanini 2006:163). The information available from the textual data is confirmed by the increasing presence of elements associated with grape processing probably linked to wine production, such as plaster basins and pits, as well as with wine consumption, such as Caliciform Ware and red burnished tall double-handled cups (i.e., the *depa amphikypella*), found at numerous sites in this broad region (Laneri 2007a; Zettler and Miller 1995). Thus, when viewed together, these elements can be interpreted as clear signs of a transformation in the economic activities of some of these northern Mesopotamian sites most probably linked to an

Figure 8.2. The Lower Town of Titriş Höyük, highlighting three residential funerary chambers (A, B, and C). (After Laneri 2004:tavola 4)

intensive use of Mediterranean polyculture that characterized the Bronze Age economy of numerous Mediterranean societies (Gilman 1981; Laneri 2007a).

However, it is from the transformation in the funerary practices between the MEBA and the LEBA that we recognize the clearest indicator of social change at Titriş Höyük. At this time, the extramural cemeteries used during the MEBA were abandoned, and residential funerary depositions of selected deceased were found inside of Titriş Höyük houses (Figures 8.2, 8.4). Most of these human depositions are found inside funerary chambers planned and constructed together with the private dwellings. The funerary chambers are usually located in a single room or inside the main courtyard, and are reachable through an entrance *dromos* composed of a few steps going down. Each private dwelling contains between one and three of these funerary chambers (Laneri 2007a).

Titriş Höyük's residential graves contain multiple depositions, with a maximum of eight individuals buried inside one tomb. The skeletons were buried inside of the funerary chamber. The analysis of the skeletal remains has not generally furnished any relevant sex and/or age distinctions among the dead placed within the intramural tombs (see charts in Hončа and Algaze 1998:table 1-2). An important element of transformation between these two archaeological phases is an increase in the mortality rate of young adults. This is probably related to poorer living and working conditions within the site during the later phase (Hončа and Algaze 1998:116–117, table 3). In terms of the skeletons' deposition within the funerary chamber, they were disposed either in an articulated, primary deposition—as commonly seen in the depositions of the Lower Town—or in the manner of a disarticulated, secondary deposition, typical of the tombs of the Outer Town. A distinction between the funerary chambers of the Lower and Outer Towns is also confirmed by richer furnishings within the tombs of the Lower Town as compared to those located in the Outer Town (Laneri 2007a:250–253).

In regards to the funerary goods discovered within the intramural tombs, the highest number of objects is represented by pottery vessels of a Syro-Anatolian tradition (e.g., the so-called Caliciform Ware [Akkermans and

Figure 8.3. An in situ plaster basin found in one of the Lower Town private dwellings at Titriş Höyük. (Thanks to Guillermo Algaze, Tim Matney, and the Titriş Höyük Photo Archive)

Schwartz 2003:246–253]), followed by semiprecious stone beads for necklaces, bronze weapons, and bronze and silver ornaments, as well as a few grinding stones and stone vessels (Laneri 2004:218–228, tavole 25–44). The presence of certain commodities or exotic materials among the furnishings of these tombs (e.g., silver objects and semiprecious stones) also suggests that the families inhabiting these private dwellings had access to economic surpluses that, according to contemporaneous Mesopotamian written sources, were exclusively owned by public authorities and private families having entrepreneurial activities (see above). Moreover, some of these commodities were definitely acquired through long-distance exchange as is also demonstrated by the presence of a tall double-handled cup, the *depas amphikypellon*, in two of the funerary assemblages (Laneri 2007a:fig. 6). As mentioned before, this type of ceramic vessel was most probably used to contain wine and represents a key element in the cultural and economic exchanges that took place during the late third millennium B.C.E. throughout a broad geographic area extending from the Aegean islands and western Anatolian regions to the middle Euphrates valley (Şahoğlu 2005).

A symbolic connection between wine production and funerary rituals is also represented by the unique deposition of human bones found on top of a plaster basin in the corner of a house in the Outer Town (Algaze et al. 2001) (Figure 8.5). Seventeen skulls and other bones of young adult males and a few bones of one infant and an adult woman, totaling 19 individuals, were found in this context (Laneri 2007a). Most of the bones show clear cut marks related to a secondary process of corpse dismemberment. As mentioned before, chemical analyses have tested that these plaster basins were used in activities associated with grape processing most probably for the purpose of wine production

Figure 8.4. An intramural funerary chamber discovered in a private dwelling of the Outer Town at Titriş Höyük. (Thanks to Guillermo Algaze, Tim Matney, and the Titriş Höyük Photo Archive)

(Figure 8.3). Thus, we can assume that a ritualistic relationship between the use of the basin as a locale for processing wine and the funerary deposition must have been involved in this unique funerary practice (Laneri 2002).

The transformation witnessed at Titriş Höyük during the second half of the third millennium B.C.E. involved the urban fabric, subsistence strategies, and funerary customs. These changes appear to have increased the economic and political importance given to private households by central authorities in producing, consuming, and trading specialized goods through the use of innovative productive techniques, such as Mediterranean polyculture. The recognition of the emerging families by the central authorities is clearly evident in the way the city is now planned with larger domestic neighborhoods that include the productive areas. In addition, and as demonstrated by the furnishing goods found in the funerary chambers of the houses at Titriş Höyük, some of these emerging families had access to important commodities (e.g., semiprecious stones, silver, and bronze) that were typically controlled by the institutional organizations.

Figure 8.5. A unique funerary deposition found on a plaster basin in the Outer Town at Titriş Höyük. (Thanks to Guillermo Algaze, Tim Matney, and the Titriş Höyük Photo Archive)

Thus, the practice of residential funerary depositions during the LEBA appears as directly linked to the consolidation of the economic and social power gained by wealthy private households in a transforming political landscape in which ancestors were buried in the house's funerary chambers and acted as "components of chains of reference" (see Gillespie, chapter 7, this volume) for solidifying the social memory of the emerging household (Jones 2007). The need to solidify the familial structure in this manner can be linked to the increased financial risk represented by changes in economic activities, such as the introduction of Mediterranean polyculture for the purpose of wine production, which requires a greater investment in time to be profitable (five to ten years for the plants to grow), but also allows for higher potential economic returns as compared to a traditional monoculture production (Gilman 1981).

The Social Memory of the Ancestors

The importance of burying selected individuals inside funerary chambers within private dwellings in order to reinforce the role of emerging social groups in ancient Mesopotamia is even more evident from the archaeological evidence available from the early second millennium B.C.E. (Jonker 1995). This archaeological phase is characterized by the establishment of local city-states in which wealthy households increased their power through their involvement in developing long-distance trade of textiles and raw materials between Mesopotamia, Anatolia, Iran, and the Gulf region. As previously noted, during this period private entrepreneurs are granted economic autonomy by the palace that, as pointed out by Goddeeris (2002:338–339), can allow for risk-taking and, consequentially, profits acquired through the use of different means (e.g., trade, land ownership, issue of loans).

This is also a period characterized by the emergence of new ethnic groups (e.g., the Amorites and the Hurrians) that begin to interact with those already inhabiting the Mesopotamian region, creating a phenomenon of interethnic relationship that validates the hypothesis of a transforming sociocultural dynamic within Mesopotamian city-states. In particular, the Amorites will solidify their social and political role in Mesopotamia during the late third and early second millennia B.C.E. and will be able to achieve prominent political and economic power in Mesopotamian societies as is witnessed by the emergence of a new royal lineage at Babylon with the figure of Hammurabi as the leading charismatic figure (Porter 2007).

For this period, cuneiform texts are also a valid source of information useful for elucidating the important role played by ancestral figures in the socioeconomic organization of both elite and non-elite groups. This is especially clear from a ritual used for the commemoration and remembrance of ancestors in which the communities of the living revisited the memory of the dead through periodic libation offerings (i.e., the *kispum*—in Akkadian—ritual [Tsukimoto 1985]).

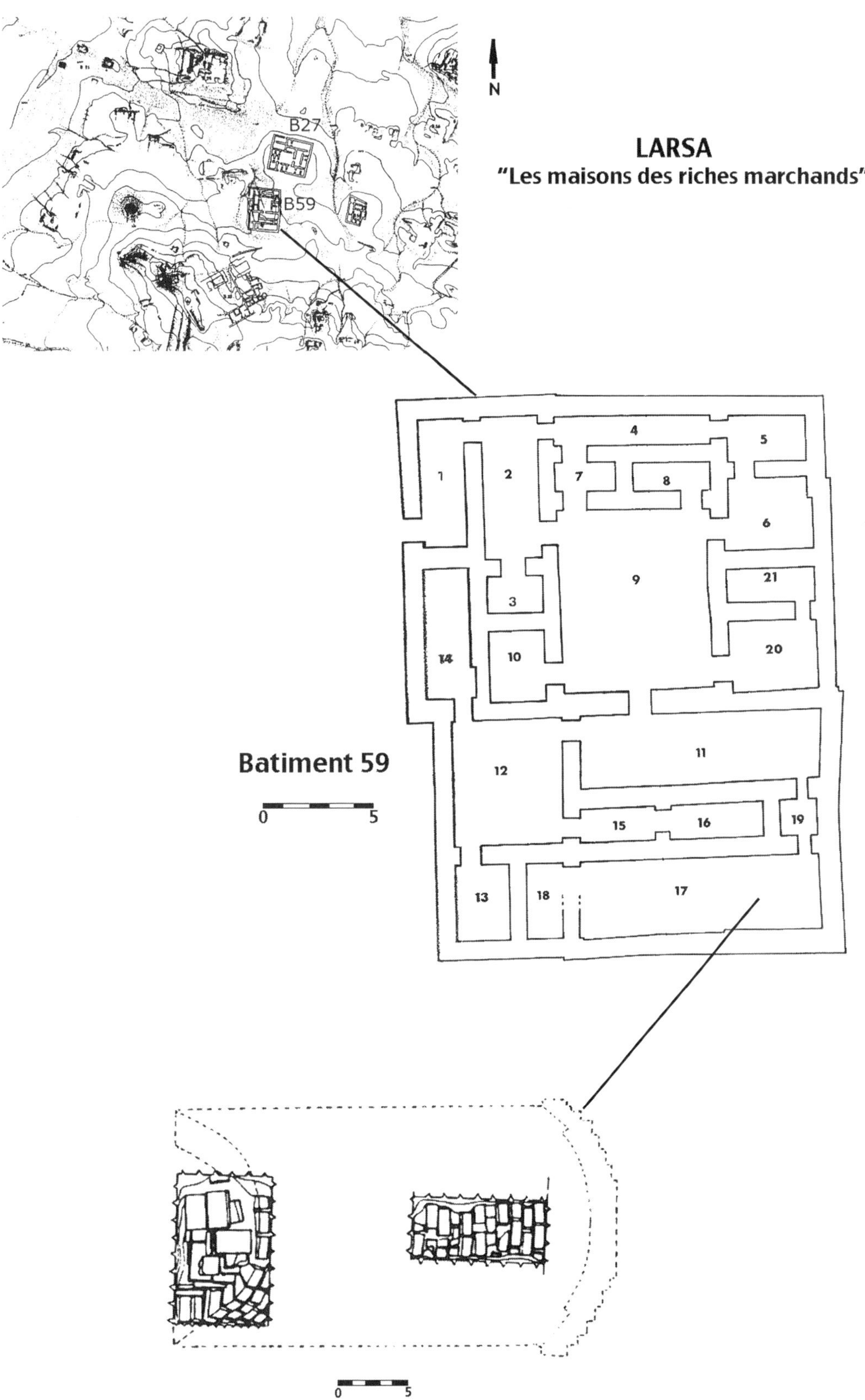

Figure 8.6. Reconstruction of the location of a residential funerary crypt found in room 17 of the Batiment 59 in the area of "Les maisons des riches marchands" at Larsa. (Based on Calvet 2003:fig. 9)

However, the importance of ancestral figures in reinforcing the structure of household lineages and affirming the power of emerging families is particularly clear from the construction of residential vaulted funerary chambers consistently planned within private dwellings found in numerous northern and southern Mesopotamian contexts. A long list of Mesopotamian and Near Eastern settlements display the use of residential funerary chambers built within private dwellings (Figure 8.6): Tell Hammam el Turkman (Thissen 1988), Tell Barri (Valentini 2003), Chagar Bazar (Mallowan 1937), Tell Mozan (Buccellati and Kelly-Buccellati 2002), Tell Mohammed Diyab (Bachelot 1992), Tell Arbid (Wygnanska in press), Tell Halawa (Yaseen 1995), Assur (Haller 1954), Ur (Woolley and Mallowan 1976), Isin (Hrouda 1987), Larsa (Calvet 1996, 2003), Sippar (Gasche 1989), and Nippur (Stone 1987), as well as the houses of the Old Assyrian merchants in the central Anatolian commercial harbor (*karum*) of Kültepe/Kanish (Özguç 2003:113–114) and private households in Iran (e.g., Susa and Tchoga-Zanbil [Ghirshman 1968a and 1968b]).

From among these examples, the residential funerary chambers unearthed at Ur and Larsa in southern Mesopotamia are the best available case studies to be used for the objectives of this chapter. At Ur, the 369 residential funerary depositions consist of both single and multiple depositions divided among pits, *pithoi*, clay coffins, and funerary chambers. These funerary depositions are found in six neighborhoods in which the archaeologists were able to define about 58 houses. Moreover, the funerary chambers are "brick-built burial-vault[s built] under the pavement of the private chapel" (Woolley and Mallowan 1976:33, fig. 2a–d). As already seen at Titriş Höyük, these funerary chambers are planned as part of the construction of the house and are usually located in the back of the medium to large-sized houses. Moreover, altars, daises, tables, chimneys, and pipes connecting to funerary chambers, as well as traces of burnt material and numerous clay votive plaques decorated with anthropomorphic motifs (Barrett 2007:35–42), are recognizable in the rooms containing the tombs, which were named by Woolley as "domestic chapels" (Woolley and Mallowan 1976:29–30, pls. 43–48). These elements reinforce the existence of postmortem rituals dedicated to the memory of the ancestors that can recall the already mentioned *kispum* ritual (Postgate 1992:96–101).

One of the most interesting elements available from the early second millennium B.C.E. context of Ur is that both written texts and archaeological data lead us towards an understanding of social differences between neighborhoods of this period (Luby 1990). In particular, the EH and EM neighborhoods are formed by houses with the presence of a few funerary chambers and "domestic chapels," and a total absence of "public shrines" (Woolley and Mallowan 1976:95–118, pls. 122, 127), whereas in the AH area is the highest density of houses with large courtyards, funerary chambers, "domestic chapels," and "public shrines" (Luby 1990; Woolley and Mallowan 1976:118–166, pl. 124). The written documents found in the EH and EM areas describe groups having close connections with the temple authorities (i.e., priests and prebendaries; Charpin 1986), whereas those unearthed from the houses located in area AH describe a population of families that have looser ties to the temple and/or palace estates and are involved in the "management of different sectors of the economy where silver was needed . . . [thus, it can be considered] the financial district of Ur" (Van de Mieroop 1992:163).

The important role played by wealthy families in the Mesopotamian economy of the early second millennium B.C.E. is further emphasized by the extensive use of the merchants' service by the palatial authority both at Ur and, later, at Larsa (e.g., collecting taxes and trading palaces' economic surpluses [Van de Mieroop 1992:203]). At Larsa, their power is evident not only in the written data, but also in the creation of a series of large houses (ca. 1790–1738 B.C.E., "Les maisons des riches marchands" [Calvet 2003:186]) located in the northeastern section of the city and built using space between the houses. In the back of two of these houses (*Batiment* 27 and *Batiment* 59), the archaeologists excavated corbelled vaulted tombs in mud brick (Calvet 2003:150–151, 157, figs. 9, 17b, 34, 35a, pls. 7b, 8a, 30–31) (Figure 8.6).[1]

In a way similar to the examples previously discussed for the late third millennium B.C.E., both the written and the archaeological data clearly show the importance given to the memorialization of ancestors within the family's house by the communities of the early second millennium (Jonker 1995). In some cases (e.g., at Ur), the prominent role embodied by the ancestors in the construction of the social memory of the family is even more evident in the creation of altars located in the room above the funerary chambers.

Thus, the act of structural and bodily *incorporation* of ancestors into the private dwellings and also the memory of the living communities are entwined with a continuous act of *commemoration* enacted through the use of rooms dedicated to the veneration of the family ancestors and, as a consequence, for "the creation of a place intended to evoke memory" (see Joyce, chapter 3, this volume).

Conclusions

The picture emerging from the data available from late third and early second millennia B.C.E. Mesopotamia is of a transforming society in which innovative productive techniques, changes in subsistence strategies, and access to precious raw materials and commodities through the control of complex networks of long-distance exchange favored the establishment of powerful households able to mobilize surpluses for institutional organizations as well as for increasing their own wealth and social position within Mesopotamian society. Thus, in a way similar to McAnany's analysis of the ritual funerary practices in Maya culture, in Mesopotamia, "the practice of ancestor veneration is linked to the entrenchment of resource rights . . . [and] was a critically important organizing force in all sectors" (McAnany 1995:7).

With this perspective in mind, the practice of disposal of the dead in residential funerary chambers in ancient Mesopotamia should be interpreted as a means for protecting and strengthening a kin-based tradition of familial descent, while the construction of funerary chambers and the differentiation in funerary goods buried with selected deceased were probably used to differentiate these emerging families from lower classes, probably more dependent on the institutional organizations, or from different ethnic groups. Within this perspective, I would also agree with Marc Van de Mieroop (1997:108) when he envisions a transformation in the social organization of families during this historical phase, in which we witness a merging of extended family ties with professional ties in the social structure of Mesopotamian society.

In conclusion, the construction of a family crypt within the private dwelling allowed the living members to locate the social memory of the "house," which also served as a source of protection during the course of daily life activities in times of socioeconomic transformation (see White and Eyre, chapter 5, this volume). Thus, the agency embodied by the memorialization and remembrance of this locale by the living members of the family must have been very strong if it had the power to open the way for a new social class composed of powerful households of merchants and entrepreneurs.

Acknowledgments

I would first like to thank the editors of this book, Ron Adams and Stacie King, for inviting me to be part of this prestigious publication. My best acknowledgments go also to Guillermo Algaze and Tim Matney for allowing me to work on the material from Titriş Höyük, to Marc Van de Mieroop for reading and commenting on a final draft of this essay, and to the anonymous reviewers for their useful comments on an earlier draft of this chapter.

Note

1. It is important to notice that, as compared to the funerary chambers discovered at Ur, those found at Larsa lack the domestic chapels (Calvet 2003).

References

Adams, Robert McC.
1974 Anthropological Perspectives on Ancient Trade. Current Anthropology 15:239–258.

Akkermans, Peter M. M. G., and Glenn M. Schwartz
2003 The Archaeology of Syria. Cambridge: Cambridge University Press.

Algaze, Guillermo
1983–84 Private Houses and Graves at Ingharra: A Reconsideration. Mesopotamia 18-19:135–194.
2008 Ancient Mesopotamia at the Dawn of Civilization: The Evolution of an Urban Landscape. Chicago: University of Chicago Press.

Algaze, Guillermo, Gulay Dinckan, Britt Hartenberger, Timothy Matney, Jennifer Pournelle, Lynn Rainville, Steven Rosen, Eric Rupley, Duncan Schlee, and Regis Vallet
2001 Research at Titriş Höyük in Southeastern Turkey: The 1999 Season. Anatolica 27:23–106.

Bachelot, Luc
1992 Une tombe construite du deuxième millénaire av. J.-C., à Mohammed Diyab. *In* Recherches en Haute Mésopotamie: Tell Mohammed Diyab, Campagnes 1990 et 1991. Jean-Marie Durand, ed. Pp. 31–38. Mémoires de N.A.B.U. 2. Paris: SEPOA.

Barrett, E. Caitlin
2007 Was Dust Their Food and Clay Their Bread? Grave Goods, the Mesopotamian Afterlife, and the Liminal Role of Inana/Ishtar. Journal of Near Eastern Religions 7(1):7–65.

Bartoloni, Gilda, ed.
2008 Sepolti tra i vivi: Atti del convegno internazionale: Evidenza ed interpretazione di contesti funerari in abitato. Roma, 26–29 Aprile 2006. Rome: Ed. Quasar.

Buccellati, Giorgio, and Marilyn Kelly-Buccellati
2002 Die Grosse Schnittstelle. Berichte über die 14. Kampagne in Tall Mozan/Urkes: Ausgrabungen im Gebiet AA, Juni–Oktober 2001. Mitteilungen der Deutschen Orient-Gesellschaft zu Berlin 134:103–130.

Calvet, Yves
1996 Maisons privées paléo-babyloniennes à Larsa: Remarques d'architecture. *In* Houses and Households in Ancient Mesopotamia. Klaas R. Veenhof, ed. Pp. 197–209. Istanbul: Nederlands Historisch-Archaeologisch Instituut.
2003 Batiments paléobabyloniens à Larsa. *In* Larsa: Travaux de 1987 et 1989. Jean-Louis Hout, ed. Pp. 143–298. Beirut: Institut Français d'Archaéologie du Proche-Orient.

Charpin, Dominique
1986 Le clergé d'Ur au siècle d'Hammurabi. École Pratique des Hautes Études IVe Section, Sciences Historiques et Philologiques II, Hautes Études Orientales 22. Paris: Librarie Droz.

Cooper, Lisa
2006 Early Urbanism on the Syrian Euphrates. New York: Routledge.

Dalley, Stephanie
2002 Mari and Karana: Two Old Babylonian Cities. Piscataway, NJ: Gorgias.

Delougaz, Pinhas, Harold D. Hill, and Lloyd Seton
1967 Private Houses and Graves in the Diyala Region. Oriental Institute Publications 88. Chicago: University of Chicago Press.

Edens, Christopher
1992 Dynamics of Trade in Ancient Mesopotamian "World System." American Anthropologist 94:118–139.

Forlanini, Massimo
2006 Étapes et itenéraires entre Assur et l'Anatole des marchands Paléo-Assyriens: Nouveaux documents et nouveaux probléms. KASKAL. Rivista di Storia, Ambienti e Culture del Vicino Oriente Antico 3:149–175.

Gasche, Hermann
1989 La Babylonie au 17e siecle avant notre ere: Approche archeologique, problemes et perpectives. Mesopotamian History and Environment, series 2, memoirs 1. Ghent: University of Ghent.

Ghirshman, Roman
1968a Tchoga Zanbil (Dur Untash), vol. 2: Téménos, temples, palais, tombes. Mémoires de la Mission Archéologique en Iran, 40. Paris.
1968b Suse au tournant du III et du II millénaire avant notre ère. Arts Asiatiques 17:3–44.

Gillespie, Susan D.
2001 Personhood, Agency, and Mortuary Ritual: A Case Study from the Ancient Maya. Journal of Anthropological Archaeology 20:73–112.

Gilman, Antonio
1981 The Development of Social Stratification in Bronze Age Europe. Current Anthropology 22:1–23.

Goddeeris, Anne
2002 Economy and Society in Northern Babylonia in the Early Old Babylonian Period (ca. 2000–1800 B.C.E.). Orientalia Lovaniensia Analect 109. Leuven: Peeters.

Haller, Arndt
1954 Die Gräber und Grüfte von Assur. Ausgrabungen der Deutschen Orient-Gesellschaft in Assur. A: Die Baudenkmäler aus assyrischer Zeit, 7. Wissenschaftliche Veröffentlichung der Deutschen Orient-Gesellschaft, 65. Berlin: Gebr. Mann.

Hodder, Ian, and Craig Cessford
2004 Daily Practice and Social Memory at Çatalhöyük. American Antiquity 69:17–40.

HONça, Deidra, and Guillermo Algaze
1998 Preliminary Report on the Human Skeletal Remains at Titriş Höyük: 1991–1996 Seasons. Anatolica 24:100–125.

Hrouda, Bartel, ed.
1987 Isin-Išan Bahriyat III: Die Ergebnisse der Ausgrabungen 1983–1984. Munich: Verlag der Bayerishen Akademie der Wissenschaften.

Jean-Marie, Marylou
1999 Tombes et Nécropoles de Mari. Mission Archéologique de Mari, Tome V. Beirut: Institut Français d'Archaéologie du Proche-Orient.

Jones, Andrew
2007 Memory and Material Culture. Cambridge: Cambridge University Press.

Jonker, Gerdien
1995 The Topography of Remembrance: The Dead, Tradition and Collective Memory in Mesopotamia. Studies in the History of Religions, 68. Leiden: E. J. Brill.

Kuijt, Ian
2001 Place, Death, and the Transmission of Social Memory in Early Agricultural Communities of the Near Eastern Pre-Pottery Neolithic. *In* Social Memory, Identity, and Death: Anthropological Perspectives on Mortuary Rituals. Meredith S. Chesson, ed. Pp. 80–99. Archeological Papers of the American Anthropological Association, 10. Arlington, VA: American Anthropological Association.

Lamberg-Karlovsky, Carl C.
1996 The Archaeological Evidence for International Commerce: Public and/or Private Enterprise in Mesopotamia. *In* Privatization in the Ancient Near East and Classical World. Michael Hudson and Baruch A. Levine, eds. Pp. 73–108. Peabody Museum Bulletin 5. Cambridge, MA: Peabody Museum of Archaeology and Ethnology, Harvard University.

Laneri, Nicola
2002 The Discovery of a Funerary Ritual: Inanna/Ishtar and Her Descent to the Nether World in Titriş Höyük, Turkey. East and West 52:1–4, 9–52.
2004 I costumi funerari della media vallata dell'Eufrate durante il III millennio a.C. Dissertationes 4. Naples: Istituto Universitario Orientale.
2007a Burial Practices at Titriş Höyük, Turkey: An Interpretation. Journal of Near Eastern Studies 66(4):241–266.
2007b An Archaeology of Funerary Rituals. *In* Performing Death: Social Analyses of Funerary Traditions in the Ancient Near East and Mediterranean. Nicola Laneri, ed. Pp. 1–15. Oriental Institute Seminars 3. Chicago: Oriental Institute.

Larsen, Morgen T.
1987 Commercial Networks in the Ancient Near East. *In* Centre and Periphery in the Ancient World. Michael Rowlands, Morgen Larsen, and Kristian Kristiansen, eds. Pp. 47–56. Cambridge: Cambridge University Press.

Luby, Edward
1990 Social Variation in Ancient Mesopotamia: An Architectural and Mortuary Analysis in the Early Second Millennium B.C.E. Ph.D. dissertation, Department of Anthropology, SUNY Stony Brook.

Lull, Vicente
2000 Argaric Society: Death at Home. Antiquity 74: 581–590.

Mallowan, Max E. L.
1937 The Excavations at Tall Chagar Bazar and an Archaeological Survey of the Habur Region: Second Campaign, 1936. Iraq 4:91–177.

Matney, Timothy, and Guillermo Algaze
1995 Urban Development at Mid-Late Early Bronze Age Titriş Höyük in Southeastern Anatolia. Bulletin of the American School of Oriental Research 99/300:33–52.

McAnany, Patricia A.
1995 Living with the Ancestors: Kinship and Kingship in Ancient Maya Society. Austin: University of Texas Press.

Michel, Cécile
2001 Correspondance des marchands de Kanish au début du IIe millénaire avant J.-C. Paris: Éditions du Cerf.

Özguç, Tahsin
2003 Kültepe/Nesha: The Earliest International Trade Center and the Oldest Capital City of the Hittites. Istanbul: Middle Eastern Culture Center in Japan.

Porter, Anne
2007 You Say Potato, I Say... Typology, Chronology and the Origins of the Amorites. *In* Sociétés humaines et changement climatique à la fin du troisième millénaire: Une crise a-t-elle eu lieu en Haute Mésopotamie? Varia Anatolica XIX. Catherine Kuzucuoğlu and Catherine Marro, eds. Pp. 69–116. Paris: De Boccard.

Postgate, Nicholas
1980 Early Dynastic Burial Customs at Abu Salabikh. Sumer 36(1-2):65–82.
1992 Early Mesopotamia: Society and Economy at the Dawn of History. London: Routledge.

Powell, Marvin G.
1999 *Wir müssen unsere Nische nutzen:* Monies, Motives, and Methods in Babylonian Economics. *In* Trade and Finance in Ancient Mesopotamia. J. G. Dercksen, ed. Pp. 5–24. MOS Studies 1. Istanbul: Nederlands Historisch-Archaeologisch Instituut.

Reade, Julian
1982 Tell Taya. *In* Fifty Years of Mesopotamian Discovery: The Work of the British School of Archaeology in Iraq 1932–1982. John Curtis, ed. Pp. 72–78. London: The British School of Archaeology in Iraq.

Ristvet, Lauren
2007 The Third Millennium City Wall at Tell Leilan, Syria: Identity, Authority, and Urbanism. *In* Power and Architecture: Monumental Public Architecture in the Bronze Age Near East and Aegean. J. Bretschneider, J. Driessen, and Karl Van Lerberghe, eds. Pp. 183–211. Orientalia Lovaniensia Analecta 156. Leuven: Uitgeverij Peeters en Departement Oosterse Studies.

Şahoğlu, Vasif
2005 The Anatolian Trade Network and the Izmir Region during the Early Bronze Age. Oxford Journal of Archaeology 24:340–345.

Stein, Gil
2004 Structural Parameters and Sociocultural Factors in the Economic Organization of North Mesopotamian Urbanism in the Third Millennium B.C.E. *In* Archaeological Perspectives on Political Economies. Gary M. Feinman and Linda M. Nichols, eds. Pp. 61–78. Salt Lake City: University of Utah Press.

Stone, Elizabeth C.
1987 Nippur Neighborhoods. Studies in Ancient Oriental Civilization 44. Chicago: Oriental Institute.
1996 Houses, Households, and Neighborhoods in the Old Babylonian Period: The Role of Extended Families. *In* Houses and Households in Ancient Mesopotamia. Klaas R. Veenhof, ed. Pp. 229–236. Istanbul: Nederlands Historisch-Archaeologisch Instituut.
1999 The Constraints on State and Urban Form in Ancient Mesopotamia. *In* Urbanization and Land Ownership in the Ancient Near East. Michael Hudson and Baruch A. Levine, eds. Pp. 203–228. Peabody Museum Bulletin 7. Cambridge, MA: Peabody Museum of Archaeology and Ethnology, Harvard University.

Thissen, Laurens
1988 The Burials. *In* Hammam et- Turkman I: Report on the University of Amsterdam's 1981–84 Excavations in Syria. Mauritius N. Van Loon, ed. Pp. 143–180. Istanbul: Nederlands Historisch-Archaeologisch Instituut.

Tsukimoto, Akjo
1985 Untersuchungen zur Totenpflege (*kispum*) im alten Mesopotamien. Alter Orient und Altes Testament 216. Neukirchen: Butzon and Bercker.

Valentini, Stefano
2003 Le pratiche funerarie e l'ideologia funeraria a Tell Barri/Kahat durante il Bronzo Medio, in relazione all'area Siro-mesopotamica settentrionale. Studi Micenei ed Egeo-anatolici 45:273–305.

Van Driel, Govert
1999 Capital Formation and Investment in an Institutional Context in Ancient Mesopotamia. *In* Trade and Finance in Ancient Mesopotamia. J. G. Dercksen, ed. Pp. 25–42. MOS Studies 1. Istanbul: Nederlands Historisch-Archaeologisch Instituut.

Van Loon, Mauritius N., ed.
2001 Selenkahiye: Final Report on the University of Chicago and University of Amsterdam Excavations in the Tabqa Reservoir, Northern Syria, 1967–1975. PIHANS, vol. 92. Istanbul: Nederlands Instituut voor het Nabije Oosten.

Van de Mieroop, Marc
1992 Society and Enterprise in Old Babylonian Ur. Berlin: Dietrich Reimer Verlag.
1997 The Ancient Mesopotamian City. Oxford: Oxford University Press.

Veenhof, Klaas R.
1999 Silver and Credit in Old Assyrian Trade. *In* Trade and Finance in Ancient Mesopotamia. J. G. Dercksen, ed. Pp. 55–83. MOS Studies 1. Istanbul: Nederlands Historisch-Archaeologisch Instituut.

Woolley, Leonard, and Max Mallowan
1976 The Old Babylonian Period. Ur Excavations 7. Publications of the Joint Expedition of the British Museum and of the Museum of the University of Pennsylvania to Mesopotamia. London: British Museum Publications.

Wygnanska, Zuzanna
In press Burial Customs at Tell Arbid (Syria) in the Middle Bronze Age. Cultural Interrelations with the Nile Delta and Levant. University of Warsaw.

Yaseen, Ghassan Taha
1995 Old Babylonian Pottery from the Hamrin: Tell Halawa. Edubba 4. London: Nabu Publications.

Yoffee, Norman
2005 Myths of the Archaic State: Evolution of the Earliest Cities, States, and Civilizations. Cambridge: Cambridge University Press.

Zettler, Richard, and Naomi Miller
1995 Searching for Wine in the Archaeological Record of Ancient Mesopotamia of the 3rd and 2nd Millennia B.C. *In* The Origins and Ancient History of Wine. Patrick E. McGovern, Stuart James Fleming, and Solomon H. Katz, eds. Pp. 123–131. Philadelphia: Gordon and Breach.

9

Practices of Place-Making, Ancestralizing, and Re-animation within Memory Communities

Patricia A. McAnany
University of North Carolina, Chapel Hill

ABSTRACT

Place-making, ancestralizing, and re-animation within memory communities are key features of residential burial. The history and ethical responsibilities of this archaeological study are considered within the discipline, particularly when control of the past has been alienated from descendant peoples. Residential burial practices create or modify a built environment, speak to the vitality of the house and community, but often minimize the message of social difference that is redolent in monumental mortuary shrines. Consideration is given to the notion that ancestralizing practices signal inalienable wealth (including the relicts of ancestors) and that such actions likely also signal a commitment to an ethos of hereditary wealth transmission. [place-making, ancestralizing, re-animation, memory communities, embodied ancestry]

> Memories themselves are young at one time . . . As soon as they are allowed to go a little mouldy, they turn into the most repulsive ghosts, oozing selfishness, vanity and lies. (Céline 1960[1932]:328)

Unlike most contemporary archaeologists, the French novelist Louis-Ferdinand Céline took a dim view of memory, critiquing the inward gaze and situated veracity of distant memories. Most of the contributors to this multiregional exploration of residential burial practices—revealed archaeologically and ethnoarchaeologically—would take issue with the nihilism of Céline; instead, they embrace memory theory and its twin theme, identity, in their interpretative narratives. In the pages to follow, I examine the theoretical framing of residential burial practice with reference to the spatial breadth and theoretical diversity of the preceding case studies and then consider residential burial in terms of place-making, ancestralizing, and re-animation among memory communities. First, I situate the study of residential burial terminologically and ethically within archaeology.

Terms, Methods, and Ethical Consequences

The term *residential burial,* as adopted by contributors to this volume, is more inclusive than related terms such as *subfloor burial* or *intramural burial* and can absorb a number of significant variations, such as burial under stilt houses (White and Eyre, chapter 5, this volume) and under shared plaza surfaces (Gillespie, chapter 7, this volume). Also included within these pages are examples of what might be termed *community burial*—in nonresidential earthen mounds in the U.S. Southeast (Sullivan and Rodning, chapter 6, this volume) and in free-standing stone tombs of West Sumba, Indonesia (Adams and Kusumawati, chapter 2, this volume). Although these community burial practices exhibit a concern with *display* that generally is not part of subfloor burial, the complex cross-referencing between burials in community spaces and residences warrants considering all of these cases as examples of residential burial practice. Methodologically, contributors consciously embrace the social significance of keeping the dead close to

ARCHEOLOGICAL PAPERS OF THE AMERICAN ANTHROPOLOGICAL ASSOCIATION, Vol. 20, Issue 1, pp. 136–142, ISSN 1551-823X, online ISSN 1551-8248. DOI: 10.1111/j.1551-8248.2011.01032.x.

the living and in several chapters—e.g., White and Eyre as well as Gillespie—authors deploy a careful reading of artifact distributions and vertical and horizontal citation of mortuary contexts to create what has been discussed elsewhere as social stratigraphy (McAnany and Hodder 2009). In doing so, authors move away from more traditional archaeological approaches to human interment that de-emphasized context and valued mortuary deposits for their (a) temporally sensitive content (generally ceramic) and (b) variable accoutrements that were interpreted as indexing status distinctions or resource monopolization (see Binford 1971; Goldstein 1981; Morris 1991; Saxe 1970). So valued, the contents interred with the dead enabled culture history during the early 20th century and then processualism through the middle decades of the century. Gillespie (this volume) provides a particularly compelling contextual analysis that points to the limitations of chronological phase-based mortuary analysis. And while status, no doubt, is encoded within burial accoutrements, there is no 1:1 relationship and much is lost analytically by ignoring significant sources of variation that are not status linked.

In the Americas, the discipline of archaeology was both nurtured by and lost its innocence as a consequence of burial excavation. The 18th-century cross-sectional drawing by Thomas Jefferson of burials within an earthen mound located on Monticello often is cited in support of the claim that Jefferson was a founding father of American Archaeology. Likewise, the 1915–26 excavation of over 2,000 residential burials by Alfred Kidder at Pecos Pueblo in the U.S. Southwest played an influential role in creating a regional chronological sequence (the Pecos Classification). Equally iconic although farther afield were excavations during the 1950s by Kathleen Kenyon at Jericho in which she discovered plastered skulls buried within residences and grappled in a sophisticated fashion with the complexities of postmortem body processing. But this emphasis on "grave digging"—difficult to avoid when houses are under excavation and residential burial practices were in effect—can take on a ghoulish scientific detachment when skeleton and artifacts are separated from their context for analysis and archived in laboratory drawers (or worse). The ethical engagement of American Archaeology and the U.S. museum community with this issue in the aftermath of the passage of NAGPRA in 1990 is now part of our institutional memory and consultation with descendant communities has become an integral protocol for professional practice within U.S. archaeology. But it is worth considering that the United States is not the only country in which burials were/are excavated that are linked ancestrally with indigenous, colonized populations. Elsewhere (McAnany 1995, 2007), I have discussed this issue in reference to the Maya region. In short, the study of residential burials—so powerfully evocative of place and embodied ancestry—is fraught with ethical land mines because burial excavation highlights the privileged position of archaeologists in reference to a past, particularly when that past has been alienated from descendant peoples by colonial and nation-building processes (McAnany and Parks in press).

Residential Burial Practices Theoretically Framed

Death brings separation as well as loss but also affords opportunities, especially if death means the loss of a senior family member. As noted by Metcalf and Huntington (1991), *deathways* are highly variable and contingent upon a host of factors—both idiosyncratic and more broadly social. From an archaeological perspective, the hermeneutics of death and the way in which the social persona of a deceased one is transformed, remembered, or forgotten reside entirely in the world of survivors (McAnany 2011). The mortuary practices by which a deceased household or community member is processed and buried are not really about the dead but about the living and how they cope with separation, loss, and new opportunities. Gillespie (this volume) refers to this by discussing burial contexts as "future-oriented projects." Most chapters comment on the fact that residential burials are positioned so as to *keep the deceased close to the daily rhythm of household activities.* In the ethnoarchaeological study of the stone tombs of West Sumba, Adams and Kusumawati (this volume) found that, in addition to reverential referencing, tomb structures were used in mundane ways. Why this intimacy and blurring in a locative sense of the resting place of the living with that of the dead? I address this question from several different perspectives.

Memory can be evoked as a compelling factor in residential burial practices and many contributors situate their study in reference to Connerton (1989), Halbwachs (1992), and archaeological studies that consider the materiality of social memory (e.g., see contributions in Mills and Walker 2008; Van Dyke and Alcock 2003). If a house can be considered history-in-the-making, as do Hodder and Cessford (2004) in reference to Çatalhöyük, then residential burials are history-making practices and part of what Julia Hendon (2010:2)—in referencing Melion and Küchler (1991:30)—calls a "political economy of memory" that is engaged by "memory communities." The selectivity of membership in "memory communities" appears to be indicated by who is interred residentially—and so remembered—as well as by the residential or community group that prepares, maintains, and refurbishes burial facilities. King (chapter 4, this volume) is concerned with age-based social difference as a selective factor of membership in memory communities within Postclassic Oaxaca. Sullivan and Rodning (this volume), on the other hand, discern a strong gendering structure to memory communities in early Cherokee burial patterns of the U.S. Southeast.

By definition, residential burial practices create or modify a built environment and some contributors consider the role of residential burial in house creation. Within Mesoamerica and elsewhere, burial placement can be a foundational event to house construction (Storey 2004; also see Gillespie, this volume); Laneri (chapter 8, this volume) states that burial chambers often were built as part of house construction in third and second millennium B.C.E. Mesopotamian houses. By way of understanding the emergence of residential burial at Puerto Escondido, Honduras, Joyce (chapter 3, this volume) makes a convincing argument that practices of incorporation and commemoration predate the interment of human remains under house floors. With this perspective, the incorporative practice of residential burial was not novel but an expansion of preexisting ways of place-making that emphasized the inalienability of things (and deceased house members) that retained their value even though or because they were hidden away. While intriguing, the specificity of the case study brings up the obvious question as to whether or not this interpretive narrative can be extended to the many other times and places in which burial practices are in evidence. The question is answerable and could profitably be explored further.

The House as a durable armature of the built environment can have tremendous staying power and ability to instantiate a residential group, their web of social connectedness, and their history. Many contributors turn to the "house model" (Joyce and Gillespie 2000) for interpretive leverage; this tactic shifts inquiry from characteristics of those interred within residences (such as biological distance or genealogical affinity) to the house itself as the principal container of meaning. A future rapprochement that integrates these two approaches would significantly advance burial studies. Although the house model often is juxtaposed against a lineage model, the two are not mutually exclusive. As Watanabe (2004) notes, house members invariably articulate a descent ideology even if co-residential members are not biologically related to each other or to house founders.

Agency and materiality loom large in these contributions, in some cases explicitly while in others the theoretical frames provide strong subtext. The study of materiality (Henare et al. 2007; Miller 2005) foregrounds the ways in which things instantiate meaning and, furthermore, interact with human actors in ways that are asserted by thing theorists such as Latour (2005), Gell (1998), and others to be fully intersubjective. This approach has traction in the study of residential burials, particularly in an area such as Mesoamerica where a cosmology of agency accorded to inanimate entities (and the dead are included here) prefigures postulates of thing theorists. The vertical network of citational deposits reconstructed by Gillespie (this volume) for Chalcatzingo includes those with and without human remains; she asserts that upper-level deposits were created in response to or because of memory of deposits that already existed in lower levels. The forward impact of materials from earlier place-making practices also is suggested in the contribution by Joyce (this volume) in which she reasons that meanings ascribed to the incorporation of nonhuman objects such as shell and jadeite within residential contexts provided a precursor to the interment of human remains. I return to this complex cross-threading between social actors and the agentive properties of things below in a consideration of ancestralizing practices.

Hierarchization is approached with skepticism by most contributors and, in some cases, is juxtaposed against more heterarchical notions of collective or community-based action. White and Eyre (this volume) assert that residential burial practices in the Metal Age of Thailand provide evidence of resistance against hierarchization and political centralization; Adams and Kusumawati (this volume) describe a decentralized political situation in which a *rato* ("man of renown") leads a community and is commemorated by interment within a stone tomb; and Laneri (this volume) notes that at the Mesopotamian city of Ur, the highest density of funerary chambers within private residences is located in neighborhoods with loose ties to temple and palace estates. While the terms *hierarchy* and *heterarchy* arguably have been overly framed typologically, contributors present empirical evidence that residential burial practices relate to social difference but not in the same way as entombment within monumental structures. This tension extends to a wary approach to the public/private dichotomy and to the question of whether residential burial informs us of personal or collective identity. In several cases described in the preceding chapters, variation in burial accoutrement and facility seems to express personal identities couched within a larger collective. Residential burials exhibit referential linkages to an entity—house or community—that is larger than a single agent. Such *agent-based affiliative dynamics* seem to be operating in the case study from Thailand presented by White and Eyre (this volume).

The *longue duree* of residential burial practices often is pronounced (over 2,000 years for some Thai Metal Age villages according to White and Eyre, this volume). One is tempted to suggest that there is demonstrative long-term stability to these practices—proven success in social reproduction measured across the many generations of social actors who built, maintained, and embellished residences with ancestral interments. On the other hand, one cannot lose sight of the loss that inevitably accompanied the death of a house member and the negotiation and contestation that likely ensued over whether or not the deceased person would join the community of remembered residents or provide fertilizer for fields and orchards, thereby joining the far larger ranks of "the forgotten." When archaeologists gaze upon the remains of a deceased house member, we are witnessing the result of memory selection. Nonetheless, even when burials are located in special above-ground shrines located outside of the house, such as the large Indonesian stone tombs described by Adams and Kusumawati (this volume), these facilities arguably speak to the vitality of the house and community/clan and often minimize the message of social difference, political privilege, and exclusion that is redolent in many monumental mortuary shrines—such as those found in the Late Classic Maya Lowlands (Fitzsimmons 2009).

As is evident from this discussion of contact points between residential burial practices and contemporary social theory, there are few topics with which this social practice does not resonate. I turn now to three practices in particular—place-making, ancestralizing, and re-animation. Within many memory communities, the materiality of these practices creates residential burial.

Practices of Place-Making, Ancestralizing, and Re-Animation

As Hendon (2010:1–31) discusses, memory does not exist in the mind, ready to be tapped when relevant environmental stimuli are present, but rather is generated and constantly reinterpreted through engagement with places, things, sounds, smells, and tactile sensations. Here, the manner in which residential places and mortuary practices entangle to generate place-based and time-phased memories is of concern. A commitment to place involves a stretching and lengthening of the temporal fabric of the residence in order to make house histories. In the case of K'axob in the Maya Lowlands, this social process was materialized in long, complex chains of burial interment that alternated with structure renovation. Houses seem little more than protective shields for ancestors who "slept" beneath the living platforms of descendants and punctuated the construction of deeply sedimented stratigraphic histories. Such ancestralizing practice is contingent upon a kind of landscape inhabitation that works well with a strongly anchored (that is, localized) ethos of place-making. In reference to ancestral Cherokee material, Sullivan and Rodning (this volume) suggest that a deepened commitment to an agricultural lifestyle played a role in this strongly locative practice. The importance of "acting local" is also manifest in the construction of West Sumba tombs. When stone was imported for tomb construction, it was considered analogous to acquiring a bride from another clan (Adams and Kusumawati, this volume). When those who are to be remembered are kept at home and not transported to a distant place to become part of an ancestral landscape, the house takes on a central role in locative meaning-making and social reproduction.

In this situation, the residence also becomes a place of active power relations and enhanced agency and accrues a significance that is quite alien to the modern experience. Sullivan and Rodning (this volume) confront the Western devaluation of the house in reinterpreting ancestral Cherokee burial patterns in which there is pronounced segregation in burial locale by gender role—with females most represented in residences and males in mound burials. This twist on residence versus community entanglement indicates how profoundly separate gender-based realms of activities, power, pedagogy, and ultimately burial placement can be. As Sullivan and Rodning note, these are deeply contextualized realms of political influence that form the ancestral heritage of localized residential groups.

Why this emphasis on interring selected members of a residential group within or near the house? Why this localization of ancestralizing practices within the residence, especially given the fact that such practices often emerged sequential to interment within the larger frame of ancestral landscape? Although social memory routinely is invoked to explain residential burial, descendant house members likely detected only subtle signals of previous interments—a patch on the floor or a slightly raised platform. Perhaps the long-term importance of residential burial practice lies in the ancestralizing practices that surround this type of interment in which a selective subset of house members was stored, guarded, and managed as part of the inalienable wealth of the residential group. Ancestors became iconic of group identity, longevity, and future possibilities. Like all valuable icons, they were treated reverentially and placed within what Hendon (2010:121) refers to as "religiously charged storehouses." Since many residential burials were concealed from all but members of the immediate memory community, this practice evokes the contemporary act of placing valuable things for which one cannot risk theft or destruction in a bank safe-deposit box. Weiner's (1992:17) notion of inalienable possessions—things that might be loaned but never given away—as constituting the oldest form of wealth and the origin of social difference is highly relevant here. If ancestralizing practices signal inalienable wealth (which includes the relicts of ancestors), then such actions likely also signal a commitment to an ethos of hereditary wealth transmission (Bowles et al. 2010). Ancestors embody—literally—one part of a larger group of inalienable possessions that includes claims on land along with sacred things that evoke ancestral connection. All are safeguarded by house members and serve to promote the distinction and renown of a house or of clan groups and to emphasize difference among groups. In the words of Weiner (1992:4), ancestors provide cosmological authentication.

Among indigenous peoples in many parts of Mesoamerica, a house was not considered complete until a dedication had been performed. The purpose of a house dedication ritual has been described as providing nourishment for the animus of the house (Monaghan 2000:30; Vogt 1976:52–55). The term *ensouling ceremony* is used by Vogt (1976:52–55), which suggests that a new house is animated in the course of the ceremony. Ensouling practices generally included the placement of valuables or valuable nourishment within a hole dug beneath the house. At ancestral Maya places such as K'axob, where long sequences of structure renovation are present, "ensouling ceremonies" (with or without human remains) often were repeated after house modification (Harrison-Buck 2004).

Death de-animates a human—socially and biologically—but ancestralizing rituals of commemoration can re-animate the spirit of a person. Hieroglyphically, ritual practices in which Classic Maya deities and ancestors were re-animated are documented in approximately 50 separate texts (Houston 2006:148). This emphasis on continued contact and consultation with ancestors suggests that—in the Maya region especially—residential burial might be a kind of supra-ensoulment of the house that included a commitment to ancestor commemoration as a key element of survival and social reproduction of the memory community. In a sense, the animus or social persona of the deceased merged with the built environment of the house. Commemorating ancestors and ensuring future prosperity of the house became one and the same endeavor. Several contributors comment on the danger to the living that is posed by forgetting the dead whose journey to an afterlife might be unsuccessful if proper rituals of passage are not observed initially and then calendrically. An unsuccessful passage—and a disquieted spirit—can only mean trouble for the living. In an ethnography about Nahua identity, Alan Sandstrom emphasizes the concern with unsettled spirits of the dead and notes that the "majority of a shaman's professional activity is spent controlling *ejecatl* spirits, usually through cleansing rituals" (Sandstrom 1991:252). *Ejecatl* spirits are the wandering souls of those who died bad deaths or have been forgotten by kinsmen. Problems among the living were linked, in this context, to poor management of the dead.

The selectivity of residential burial practices indicates that many of the deceased house members were forgotten or were commemorated only in a vague and general way, but those who were interred within the residence were positioned to be remembered. Pre-hispanically, memory work in the Maya region included re-animation that occurred through structure renewal, burning of incense and other smoke-producing substances near burial interments, and dance performance. Archaeological evidence of smoking, burning, and re-entry of burial facilities appears within domestic as well as monumental contexts and indicates variable and overlapping networks of memory communities. In this way, place-making, ancestralizing, and re-animation were entangled with the practice of enshrining the relicts of select house members within the residence.

Despite the dim view of memory voiced by the French novelist Céline, I believe that the contributions to this volume make significant strides towards the interpretation of residential burial practices within the context of memory communities. My thanks to the editors and chapter contributors for producing a stimulating and path-breaking set of essays that will play a definitive role in reshaping the topic of mortuary studies.

References

Binford, Lewis R.
1971 Mortuary Practices: Their Study and Their Potential. *In* Approaches to the Social Dimensions of Mortuary Practices. J. A. Brown, ed. Pp. 6–29. Memoirs of the Society for American Archaeology, 25. Washington, DC.

Bowles, Samuel, Eric Alden Smith, and Monique Borgerhoff Mulder
2010 The Emergence and Persistence of Inequality in Premodern Societies. Current Anthropology 51:7–17.

Céline, Louis-Ferdinand
1960 [1932] Journey to the End of the Night. John H. P. Marks, trans. New York: New Directions Books.

Connerton, P.
1989 How Societies Remember. Cambridge: Cambridge University Press.

Fitzsimmons, James L.
2009 Death and the Classic Maya Kings. Austin, TX: University of Texas Press.

Gell, Alfred
1998 Art and Agency: An Anthropological Theory. Oxford: Clarendon Press.

Goldstein, Lynne G.
1981 One-Dimensional Archaeology and Multi-Dimensional People: Spatial Organisation and Mortuary Analysis. *In* The Archaeology of Death. R. Chapman, I. Kinnes, and K. Randsborg, eds. Pp. 53–69. Cambridge: Cambridge University Press.

Halbwachs, Maurice
1992 On Collective Memory. L. A. Coser, trans. Chicago: University of Chicago Press.

Harrison-Buck, Eleanor
2004 Nourishing the Animus of Lived Space through Ritual Caching. *In* K'axob: Ritual, Work, and Family in an Ancient Maya Village. P. A. McAnany, ed. Pp. 65–85. Cotsen Institute of Archaeology, Monumenta Archaeologica 22. Los Angeles: University of California.

Henare, Amiria, Martin Holbraad, and Sari Wastell, eds.
2007 Thinking Through Things: Theorising Artefacts Ethnographically. London: Routledge.

Hendon, Julia A.
2010 Houses in a Landscape: Memory and Everyday Life in Mesoamerica. Durham, NC: Duke University Press.

Hodder, Ian, and Craig Cessford
2004 Daily Practice and Social Memory at Çatalhöyük. American Antiquity 69:17–40.

Houston, Stephen D.
2006 Impersonation, Dance, and the Problem of Spectacle among the Classic Maya. *In* Archaeology of Performance: Theaters of Power, Community, and Politics. T. Inomata and L. S. Coben, eds. Pp. 135–155. Lanham, MD: AltaMira.

Joyce, Rosemary A., and Susan D. Gillespie, eds.
2000 Beyond Kinship: Social and Material Reproduction in House Societies. Philadelphia: University of Pennsylvania Press.

Latour, Bruno
2005 Reassembling the Social: An Introduction to Actor-Network Theory. Oxford: Oxford University Press.

McAnany, Patricia A.
1995 Living with the Ancestors: Kinship and Kingship in Ancient Maya Society. Austin: University of Texas Press.
2007 A View from Mesoamerica. Cambridge Archaeological Journal 17(2):19–22.
2011 Toward a Hermeneutics of Death: Commentary on Seven Essays. *In* Living with the Dead: Mortuary Ritual in Mesoamerica. James L. Fitzsimmons and Izumi Shimada, eds. Pp. 231–239. Tucson: University of Arizona Press.

McAnany, Patricia A., and Ian Hodder
2009 Thinking about Stratigraphic Sequence in Social Terms. Archaeological Dialogues 16(1):1–22.

McAnany, Patricia A., and Shoshaunna Parks.
In press Casualties of Heritage Distancing: Children, Ch'orti' Indigeneity, and the Copán Archaeoscape. Current Anthropology.

Melion, Walter, and Susanne Küchler
1991 Introduction: Memory, Cognition, and Image Production. *In* Images of Memory: On Remembering and Representation. S. Küchler and W. Melion, eds. Pp. 1–46. Washington, DC: Smithsonian Institution Press.

Metcalf, Peter, and Richard Huntington
1991 Celebrations of Death: The Anthropology of Mortuary Ritual. 2nd edition. Cambridge: Cambridge University Press.

Miller, Daniel
2005 Materiality: An Introduction. *In* Materiality. D. Miller, ed. Pp. 1–50. Durham, NC: Duke University Press.

Mills, Barbara J., and William H. Walker, eds.
2008 Memory Work: Archaeologies of Material Practices. Santa Fe, NM: School for Advanced Research Press.

Monaghan, John D.
2000 Theology and History in the Study of Mesoamerican Religions. *In* Supplement to the Handbook of Middle American Indians, vol. 6: Ethnology. J. D.

Monaghan, ed. Pp. 24–49. Austin: University of Texas Press.

Morris, Ian
1991 The Archaeology of Ancestors: The Saxe/Goldstein Hypothesis Revisited. Cambridge Archaeological Journal 1:147–169.

Sandstrom, Alan R.
1991 Corn Is Our Blood: Culture and Ethnic Identity in a Contemporary Aztec Indian Village. Norman: University of Oklahoma Press.

Saxe, Arthur A.
1970 Social Dimensions of Mortuary Practices. Ph.D. dissertation, Department of Anthropology, University of Michigan.

Storey, Rebecca
2004 Ancestors: Bioarchaeology of the Human Remains of K'axob. *In* K'axob: Ritual, Work, and Family in an Ancient Maya Village. P. A. McAnany, ed. Pp. 109–138. Cotsen Institute of Archaeology, Monumenta Archaeologica 22. Los Angeles: University of California.

Van Dyke, Ruth M., and Susan E. Alcock, eds.
2003 Archaeologies of Memory. Malden, MA: Blackwell.

Vogt, Evon Z.
1976 Tortillas for the Gods: A Symbolic Analysis of Zinacanteco Rituals. Cambridge, MA: Harvard University Press.

Watanabe, John M.
2004 Some Models in a Muddle: Lineage and House in Classic Maya Social Organization. Ancient Mesoamerica 15(1):159–166.

Weiner, Annette B.
1992 Inalienable Possessions: The Paradox of Keeping-While-Giving. Berkeley: University of California Press.

List of Contributors

About the Editors

Ron L. Adams is an Adjunct Professor in the Department of Archaeology at Simon Fraser University. His research interests include ethnoarchaeology and the archaeology of complex societies in East Asia and Northwestern North America.

Stacie M. King is an Assistant Professor in the Department of Anthropology at Indiana University. Her research interests include everyday social relations, social identity, conquest, and colonialism in Oaxaca, Mexico.

The cover image shows a plan view of Structure 8-8b, Operation B, Río Viejo.

Ron L. Adams
Department of Archaeology
Simon Fraser University
8888 University Dr.
Burnaby, BC V5A 1S6
ron.l.adams73@gmail.com

Chureekamol Onsuwan Eyre
University of Pennsylvania Museum
3260 South St.
Philadelphia, PA 19104-6324
onsuwan@sas.upenn.edu

Susan D. Gillespie
University of Florida, PO Box 117305
Gainesville, Florida 32611-7305
sgillesp@ufl.edu

Rosemary A. Joyce
Professor of Anthropology
University of California, Berkeley
Kroeber Hall #3710
Berkeley, CA 94720-3710
rajoyce@berkeley.edu

Stacie M. King
Department of Anthropology
Indiana University
Bloomington, IN 47405
kingsm@indiana.edu

Ayu Kusumawati
Balai Arkeologi Denpasar
Jl. Raya Sesetan No. 80
Denpasar 80223
Bali, Indonesia

Nicola Laneri
Istituto Italiano per l'Africa e l'Oriente
Via. U. Aldrovandi 16
00197 Rome, Italy
nicolalaneri@hotmail.com

Patricia A. McAnany
Department of Anthropology,
Campus Box 3115
University of North Carolina,
Chapel Hill
Chapel Hill, NC 27599
mcanany@email.unc.edu
www.machiproject.org

Christopher B. Rodning
Department of Anthropology
Tulane University
101 Dinwiddie Hall
New Orleans, LA 70118 USA
crodning@tulane.edu
http://www.tulane.edu/~crodning/

Lynne P. Sullivan
Frank H. McClung Museum
University of Tennessee
Knoxville, TN 37996-3200
lsulliv2@utk.edu
http://mcclungmuseum.utk.edu/

Joyce White
University of Pennsylvania Museum
3260 South St.
Philadelphia, PA 19104-6324
banchang@sas.upenn.edu

Haa Léelk'w Hás Aaní Saax'ú

Our Grandparents' Names on the Land